BEST PRACTICE IN MOTIVATION AND MANAGEMENT IN THE CLASSROOM

ABOUT THE AUTHORS

DENNIS GENE WISEMAN holds the Ph.D. and M.A. degrees from the University of Illinois at Urbana-Champaign (1974, 1970) and the B.A. degree from the University of Indianapolis (1969). He is the Director of the Biddle Center for Teaching and Learning in the Spadoni College of Education at Coastal Carolina University, Conway, South Carolina. Dr. Wiseman has taught with the Champaign, Illinois, and Indianapolis, Indiana, public school systems. He is co-author of *Effective Teaching: Preparation and Implementation; The Middle Level Teachers' Handbook: Becoming a Reflective Practitioner; The Modern Middle School: Addressing Standards and Student Needs; and Teaching at the University Level: Cross-Cultural Perspectives from the United States and Russia,* author of numerous articles in professional journals, and actively involved in collaboration activities between PreK-12 and higher education. His teaching specialization areas are curriculum and instruction and educational psychology.

GILBERT HARRISON HUNT holds the Ph.D. and M.Ed. degrees from the University of North Carolina at Chapel Hill (1975, 1971) and the B.S. degree from Campbell University (1969). He is Dean of the Spadoni College of Education at Coastal Carolina University, Conway, South Carolina. Dr. Hunt has taught at the middle school level with the Harnett County, North Carolina, public school system. He is co-author of *Effective Teaching: Preparation and Implementation; The Middle Level Teachers' Handbook: Becoming a Reflective Practitioner; The Modern Middle School: Addressing Standards and Student Needs; and Teaching at the University Level: Cross-Cultural Perspectives from the United States and Russia,* author of numerous articles in professional journals, and is a member of Phi Delta Kappa, Kappa Delta Pi, National Middle School Association, and Association of Teacher Educators.

Second Edition

BEST PRACTICE IN MOTIVATION AND MANAGEMENT IN THE CLASSROOM

By

DENNIS G. WISEMAN, Ph.D.

and

GILBERT H. HUNT, Ph.D.

Coastal Carolina University
Conway, SC

CHARLES C THOMAS • PUBLISHER, LTD.
Springfield • Illinois • U.S.A.

Published and Distributed Throughout the World by

CHARLES C THOMAS • PUBLISHER, LTD.
2600 South First Street
Springfield, Illinois 62704

©2008 by CHARLES C THOMAS • PUBLISHER, LTD.

ISBN 978-0-398-07786-0 (hard)
ISBN 978-0-398-07793-8 (paper)

Library of Congress Catalog Card Number: 2007039158

With THOMAS BOOKS *careful attention is given to all details of man-
ufacturing and design. It is the Publisher's desire to present books that are satisfactory as to their physical qualities and artistic possibilities and appropriate for their particular use.* THOMAS BOOKS *will be true to those laws
of quality that assure a good name and good will.*

Printed in the United States of America
CR-R-3

Library of Congress Cataloging-in-Publication Data

Wiseman, Dennis.
  Best practice in motivation and management in the classroom / by
Dennis G. Wiseman and Gilbert H. Hunt. -- 2nd ed.
      p. cm.
  Includes bibliographical references and index.
  ISBN 978-0-398-07786-0 (hard) -- ISBN 978-0-398-07793-8 (pbk.)
  1. Motivation in education. 2. Classroom management. 3. Effective
teaching. I. Hunt, Gilbert. II. Title.

LB1065.W57 2008
371.102'4--dc22

                                                          2007039158

This text is dedicated to those students who enter schools each day and bring with them, or encounter there, problems in motivation and management and to the many dedicated teachers who continue to seek ways to meet both the personal and learning needs of these students.

PREFACE

There is no question that teachers today must have an in-depth understanding of the subjects that they teach. Students cannot be expected to achieve at high levels without teachers who are expert themselves in the subject matter that they are charged to teach to their students. Knowledge of subject matter alone, however, is not sufficient to ensure that teachers will be effective and that students will be successful in their learning. Teachers interact with students in their classrooms on a daily basis who often see little value in what they are being taught and feel uncomfortable or out of place in the schooling environment that frequently is so very different from that of their homes and communities. Many of these students have difficulty controlling their own behaviors and focusing on what is expected of them in the classroom. Many bring with them a host of issues and concerns about who they are today as well as who they will become in the future.

Teachers today are expected to provide services to all of their students, schools, and communities that would never have been considered and/or discussed even ten years ago. Likewise, teachers are held accountable for their own performance and the performance of their students in ways and through means that also would not have received serious consideration in years past. The demand for additional services and higher levels of performance and accountability comes at a time when the challenges that teachers face each day in their schools and classrooms are greater than at any previous time in the history of the teaching profession.

Beyond the need to have an in-depth understanding of their subject matter, teachers have an equally or perhaps greater need to be able to teach this subject matter in ways that their students find understandable, interesting, relevant, and engaging. If students do not see what they are learning as being of value, if they do not recognize it as being relevant to their lives either now or in the future, if they are not meaningfully connected to it, and if they do not view it as being understandable to the degree that they can be successful, they will not achieve at their greatest potentials. In today's classrooms and schools, teachers are expected to achieve at high levels in getting their students to learn, and students are expected to achieve at high levels in demonstrating what they have learned.

To be effective, teachers also must have an understanding of their students' interests, styles of learning, and backgrounds, both academic and personal. Teachers cannot meet the unique needs of their students if they do not know their unique needs. Having the ability to manage the learning environment, motivate students in the environment, and offer instruction that itself is motivating and which contributes to students learning what they need to learn and acquiring skills they need to acquire characterizes effective teachers. To meet the expectations held for them, teachers must have highly developed skills as instructional specialists, motivators, managers, and problem solvers.

This text offers practical information and vicarious practice for both beginning as well as veteran teachers to become more knowledgeable, skilled, and effective in their work. Through study, application of what has been studied, and the analysis and evaluation of the end result of this application, teachers who care to improve can improve. And, teachers who are already successful in their teaching can be even more successful. Effective teachers are active learners themselves. This text provides a specific context and focus for this active learning in the areas of student motivation and classroom management which are considered critical for best practice in teaching in classrooms today.

D.G.W.
G.H.H.

CONTENTS

BEST PRACTICE IN MOTIVATION AND MANAGEMENT IN THE CLASSROOM

Chapter 1

MOTIVATION AND MANAGEMENT:
TWO SIDES OF THE SAME COIN

When a classroom population ranges from twenty to forty students from disparate backgrounds, peaceable and productive learning environments depend on the management of explicit standards and expectations to which all adhere. Schools need to set up management structures that promote prosocial behaviors and educators must be prepared to teach replacement behaviors that are prosocial. A major flaw in school management has been that of erasing negative behaviors without teaching prosocial replacement behaviors. (Froyen & Iverson, 1999, p. 6)

The knowledge base of motivation is so extensive that the crucial factor is making the best choice for a particular problem. If we have not learned the extensive motivational knowledge base, then our choices are limited. (Alderman, 2004, pp. 15–16)

THE INTERRELATEDNESS OF MOTIVATION
AND MANAGEMENT

Annual polls conducted by the Gallup organization, in conjunction with Phi Delta Kappa, have for years identified classroom management among the most critical concerns of those held by veteran and novice teachers alike. Beginning almost forty years ago, from 1968 to 1986, *discipline* was identified as the most important problem that teachers face. From 1986 to 1992, *discipline* ranked third only to *drugs* and *inadequate funding* as the most significant problem. In 1994 and 1995, *discipline* again was the number one problem (Elam & Rose, 1995); second to *drug abuse* in 1996 (Elam, Rose, & Gallup, 1996); tied for first with *lack of financial funding* in 1997 (Rose, Gallup, & Elam, 1997); second to *fighting, violence* and *gangs* in 1998 (Rose & Gallup, 1998); first again in 1999 (Rose & Gallup, 1999); and second to *lack of financial support* in 2000 (Rose & Gallup, 2000). In more recent years, the most significant problem identified with America's public schools has been lack of financial support and funding followed by *discipline* or

3

overcrowded schools being second or third in importance. Each poll also identified *fighting, violence* and *gangs*, and *use of drugs* as being among the top five concerns that teachers face (Rose & Gallup, 2003; Rose & Gallup, 2004; Rose & Gallup, 2005; Rose & Gallup, 2006). With the question asked being "What do you think are the biggest problems with which the public schools of your community must deal?", *discipline* and now *violence* are being rated on a consistent basis as two highly significant problems. Educators must give greater attention than ever before to addressing what clearly is a significant national issue.

Problems of discipline and management in schools and classrooms are no longer problems of only public perception; they now impact teacher recruitment and retention as well. It is commonly accepted that the student behavior problems that teachers face in their schools and classrooms are directly related to the teacher shortage problems also being faced by states and school districts as these problems have contributed to the reduction in the number of teachers entering the profession. Such problems also are believed by many to be a part of the reason for the shorter length of time that many teachers stay in teaching. Basically, why would anyone desire to enter a work environment on a daily basis that reflects stress, frustration, and, in some cases, fear? While teacher preparation programs are dedicating more and more time to the study of classroom management, such programs alone cannot successfully address the problem. Teachers themselves, after they have entered the profession, must remain active learners and continue to develop their skills in working with their students and classrooms to establish active, positive, safe, and successful learning environments. Whether from a student achievement or school staffing perspective, managing student behavior is a problem of critical importance to the teaching profession.

Being confronted with problems of managing student behavior also has been identified as one of the most important concerns of preservice teachers or those preparing to enter the teaching profession. Beginning teachers share many common concerns such as being able to maintain classroom discipline, motivate students, accommodate for differences among students, appropriately evaluate student work, work with parents, and develop positive relationships with other teachers (Conway & Clark, 2003; Veenman, 1984). Historically, preservice and beginning teachers have felt least well prepared to deal with issues related to classroom management and discipline (Kher-Durlabhji, Lacina-Gifford, Jackson, Guillory, & Yandell, 1997).

Over the past few years, managing student behavior has gone beyond being an issue associated only with engaging students in effective instruction to represent an issue that is also associated with classroom and school safety. School-based tragedies across the country involving student violence have captured the national attention with outcries for immediate action and demands for safer schools. Beginning teachers are faced with the daunting challenge of offering instruction of high quality in what are often very unpredictable and, at times, unsafe environments. Clement (1998) reports on the ten most common problems faced by first-year teachers with student motivation and classroom management and discipline being first and third on the list respectively. It should also be noted that problems two, four, six, seven, eight, and nine can all impact concerns associated with student motivation and classroom management.

1. student motivation,
2. handling students' social and emotional problems,
3. maintaining classroom management and discipline,
4. overenrolled classrooms,
5. book and supply shortages,
6. uncomfortable classroom environments (size, temperature, cleanliness),
7. working with special education or inclusion students,
8. grading students' work,
9. communicating with parents, and
10. school or district administration.

Although problems of student behavior in schools are easily documented, the major tenet of this text does not view the management of student behavior as a stand-alone issue. Rather, problems of student behavior management must be looked at more broadly as these problems relate to student motivation and effective teaching practice. Because of their special relationship, it is not advisable to separate problems of student management from the challenge of student motivation and the importance of effective teaching. Efforts to do so only serve to oversimplify the understanding of each area as an important concern for teachers and their responsibility to establish successful learning environments in classrooms and schools. While it is possible to study student management separately from student motivation and effective teaching, treating the three in isolation from one another misdirects their most meaningful, synergistic understanding. This understanding and their importance to school settings go together, and, in fact, rely on one another. Jones and Jones (2007) note that teachers need to acknowledge that the relationship between classroom management and instruction is inseparable. Lessons that encourage students' active participation and that address their interests, needs, and backgrounds are not only more likely to foster academic achievement, they also are more likely to generate the good will, respect, and cooperation that is needed for a productive learning environment.

All too frequently, the problems that teachers have in managing student behavior are fundamentally problems of student motivation, or, at least, management and motivation problems occurring simultaneously. And, effective teaching practices are closely related to both management and motivation. This text explores student management and student motivation as they directly relate to each other, and influence each other, rather than as discretely separate aspects of the teaching and learning process. No teacher should leave school at the end of the day lamenting how difficult it was to manage his or her students without also exploring how he or she might become better able to motivate them. In most cases, though perhaps not in all, in classrooms where there are problems in managing student behavior, there also is the absence of needed levels of student motivation. It has been reported that some teachers spend as much as 30 to 80 percent of their time addressing discipline problems (Levin & Nolan, 2007). This figure simply serves to reinforce the special relationship that exists between motivation, management and teaching and learning. To be successful, teachers must be able to establish appropriate student behavior in their classrooms in order to maximize the time that they and their students spend on learning.

ESTABLISHING A COMMON LANGUAGE FOR THE STUDY OF MOTIVATION AND MANAGEMENT

Because understanding the relationship between student motivation and student management is so important to establishing successful teaching practices, having a clear meaning of both concepts as they relate to the work of the teacher in the classroom is essential. Though the terms are used frequently, they are often used in different ways with different meanings. Additionally, it is also important to address the meaning of student *discipline* as the term discipline is often used interchangeably with *management*. This is unfortunate as the two are not the same. As clear communication and understanding are key to effective teaching practice, so are they key to the successful understanding and study of that practice.

The following are popular definitions of the concepts *motivation* and *management* found in the literature today.

Motivation

- processes that can arouse and initiate student behavior, give direction and purpose to behavior, help behavior to persist, and help the student choose a particular behavior (Burden, 2003);
- an energizing or activating of behavior, a directing of behavior, and a regulating persistence of behavior (Alderman, 2004);
- an inner drive that focuses behavior on a particular goal or task and causes the individual to be persistent in trying to achieve the goal or complete the task successfully (Levin & Nolan, 2007);
- an internal state that arouses one to action, pushes one in a particular direction, and keeps one engaged in certain activities (Elliott, Kratochwill, Cook, & Travers, 2000);
- an internal state that arouses, directs and maintains behavior (Woolfolk, 2007).

Management

- strategies that create and maintain productive learning environments (Eggen & Kauchak, 2007);
- all things that a teacher does to organize students, space, time, and materials so that instruction in content and student learning can take place (Wong & Wong, 2005);
- teacher actions to create a learning environment that encourage positive social interaction, active engagement in learning, and self-motivation (Burden & Byrd, 2007);
- the use of rules and procedures to maintain order so that learning may result (Elliott et al., 2000);

- teacher actions to create a learning environment that encourages positive social interaction, active engagement in learning, and self-motivation (Burden & Cooper, 2004).

Based on the definitions presented here, *management* may be looked upon as an action or actions that the teacher takes in relation to the classroom environment in order to make optimum levels of student achievement possible. *Motivation*, on the other hand, may be seen as that which the teacher initiates, or seeks to bring about, so that students become and stay positively engaged in the teacher's learning activities. Management and motivation go hand in hand. For the purposes of this text, **management** is *a system of organization that addresses all elements of the classroom (i.e., students, space, time, materials, and behavioral rules and procedures) that enables the teacher to reach optimum levels of instruction and establish a foundation for student learning.* **Motivation** is *an internal state that arouses students to action, directs them to certain behaviors, and assists them in maintaining that arousal and action with regard to behaviors important and appropriate to the learning environment.* Following these observations, how does student discipline relate to student motivation and management? The following are common definitions of the concept discipline:

Discipline

- teacher responses to student misbehavior (Eggen & Kauchak, 2007);
- the required action by a teacher or school official, toward a student (or group of students), after the student's behavior disrupts the ongoing educational activity or breaks a pre-established rule or law created by the teacher, the school administration, or the general society (Wolfgang, 1999);
- what teachers do to help students behave acceptably in school (Charles, 2005);
- the process of enforcing standards and building cooperation so that disruptions are minimized and learning is maximized (Jones, 1987);
- the act of responding to misbehaving students in an effort to restore order (Burden, 2003).

In considering these definitions, discipline is what the teacher engages in when efforts to motivate students and manage the classroom have not been successful. While the terms discipline and punishment are at times used interchangeably, they are not the same (Coloroso, 1994). Punishment is considered to be adult oriented, imposes power from without, can arouse anger and resentment, and invite conflict. Punishment can wound rather than heal by focusing on blame and pain and demonstrates the teacher's ability to control a student. Discipline and punishment are not synonymous. The process of discipline, for example, does four things that the act of punishment cannot do (Coloroso, 2000). Discipline:

1. shows students what they should have done,
2. gives students as much ownership of the problem as they are able to handle,
3. gives students options for solving the problem, and
4. leaves students with their dignity in tact.

For purposes of this discussion, **discipline** is an *action taken on the part of the teacher to enforce rules and respond to student misbehavior.* Misbehavior is behavior that is considered to be inappropriate and includes any student behavior that is perceived by the teacher to compete with or threaten the academic actions at a particular moment (Burden & Byrd, 2007). Misbehavior creates disruptions in the progress of planned classroom activities. Classroom misbehavior occurs intentionally, not inadvertently (Charles, 2005). In exhibiting misbehavior, students do things on purpose that they know they should not do. Five broad types of misbehavior are identified here in descending order of seriousness:

1. **Aggression:** physical and verbal attacks on the teacher or other students.
2. **Immorality:** acts such a cheating, lying, and stealing.
3. **Defiance of authority:** refusal to do what the teacher requests.
4. **Class disruptions:** talking loudly, calling out, walking about the room, clowning, tossing objects.
5. **Goofing off:** fooling around, out of seat, not doing assigned tasks, dawdling, daydreaming.

While it is important for the teacher to be prepared for discipline problems when they arise, it should be recognized that, when the teacher uses strategies to discipline students, the teacher has entered into more of a reactive than proactive mode of behavior. As with exhibiting good teaching practice, the teacher needs to be poised, confident, capable, and focused when using discipline strategies in response to student misbehavior. When the teacher uses discipline strategies, one likely reason for this is that the teacher's approach(es) to student motivation and management were less than fully effective.

Management issues/problems are a very real part of schools and classrooms today. In a survey of the American Federation of Teachers (AFT), 17 percent of the teachers surveyed indicated that they had lost four or more hours of teaching per week due to disruptive students and 19 percent reported having lost two to three hours (Walker, Ramsey, & Gresham, 2004). Forty-three teachers said they had students in their classes with discipline problems. While disruptive students engage in antisocial behavior, they, in fact, represent a rather small percentage of students in schools. However, aggressive, disruptive behavior wastes teaching time, disrupts the learning of all students, threatens safety, and overwhelms teachers. Although direct early intervention is often rare, early intervention can make a difference. When dealing with disruptive, antisocial behavior, a combination of the following strategies is strongly advised in order to successfully bring about desired behavior change: (1) a consistently enforced schoolwide behavior code, (2) social-skills training, (3) appropriately-delivered adult praise for positive behavior, (4) reinforcement contingencies and response costs, and (5) time-out. This proactive approach to dealing with disruptive behavior can make a difference and have a successful impact on student actions and classroom environment.

BEST PRACTICE IN MOTIVATION AND MANAGEMENT

Teachers who are able to maximize student learning minimize student misbehavior. Acknowledging this, the relationship between best practice in teaching and best practice in motivation and management cannot be ignored. Why is it that effective teachers typically have many fewer discipline problems to address when compared to ineffective teachers? The primary reason is not particularly complicated.

The answer to this question lies in the teacher's attitude, readiness and preparedness, and ability to manage the learning environment and offer meaningful and relevant instruction to all students. Teachers who are well prepared for their teaching, motivating, and managing, have fewer classroom problems than those who are not. It has been observed that half of what a teacher will accomplish in a day is determined before the teacher even leaves home; three-fourths of what will be accomplished will be determined before the teacher enters the school door (Wong & Wong, 2005). Being prepared is the key to success for any teacher. Effective teachers have their rooms ready, their work ready, and themselves ready.

In a classic study, Kounin (1970) identified that effective teachers really are no different from ineffective teachers in their ability to respond to and deal with student misbehavior *after the misbehavior has occurred.* Significant differences are apparent, however, in the behaviors of effective and ineffective teachers *before the misbehavior took place.* Kounin found that it was the ongoing behavior of teachers in carrying out their instruction that determined whether they were effective or ineffective. Kounin's research pointed out that ineffective teachers simply were not fully ready for all that was expected of them or needed to occur in their classrooms. Lack of readiness led to confusion, confusion led to uncertainty, uncertainty led to mixed messages with lack of clarity in communication and understanding of expectations, and all of these, in total, led to student misbehavior. The ineffective teachers, virtually daily, became more and more stressful, disorganized, frustrated, negative, and held others responsible for the problems that they were experiencing. Kounin concluded from his research that the key to maintaining orderly classrooms lies not in the teacher's ability to handle inappropriate student behavior once it occurs, but in the teacher's ability to prevent behavior problems from occurring in the first place. This observation led to the separation of the concept *classroom management,* which represents the teacher's organized system and strategies used to create and maintain an orderly learning environment, and the concept *discipline,* which represents the teacher's reactions to and ways of dealing with student misbehavior.

Effective teachers are prepared for the many things, some predictable and some unexpected, that come into play in the job of teaching. The classroom is ready, meaningful learning activities are ready, and the students are ready to learn when they enter the classroom.

Effective teachers, in fact, are so well prepared through their prior practices and planning that they are able to prevent most student misbehaviors, certainly most serious misbehaviors, from ever occurring. It perhaps sounds all too simple. The reason that effective teachers are effective is that they have fewer student behavior problems and, consequently, are better able to get their students to work (be engaged), stay on task, and achieve. In turn, effective teachers incur less stress as a consequence of having to deal with fewer behavior problems. They are able to leave school each day having been more productive and feeling more satisfied with their work than those teachers who are seen as being not effective. Kounin's conclusions have been validated over the years by other educators and researchers (Brophy & Evertson, 1976; Evertson, 1980).

Most textbooks on teaching methodology include a section on the need for the teacher to be prepared and ready when entering the classroom. Being ready for teaching often is explored with respect to the teacher being well planned to teach lessons to students. The term *plan* typically is used in the context of the teacher's plan for instruction. It is important, however, to expand this outlook toward planning and not be limited to only instructional planning. In pursuit of the well-managed classroom and motivated students, three additional types of plans should be considered. These are (1) the teacher's motivation plan, (2) the teacher's management plan, and (3) the teacher's discipline plan. While it may sound somewhat awkward to think of the teacher as a discipliner, it is not at all awkward to think of the teacher as a motivator and a manager. The effective teacher is a motivator with a plan to motivate and a manager with a plan to manage. The effective teacher also is someone capable of dealing with student misbehavior or discipline problems if or when they arise. In following this line of thought, then, the effective teacher is someone with a plan to discipline. Not only do effective teachers have such plans, they also have the ability to implement them and be successful in their use.

THE TEACHER AS A MOTIVATOR

Many different qualities come to mind when thinking of the characteristics of effective teachers. Effective teachers are organized, flexible, have a deep knowledge of the subjects that they teach, are clear in their communications, task-oriented, enthusiastic and energetic, and dynamic in their work. Included in such a listing of characteristics of effective teachers is the teacher's ability to create positive learning environments where students are actively engaged in their own learning. Teachers are able to enrich their teaching and the learning of their students by establishing positive climates/environments in their classrooms. School climate encompasses the feelings that students and staff have about the school environment over a period of time (Peterson & Skiba, 2001). These feelings have to do with how comfortable each individual feels in the environment and whether the individual feels that the environment is supportive of learning, teaching, appropriately organized, and safe. Comfortable and supportive feelings help to provide a foundation for effective and efficient learning and teaching as well as positive student behavior and attitudes. Educational research identifies that effective teachers are able to motivate students and establish motivating learning environments. Above all else, effective teachers are characterized as being motivational in their approaches to teaching. The main constraint in assisting students to achieve is not with respect to some fixed capacity that they bring with them to the classroom or school, but with respect to the degree to which they are purposefully engaged in working on their learning (Sternberg, 1999, 1985). This also involves the degree to which their teachers are actively engaged in helping them. Working toward achievement involves experiences with effective instructional practices, active participation on the part of the student, role modeling on the part of the teacher, and reward. Sternberg (1999) identifies a model for developing expertise and achievement in students with five key elements: (1) metacognitive skills, (2) learning skills, (3) thinking skills, (4) knowledge, and (5) motivation. All of these elements are dependent on the context for learning that has been established. Critical to these elements is motivation. In the absence of motivation, nothing happens. Motivation helps to bring about the development of metacognitive skills, which then influences the development of learning and thinking skills. Learning and thinking skills provide feedback for the further development of metacognitive skills, enabling the student's level of understanding to increase. Motivation is central to this process.

One of the myths associated with motivation is that teachers really do motivate students (Elliott et al., 2000). The best that teachers can do, some believe, is to establish conditions for learning which are as attractive and stimulating as possible and that match learning tasks to student abilities and interests. When these conditions have been established, students will be motivated. It may be the conditions, then, that create the motivation, not the teacher. Regardless of the source of the motivation, whether students are motivated by the conditions found in the classroom environment or by the teacher in the process of teaching and in establishing the conditions, motivation, without question, is an especially critical part of the learning process.

Considering the myriad challenges that teachers face in schools today, the learning-focused classroom represents the kind of environment most suitable for promoting student motivation (Eggen & Kauchak, 2007). **Learning-focused environments** focus on effort, continuous improvement, and understanding. This is as opposed to **performance-focused environments** that emphasize high grades, public displays of ability, and performance and achievement compared to others. The important consideration in this analysis is on the relationship between the learning-focused classroom and student motivation. Student motivation increases when teachers establish classrooms that have students at the center of all learning activities. Special qualities of (1) self-regulated students, (2) teacher characteristics, (3) climate variables, and (4) instructional variables characterize the learning-focused classroom environment:

Self-Regulated Students

- **Setting Goals:** students have meaningful opportunities to set goals for themselves and participate in the goal setting in the classroom.
- **Monitoring Goals:** students have and are expected to take responsibility for monitoring their own progress.
- **Metacognition:** students are aware of the way they study and learn, monitor the effectiveness of their efforts, and adapt when necessary.
- **Strategy Use:** students learn and use learning strategies that are effective and which assist them in the learning process.

Teacher Characteristics

- **Personal Teacher Efficacy:** the belief that teachers can have an important, positive effect on student learning; the more this is believed, the more it will happen.
- **Modeling and Enthusiasm:** teachers present information enthusiastically resulting in increased student self-efficacy, attributions of effort and ability, self-confidence, and achievement, and through their own behaviors display or project positive learning models.
- **Caring:** teachers empathize with, and invest in, the protection and development of the student.
- **Positive Expectations:** teacher expectations tend to be self-fulfilling; the expression of low expectations by differential treatment can inadvertently lead children to believe less in their abilities and perform more poorly.

Climate Variables

- **Order and Safety:** students see the learning environment as physically and psychologically safe.
- **Success:** achievement on meaningful and appropriately challenging tasks is essential; opportunities for student success are maximized.
- **Task Comprehension:** students understand what they are to be learning and why they are to be learning it.
- **Challenge:** success occurs in moderately difficult or challenging tasks.

Instructional Variables

- **Introductory Focus:** lesson beginnings attract student attention and offer a framework for the entire lesson.
- **Personalization:** lessons and topics are seen as personally meaningful and intellectually and/or emotionally relevant.
- **Involvement:** instruction actively involves students in the learning activity.
- **Feedback:** students receive information on their own personal progress and receive this information on a regular basis.

For further analysis, the following table shows a comparison of the characteristics of learning-focused and performance-focused classrooms.

Learning-Focused and Performance-Focused Characteristics

Characteristics	Learning-Focused	Performance-Focused
Success defined as-	Mastery, improvement	High grades, doing better than others
Value placed on-	Effort, improvement	High grades, demonstration of high ability
Reasons for satisfaction-	Meeting challenges, hard work	Doing better than others, success with minimum effort
Teacher oriented toward-	Student learning	Student performance
View of errors-	A normal part of learning	A basis for concern and anxiety
Reasons for effort-	Increased understanding	High grades, doing better than others
Ability viewed as-	Incremental, alterable	An entity, fixed
Reasons for assessment-	Measure progress toward preset criteria, provide feedback	Determine grades, compare students to one another

Source: Eggen and Kauchak. (2007). *Educational psychology: Windows on classrooms*, 7th ed., Pearson Education, Inc., p. 337.

Beyond the classroom environment itself, the recommendations that follow identify desirable teacher behaviors in motivating students to learn (Snowman & Biehler, 2006). These recommendations include teacher actions, student perceptions, and environmental concerns. Each recommendation is presented in the form of a teacher behavior. The teacher should:

1. use behavioral techniques to help students exert themselves and work toward remote goals,

2. make sure that students know what they are to do, how to proceed, and how to determine when they have achieved their goals,
3. encourage low-achieving students to attribute success to a combination of ability and effort and failure to insufficient effort,
4. encourage students to think of ability as a set of cognitive skills that can be added to and redefined, rather than as a fixed entity that is resistant to change, by praising the processes they use to succeed,
5. encourage students to adopt appropriate learning goals,
6. maximize factors that appeal to both personal and situational interest, and
7. try to make learning interesting by emphasizing activity, investigation, adventure, social interaction, and usefulness.

The organization of teaching strategies related to student motivation in learning by Woolfolk (2007) provides a schema for considering teacher behaviors specifically in the context of improving student motivation. The desired end result of using these strategies, and in displaying certain recommended teacher behaviors, is a classroom environment where students are motivated to learn. As the teacher is responsible for his or her own teaching behaviors, in fulfilling this responsibility the teacher is able to take responsibility for the development of the motivational richness of the learning environment.

Meet Basic Requirements

Provide a organized class environment free from constant interruptions and disruptions.
Be a patient, supportive person who never embarrasses students for mistakes.
Assign challenging but reasonable work.
Make tasks authentic, influenced by the culture.

Build Confidence and Positive Expectations

Begin work at the students' level and move in small steps.
Make learning goals clear, specific, and possible to reach in the near future.
Stress self-comparison, not comparison with others.
Communicate that academic ability is improvable.
Model good problem solving.

Show the Value of Learning

Tie class activities to student interests.
Arouse curiosity.
Make the learning task fun.
Make use of novelty and familiarity.

Help Students Stay Focused on the Task

Give students frequent opportunities to respond.
When possible, have students create a finished product.
Avoid heavy emphasis on grades and competition.
Reduce the task risk without oversimplifying the task.
Model motivation to learn for students.
Teach the learning tactics that students will need to master the material.

In addition to classroom and teacher strategy analysis, a part of the reason for poor student motivation, at times, can be found in problems in the relationship that exists between the teacher and the student (Glasser, 1997). A positive student-to-teacher relationship rests, in part, on the perception held by the student as to whether or not the teacher actually cares for him or her. Students who are destined to fail, and in many cases destined to be unmotivated, often believe that no one (in this discussion their teachers) cares about them as individuals. This is based on their own analysis of the teacher behaviors that they observe. The classroom environment needs to reflect sensitivity through positive interpersonal relationships. A poll by the Association for Supervision and Curriculum Development (2007) asked the question "What's the most effective way for schools to be safe and secure?" with the top three responses being: (1) connect every student with a caring adult, (2) ensure staff emphasizes and models mutual respect, and (3) foster identity/community by listening to kids. Establishing these three qualities in schools not only will help to create safer schools, but also will help to create a relaxed learning atmosphere that will instill confidence in students, making them emotionally equipped and ready to be actively involved in the learning process (Nissman, 2006).

DiGiulio (2000) offers a good explanation of the relationship between motivation, management, and student success while noting that teachers make success definite when they make failure impossible. Teachers can help to ensure success when they know their students' strengths, their weaknesses, what interests and what does not interest them, and when they establish a positive relationship with them. The three axioms below are offered as a guide for ensuring student success.

1. Students who feel successful are seldom behavior problems.
2. To feel successful, students must actually be successful.
3. To actually be successful, a student must first do something of value.

THE TEACHER AS A MANAGER

It would be naïve to suggest that if a teacher has a plan for establishing a well-managed classroom that this by itself will guarantee that student behavior problems will never occur. No such guarantee is possible. Nevertheless, teachers can establish and manage the learning environment in such a way as to greatly diminish the possibility of problems with student misbehavior. In order to do this, teachers must be able to develop as well as implement well-conceived management plans. The effectiveness of such plans, and their implementation, rests, to a large extent, on the teacher having a good understanding of the characteristics of positive learning environments and having the necessary skills to create them. Classroom management, historically, has been seen largely as controlling students and getting them to respond to teacher demands, needs, and goals (McCaslin & Good, 1998). For many teachers, the control of student behavior remains the primary foundation of good classroom management. Though this view may still be quite prevalent, it is not the proper foundation for classroom management. Rather than focus on control of the environment, teachers should focus on promoting the goal of students developing their own capacity for self-regulation. Self-regulation was one of the four components of the learning-focused environment presented earlier in conjunction with student motivation. **Self regulation** is *the process of taking responsibility for one's own learning by using one's own thoughts and actions to identify goals, develop strategies for reaching them, and monitor progress toward their attainment.* Students should not behave in certain ways or be regulated merely as a response to a control system that the teacher has created. Reinforcing its complexity and multi-dimensional nature, classroom management may be seen as a gestalt (ASCD, 2006), dependent on several interdependent components such as: (1) an engaging curriculum; (2) working with anger, projection, and depression; (3) students as responsible citizens; (4) the teacher as a self-knowing model; (5) classroom management skills; (6) working with resistance, conflict, and stress; and (7) robust instruction. Marzano and Marzano (2003) identify that the quality of the teacher-student relationships in the classroom is the key for all other aspects of classroom management. Although some may see the foundation of teacher-student relationships as being the student's view of the teacher as a person (e.g., a friend, nice person, sociable), the most effective teacher-student relationships are characterized by specific teacher behaviors such as exhibiting appropriate levels of dominance, showing appropriate levels of cooperation, and being aware of high-needs students. The most effective classroom managers do not treat all students the same but tend to use different strategies with different types of students. Essentially, they use what the situation calls for in terms of the student and the student's needs.

In considering the classroom environment with respect to student behavior management, it is essential that teachers be proactive in their work and able to clearly define and communicate the expectations that they hold for their students (Gathercoal, 1993). The importance of clarity and consistency in communicating rules and expectations to students cannot be overstated. If students do not know what their teachers expect of them, there is little reason to believe that they will be consistent in exhibiting those behaviors that their teachers desire.

Rules help to clarify the expectations that teachers have for students and the clear statement of even a few important rules of conduct can contribute to the prevention of many student behavior problems. Hensen and Eller (1999) offer eight guidelines to aid teachers with respect to identifying and listing classroom rules.

1. Establish the list during the first few class meetings.
2. Keep the list short.
3. State each rule simply in language the students can understand.
4. Include only those rules that are considered necessary and be prepared to explain why each rule is needed.
5. Involve students in setting rules.

6. Focus on student behavior needed to achieve lesson goals.
7. State consequences for breaking rules so that students will know what will happen if rules are broken.
8. State rewards for following rules.

It is commonly accepted that the characteristics of a well-managed classroom need to be acknowledged or agreed upon by students as well as teachers and not complicated to understand (Wong & Wong, 2005). Simplicity in the characteristics is seen as a strength. Consider the following characteristics of a well-managed classroom:

- students are deeply involved with their work, especially with academic, teacher-led instruction,
- students know what is expected of them and are generally successful,
- there is relatively little wasted time, confusion, or disruption, and
- the climate of the classroom is work-oriented but relaxed and pleasant.

The well-managed classroom has a positive climate and is physically arranged to facilitate productive work. Students are on task, cooperative and respectful of one another. All of these dimensions are within the sphere of control of the teacher and should be established early in the school year.

While many different rules are possible, there is no need for a long laundry list of rules to ensure a well-organized and well-managed classroom. A set of around five or six normally is sufficient to cover most important areas of behavior (Emmer, Evertson, & Worsham, 2006). The following general rules that encompass many classroom behaviors are often found in well-managed classrooms.

1. Bring all needed materials to class.
2. Be in your seat and ready to work when the bell rings or when the class begins.
3. Respect and be polite to all people.
4. Listen and stay seated when someone is talking.
5. Respect other people's property.
6. Obey all school rules.

In their analysis of common teacher problems in establishing well-managed classrooms, McCaslin and Good (1998) conclude that students, and the classroom in general, often suffer from inconsistent messages that teachers send to their students. Teachers frequently manage for obedience while professing to be teaching for exploration and risk taking.

> Educators have created an oxymoron: a curriculum that urges problem solving and critical thinking and a management system that requires compliance and narrow obedience. The management system at least dilutes, if not obstructs, the potential power of the curriculum for many of our students. Students are asked to think and understand, but in too many classrooms they are asked to think noiselessly, without peer communication or social exchange. And the problems they are asked to think about must be solved, neatly, within (at most) forty-five minute intervals. In the problem-solving curriculum, in too many cases, the teacher sets the performance goals, identifies relevant resources, establishes criteria for evaluation, and eventually announces winners and losers. Students generally gain recognition and approval by paying close attention to recommended procedures and by taking few academic risks (e.g., reading and extensively footnoting fifteen secondary sources rather than venturing their own informed opinions). (McCaslin & Good, 1998, p. 173)

The conflict that can be seen in this observation between what teachers say and what they do is obvious. If teachers desire that students develop successful work habits and certain behavior characteristics, it is necessary for them to have the opportunity to meaningfully think about and explore how they learn and to actively participate in their own learning; this includes participating in the development of classroom rules.

While they are different, it is clear that there is a close relationship between classroom management and discipline. Teachers are reacting to student behavior problems when they engage in the use of discipline strategies and seeking to prevent them when they develop their systems of management. In the popular *The First Days of School,* Wong and Wong (1991) identify the following Principles of Effective Discipline as a framework for both addressing student problems as well as establishing an environment to prevent their occurrence. The principles themselves reinforce this relationship.

1. Treat students with dignity and respect.
2. Effective teaching reduces discipline problems.

3. Students need a limited say in what happens in the classroom.
4. It takes time to develop an effective discipline plan and style.
5. Teachers create most of their discipline problems by how they teach and treat people.
6. Bored students become discipline problems.
7. Lack of self-esteem is the major reason why students act up.
8. No one wants or likes to fail; a student would rather be bad than be stupid.
9. Anything a teacher can do to make students feel good about themselves will help to minimize discipline problems.
10. Students who feel powerless will find ways of expressing their lack of power (e.g., not knowing what has been assigned to them).
11. Teachers deny most the students who need to learn responsibility by denying them the experience to have responsibility (e.g., student council, athletics, music, etc.).

Additional important principles of classroom management are identified by Levin and Nolan (2007, pp. 9–15). While some are specific, others are more general. Each offers an important perspective and direction to the better understanding of the role of the teacher as a classroom manager.

The Basics

- The single most important factor in determining the learning environment is teacher behavior. Intentionally or unintentionally, teachers' verbal and nonverbal behaviors influence student behaviors.
- Teachers have the professional responsibility for assuming the role of instructional leader, which involves employing techniques that maximize student on-task behavior.
- Teachers who have clearly developed ideas of (a) the relationship between teaching and discipline; (b) the factors motivating student behavior; (c) their own personal expectations for student behavior; and (d) a systematic plan to manage misbehavior have classrooms characterized by a high percentage of on-task student behavior.
- A preplanned decision-making hierarchy of intervention strategies increases the likelihood of appropriate student behavior.

The Nature of the Discipline Problem

- A discipline problem exists whenever a behavior interferes with the teaching act; interferes with the rights of others to learn; is psychologically or physically unsafe, or destroys property.
- For effective teaching to take place, teachers must be competent in influencing appropriate student behavior so as to maximize the time spent on learning. Such teachers enjoy teaching more and have greater confidence in their ability to affect student achievement.

Understanding Why Children Misbehave

- An awareness of the influences of misbehavior, which are often beyond the schools' control, enables teachers to use positive intervention techniques rather than negative techniques, which stem from erroneously viewing misbehavior as a personal affront.
- Satisfaction of basic human needs such as food, safety, belonging, and security is prerequisite for appropriate classroom behavior.
- The need for a sense of significance, competence, virtue, and power influences student behavior.
- Cognitive and moral developmental changes result in normal student behavior that often is disruptive in learning environments.
- Instructional competence can lessen the effects of negative outside influences as well as prevent the misbehavior that occurs as a result of poor instruction.

Philosophical Approaches to Classroom Management

- Theoretical approaches to classroom management are useful to teachers because they offer a basis for analyzing, understanding, and influencing student and teacher behavior.
- As social agents, teachers have access to a variety of power bases that can be used to influence student behavior.
- The techniques a teacher employs to influence student behavior should be consistent with the teacher's beliefs about how students learn and develop.

Structuring the Environment

- When environmental conditions are appropriate for learning, the likelihood of disruptive behavior is minimized.
- Students are more likely to follow classroom guidelines if the teacher models appropriate behavior; explains the relationship of the guidelines to learning, mutual student-teacher respect, and protection and safety of property and individuals; and obtains student commitment to follow them.
- Enforcing teacher expectations by using natural and logical consequences helps students to learn that they are responsible for the consequences of their behavior and thus are responsible for controlling their own behavior.
- When classroom guidelines and rules match the culture of students' homes and communities, the likelihood that students will behave appropriately is increased.
- When the teacher creates group norms that are supportive of engagement in learning activities, the likelihood that students will behave appropriately is increased.
- Student learning and on-task behavior are maximized when teaching strategies are based on what educators know about student development, how people learn, and what constitutes effective teaching.

Coping with Common Behavior Problems: Nonverbal and Verbal Interventions

- Classroom management techniques need to be consistent with the goal of helping students to become self-directing individuals.
- Use of a preplanned hierarchy of remedial interventions improves the teacher's ability to cope with misbehavior and influence appropriate behavior.
- The use of a hierarchy that starts with nonintrusive, nonverbal teacher behaviors gives students the opportunity to exercise self-control, minimizes disruption to the teaching/learning process, reduces the likelihood of student confrontation, protects students' safety, and maximizes the teacher's alternative interventions.
- An intervention hierarchy that consists of nonverbal intervention, followed by verbal intervention, and application of logical conse-

quences, when necessary, seems most effective in coping with common behavior problems.

- Some forms of verbal intervention defuse confrontation and reduce misbehavior; other forms of verbal intervention escalate misbehavior and confrontation.

Interventions for Chronic Behavior Problems

- When dealing with students who pose chronic behavior problems, teachers should employ strategies to resolve the problems within the classroom before seeking outside assistance.
- Breaking the cycle of discouragement in which most students with chronic behavior problems are trapped increases the likelihood that the problems can be resolved within the classroom.
- When teachers talk with students privately and use effective communication skills with students who have chronic behavior problems, the likelihood that the problems can be resolved within the classroom increases.
- Interventions that require students to recognize their inappropriate behavior and its impact on others increase the likelihood that the problems can be resolved within the classroom.
- Interventions that require students who exhibit chronic behavior problems to be accountable for trying to control their behavior on a daily basis increase the likelihood that the problems can be resolved within the classroom.

Seeking Outside Assistance

- Professional teachers recognize that some chronic misbehavior problems are not responsive to treatment within the classroom or are beyond their expertise and necessitate specialized outside assistance.
- When outside assistance must be sought to manage a chronic misbehavior problem adequately and appropriately, the use of a multidisciplinary team is the most effective approach.
- Parental support and cooperation with the school is critical when attempting to influence a student who exhibits chronic behavior problems. Careful planning and skilled conferencing techniques are essential in developing a positive home-school working relationship.

Effective teachers have their own individual plans for handling management problems in the classroom. Not having a well-conceived and workable plan will stymie the teacher in reaching the primary goal in teaching, this being to assist and guide students as they advance in the learning process. When management problems emerge, they stand in the way of the teacher being successful in meeting this goal. It is interesting to note that three of the five elements of the suggested management plan that follows deal specifically with motivating students. Koenig (2000) notes that, to be effective, a plan for handling student behavior needs to have five major characteristics.

1. Be individualized to fit each teacher's teaching style and personality.
2. Prevent misbehaviors and encourage cooperation.
3. Motivate a student to stop disruptive behaviors.
4. Motivate a student to want to learn.
5. Be quick and easy to use.

It is important for teachers to carefully analyze the characteristics of student motivation, classroom management, and discipline as they prepare to be effective teachers and problem solvers in their classrooms. Effective behavior management, ultimately, is represented by teachers understanding and appropriately selecting from an array of interventions created to help them influence the behavior of their students and teach them to behave in positive and safe ways (Danforth & Boyle, 2000). In the end, it will be the ability to resolve problems (instructional, motivational, and managerial) that determines the true measure of the teacher's effectiveness, in particular as successful resolutions to problems inform the teacher's practice, thus reducing the likelihood of similar problems occurring in the future.

THE TEACHER AS A REFLECTIVE PRACTITIONER

Teachers make assumptions about teaching and learning and depend on what they know and believe as they carry out their daily teaching activities (Wilen, Ishler, Hutchison, & Kindsvatter, 2000). Assumptions tend to be more informal where beliefs are more structured; both develop from one's experiences. The more that teachers

have learned from their experiences, the better grounded their assumptions and beliefs will be. As professionals, teachers must make
decisions and take action based on the most current information that
is available and continually seek to add to their information base. For
teaching to be viewed as a profession, teachers must look upon their
work as knowledge- or information-based and develop habits of deep,
substantive thinking and reflection (Darling-Hammond & Goodwin,
1993). Of the many important teaching skills, decision making is the
most significant of all (Shavelson, 1973). Given the challenges of in-
structing, motivating, and managing children in today's schooling
environments, it is difficult to argue that this is not the case.

There is no doubt that teaching involves many highly complex
processes. Effective teachers must be well informed regarding current
teaching principles and able to make use of this information to strengthen and advance their practice. As reinforced throughout this book,
teachers must be able to make sound decisions on a daily basis, and,
in fact, many times each day. These decisions need to be based on the
most current and accurate information available. Reasoned, reflective
decision making is at the heart of good teaching and, when developed,
will help ensure the highest possible levels of effective practice (Wilen
et al., 2000).

Reflection is a cornerstone of professional competence (York-Barr,
Sommers, Ghere, & Montie, 2005). To learn and make appropriate
change requires that a person reflect on past practice. **Reflection** is *a
way of thinking about educational matters that involves the ability to make
rational choices and to assume responsibility for those choices; it requires that
the teacher be introspective, open-minded, and willing to accept responsibility
for decisions and actions.* Reflection facilitates learning and continued
professional growth and is a key factor in the ability of teachers to be
effective throughout their careers (Burden & Byrd, 2007).

However, even if a teacher has a deep understanding of the concepts of motivation and management and plans for each, this will not
ensure that students will always be well motivated and the classroom
will always be well managed. The teacher must know how to make use
of this knowledge and utilize sound decision-making skills in applying
it in whatever context it is needed. While teachers need to know how
to establish positive learning environments, they also need to be able
to make appropriate adjustments to these environments as necessary,
in particular when student behavior problems arise. A critical element

here is the teacher's ability to reflect and be an informed decision maker. Whether a classroom problem is one of motivation, management, or teaching, or all three together, it is essential that the teacher has the ability to make sound decisions based on relevant and accurate information so that, when made, these decisions will result in effective classroom instruction, motivated students, and a safe, well-managed environment. If effective instruction is not occurring, and if student motivation and management are not as they are desired, the teacher must be able to alter what is taking place in the classroom in some meaningful way so that student motivation and management will be the end result.

A one-size-fits-all approach to management cannot appropriately serve teachers who seek to create calm and safe learning environments in their classrooms and, in so doing, meet the needs of all of their students (McEwan, 2000). Establishing positive classroom behavior necessitates determining exactly what students expect from teachers and what teachers expect from students. When students elect to relate to teachers through misbehavior, teachers need to be able to recognize the purpose or the goal of the misbehavior and know how to respond to it immediately and in the long term. Teachers have enormous power in influencing student behavior. As an example, the *Cooperative Discipline* system is an approach to student behavior management designed to bring about the type of learning environment that both teachers and students need and desire (Albert, 1996). In this management system, emphasis is placed on cooperation and, through it, two important achievements are possible. First, the classroom environment is a safe, orderly and inviting place where teachers can teach and students can learn. Second, student self-esteem increases, which is necessary if teachers desire for their students to behave responsibly and achieve academically. The system offers a process for management that is corrective, supportive, and preventive. Regardless of the approach adopted or developed, the key for the teacher when dealing with instances of student misbehavior is in determining the cause of the behavior being exhibited, deciding thoughtfully and knowledgeably what to do about it, and then taking appropriate action.

The following case studies (Brubaker, Case, & Reagan, 1994) represent first-year teachers who are faced with decisions to make based on problems of student behavior that they have experienced in their classrooms.

Seth's Confidence

Seth is a first-year teacher in a first-grade classroom. He completed his student teaching last year in a neighboring school with an experienced teacher near the end of a long, excellent career. Although Seth respected her, he often felt she was rather old-fashioned and knew less about modern techniques than he himself knew. By the end of his student teaching experience, Seth rarely took advice from anyone; he was confident that he knew what there was to know about teaching first-graders. He found, though, that he still had much to learn. On one particular day early in the year, the children were especially disruptive, and in spite of his many efforts, the noise level in the classroom continued to grow. It seemed as though the children were consistently up and doing things that were inappropriate. This type of behavior frustrated Seth and he began making mistakes as a result. At one point, the students even teased him and laughed at his clumsy errors. After school he went home and shared his day with his wife who was sympathetic and soothing. Seth began to feel better about things and even laughed at his own silly mistakes. He felt sure that he would do better the next day and that the children would settle down more as the school year progressed. He felt it would help if he tried to be more humorous while teaching. Seth decided that the best thing for him to do was to take each day as it came because worrying about it would only be extra stressful on him and take away from his ability to do his best.

Susan's Problem Ownership

Susan did her student teaching last year, in a ninth-grade setting, where she taught pre-algebra and algebra I. However, this year she was hired in the same school system but was assigned to teach sixth grade in a middle school on the other side of the district. Susan liked the area so she took the new position thinking that she could soon transfer to another school with more mature students when such a position came open. Susan had had a few difficult days early on, but today was an absolute disaster. Students were talking out of turn and not cooperating as she taught. Soon the conditions in the classroom deteriorated to the point where some students were actually arguing with one another across the room and in one case a student even showed defiance to Susan. Susan lost control of herself as a result of what she considered her students' petty, childish behavior. She made several threats about after school detention and parent conferences, but, by the day's end, had failed to follow through on any of them. As she drove home in her car, she thought about her unfortunate circumstances during the day. It was obvious that her mentor teacher and her principal were not helping her enough. The parents of her students were, in her opinion, not doing their jobs either. The school district itself had made a mistake, she felt, in even assigning her to a position teaching such immature students. By the time she arrived home, she had begun to feel better. She believed that things would work themselves out and, if they didn't, she would find a position elsewhere next year where the students behaved as they should and really wanted to learn mathematics.

Tameka's Planning and Analysis

Tameka is a first-year art teacher in the same high school where she had completed her student teaching the year before; in fact, she was hired to replace her former cooperating teacher, Ms. Smith, who moved with her family to another state. Ms. Smith and Tameka had become very close, yet Ms. Smith was a very strong individual who made most of the decisions in the classroom unilaterally. Ms. Smith, who had excellent control of her classroom, was almost more like a mother to Tameka than a mentor. On this particular day, Tameka had set up sixteen work stations in her classroom complete with easels, paint, and other necessary materials. She had arranged the stations neatly giving each student adequate space to prevent students from interfering with one another while working. Ms. Smith had correctly taught her the importance of having everything prepared before the students' arrival in order to not waste valuable instructional time. When the first class began, Tameka was ready to teach; however, some problems arose almost immediately. Ray and Becky had been feuding all week, and Ray came into the classroom and selected the workstation closest to the one where Becky was working. Very soon Ray and Becky were arguing and everyone was watching them instead of working on their projects. Bill, who liked Becky, walked past Ray's station and bumped into it knocking Ray's supplies on the floor. Two of the other boys in the classroom had to separate Ray and Bill to prevent a fight. Sally, another student, began laughing and making loud remarks. This was too much for Tameka who raised her voice and scolded Sally in front of the entire class. Finally, the bell rang and the students left; Tameka was totally depressed. During her planning session she got out her lesson plans and made some diagnostic notes which was one of the techniques that she had learned from Ms. Smith. As she reflected on the class that she had just finished, Tameka realized she had made some mistakes that needed correcting. She listed each mistake she could think of and then wrote beside each error what she could do to correct it in the future. For example, when you know certain students do not get along well together, you should assign their work stations in a way as to avoid the kind of problem she had had with Ray and Becky. She felt that she needed to have a conference with her first-year mentor who might have additional ideas to help her avoid some other problems she noted in terms of motivating her students to stay on task. She wondered if some type of a reward system might help. Finally, she was concerned that she had mishandled the situation with Sally in front of the class. The next day she would make a point of interacting positively with Sally where all other students could see.

These three case studies provide real-life situations for analysis and represent three different ways that the teachers involved chose to approach the problems that they were having with student behavior in their classrooms. Each took a different approach with only one, Tameka, taking an approach that was systematic in terms of breaking down the events of the day for specific review, acknowledging ownership of the problem and of the responsibility for seeking a solution, and preparing a strategy or plan to follow when the class next met. Seth took a general and less thorough approach to analyzing the problems he encountered by talking to only one other individual (his wife) about them and concluding that he should try to be more humorous in the classroom and to not worry but take each day as it came. A plan for problem resolution was not developed. Susan appeared to feel no responsibility for the problems that had developed in her classroom and was prepared to return to school the next day without recognizing the need for any specific adjustments in her approach to teaching her students or managing her classroom. She held others responsible for the problems that she was having, e.g., the students, their parents, her principal, her mentor. Like Seth, she also did not develop a plan for problem resolution nor saw a need to do so. Tameka was the only one of the three teachers who accepted responsibility for the problems that had occurred, specifically analyzed them, and formulated a plan to deal with them.

The Model for Reflection and Inquiry in Figure 1.1 is offered as a guide for teachers to systematically analyze both motivation and management problems in the classroom. The teachers identified in the three case studies just presented would find using the model beneficial as a strategy to improve their respective classroom situations. The model can play an important role in helping teachers organize pertinent information and make decisions regarding the use of initial strategies and plans to motivate students and manage the classroom. It can also be beneficial in analyzing problems related to motivation and management once they have occurred. The model represents a logical problem solving process for teachers to follow in reflecting on and making decisions in a variety of areas regarding student motivation, classroom management. and instruction While use of the model cannot guarantee motivated students or well-managed classrooms, its use will ensure that the teacher will be approaching issues in these areas in a logical and reasoned way. This, in turn, will enhance the likelihood of a higher level of student motivation and a better managed classroom in the future.

Many see solving student behavior problems in the classroom as a process of trial and error decision making. If this is the case, and to some degree when dealing with problems involving human beings it

---

Model for Reflection and Inquiry

1. Statement of the Problem

The problem is identified and clarified; the problem should be meaningful and manageable.

2. Development of a Hypothesis(es)

A hypothesis, i.e., educated guess, regarding a solution to the problem is formulated; there may be more than one hypothesis.

3. Collection of Relevant Data

Data or pertinent information relevant to the problem is collected and/or identified; references or sources of information are considered and reviewed.

4. Analysis of Data

Clarifications are made as to information collected; sources of data are considered and perhaps reconsidered. Relationships should be identified among data collected and data should be clearly organized and analyzed as to how this information relates to the problem.

5. Interpretation and Reporting of Results, Drawing Conclusions and Making Generalizations

Conclusions should be drawn and relevant generalizations made related to the accuracy of the original hypothesis.

Figure 1.1. Model for Reflection and Inquiry.

is, the use of an approach such as the Model for Reflection and Inquiry can be even more important. The model can serve to guide the teacher's thinking processes and problem solving efforts by ensuring the use of more systematic decision making with respect to what problem solving strategies are used and how they are evaluated. Over time, a better match between typical problems and effective solutions will develop. This, then, will reduce the "starting from the beginning" approach that many teachers follow when they have not systematically observed and learned from their past efforts. In becoming more knowledgeable with respect to what problem solving strategies to use in certain situations, the teacher will be able to solve problems of student motivation and classroom management more quickly and effectively when called upon to do so. Classrooms will run more smoothly and efficiently. Students will see themselves more positively as learners, and teachers will see themselves as being more effective as teachers. All of this will result in greater attention being given to the instructional program that the teacher has established and higher levels of student learning taking place.

CLASSROOM PROBLEMS ANALYSIS

Read through the following situations and (1) identify the problem, (2) decide whether the problem is one of student management or motivation, or both, and (3) formulate an initial hypothesis that could apply to successful problem resolution.

1. Bailey and Jadon are students in the third grade who sit next to each other at the back of the classroom. Day after day they seem to continually talk to each other when the teacher is teaching the class. Neither becomes involved in small group activities nor in individual seat work when these strategies are used.

2. Alexis is an eighth grade student who frequently appears uninterested in becoming involved in the activities of the class. During the teacher's lessons she typically either stares out the window of the classroom or draws in her notebook. She seldom turns assigned homework in to her teacher and often seems to be far away and daydreaming.

3. Carson is in the eleventh grade for the second year and seems to have all but given up on ever graduating from high school. He rarely brings books or writing utensils to class. When the teacher is trying to teach, he often speaks out loudly to those around him or even directly interrupts the teacher during the lesson. The teacher seldom calls on him for fear of what he might say or how he might say it.

4. Devlin is a fifth grade student who has been identified as very capable academically. However, he seldom answers questions when they are asked in class. When he is returning from lunch, sharpening a pencil, or going back to his seat from the teacher's desk, he often punches students as he walks by them or even marks on their papers or desks. He does not associate with any particular student in the class and keeps to himself most of the time.

5. Koby is in the ninth grade and has only been in the school for a few weeks. When the teacher is conducting the lesson, he often calls out answers to questions without being called on or makes comments about what the

teacher has said. When he does this, other students turn to him and make derogatory comments. This, in turn, results in Koby making derogatory remarks back to them. He seems to have no friends.

Whether classified as representing a motivation or management problem, or both, each of these situations represents problems found frequently in schools today. Each also illustrates the difficulty in identifying situations as being grounded in only student motivation or management issues. The Model for Reflection and Inquiry can help to direct the teacher to more immediate and effective solutions to problems such as these by offering a systematic approach to analyzing each situation. The first step in using the model involves clearly identifying and understanding the nature of the problem. Consider each situation and identify the problem that the teacher is dealing with. Then, go to the second step of the model and hypothesize what the teacher might do about it. The purpose here is not to "solve" any individual problem, but, to logically explore the interplay between motivation and management and accurately identify the problem and a possible approach to its resolution.

In the first situation, Bailey and Jadon obviously represent a management problem. They are inattentive to the teacher as they continually talk to one another while the teacher is teaching and do not become involved in the teacher's planned activities. It also can be observed that neither student is motivated by the learning activities that the teacher has used. Both are more motivated by their desire to interact with each other than they are to engage in the activities that the teacher has planned. Recognizing this, the teacher might begin to solve the problem by no longer allowing them to be seated next to each other and to begin to work with them individually to get them involved in the classroom lessons. The teacher might also use the management strategy of proximity control and move around the room when teaching and stand close to them whenever possible.

In the second situation, Alexis's behavior appears initially to represent more of a motivation problem than a problem of management. She does not participate in the activities of the class, but does not outwardly cause trouble either. The teacher, however, should not conclude that Alexis's behavior might not also represent a problem of management just because she is not outwardly misbehaving. Alexis's situation represents a motivation problem as she is not engaged in the academic program that the teacher has established in the classroom and a management problem for this same reason. It is recommended that the teacher set up a time to personally meet with and "interview" Alexis with respect to what interests her and what she likes to do when not in school. The teacher needs to understand Alexis better and should also take the time to ask her how she thinks the class is going and what she thinks about the activities that have been used.

In the third situation, Carson's behavior reflects a management problem for the teacher in that he is loud and not engaged in the teacher's instructional activities. Given that he is repeating the eleventh grade, he also represents a motivational challenge. Perhaps not, but Carson may have concluded that his graduation from high school is unlikely. If this is the case, the classic strategy used by many teachers to motivate students, their receiving good grades or moving from grade to grade, may be less effective in this situation. The teacher should be mindful of the theories of William Glasser (1997) and take the time to establish a personal relationship with Carson. Many students have problems, in large part, because they feel that no one cares about them personally. The teacher needs to find out what Carson hopes to do after he finishes high school. In doing this, the teacher will help Carson see that he cares about him, but, it will also allow the teacher to discover more about Carson's interests and the problems that he has encountered earlier in his high school career.

In the fourth situation, Devlin's misbehavior is obvious but may actually reflect that the teacher's primary difficulty really is in motivating him. His lack of involvement in, or possibly disinterest in, the activities of the class has led to management problems. Although Devlin is identified as academically able, he has not become involved in the lessons and activities that the teacher has presented and his behavior has become a disruption and a management concern because of this. The teacher should recognize that a part of the problem could be that Devlin does not find what goes on in the classroom challenging, interesting, or meaningful. The teacher needs to know how Devlin truly sees what is taking place in the classroom in terms of how and what the teacher teaches.

In the final situation, Koby exhibits the typical management problem of a student who does not feel connected to the classroom or the student group. Given that he is new to the school and has not established any meaningful friendships, he has selected attention-getting behaviors in order to be recognized. Koby has created management problems for the teacher in that he exhibits inappropriate behaviors in the classroom. The teacher should review the instructional activities that have been used to determine if it might be possible for cooperative learning or group activities to be implemented if they have not been. Koby's problems, to some degree, rest on his not having positive relationships with any of his classmates. These problems could partly be addressed by the teacher making sure that, through the use of certain instructional activities, he meets and gets to know more students and works with them in a mutually reliant way.

Specific plans can and should be developed to address each of these situations. After clearly identifying the problem(s), the teacher must then formulate an idea or a plan with strategies for problem resolution. Initial ideas (hypotheses) have been made here. As a part of doing this, the teacher needs to learn more about the individual students involved, their interests, their styles of learning, their strengths, what distracts them, what successes they value, etc. With this knowledge, and having a clear understanding of the problem, the teacher can then develop a workable plan for each situation so that each student becomes more motivated and connected to the learning experiences in the classroom and feels more successful when involved in them.

Problem solving to improve student motivation and classroom management is difficult and, at times, uncertain work. Without using a systematic approach to it, however, the success of the teacher in meeting individual student needs will be even more uncertain. The Model for Reflection and Inquiry offers a system for reflecting on, logically analyzing, evaluating, and developing solutions for problems of student motivation and classroom management and, if applied consistently, will result in improved learning conditions for students and improved teaching conditions for teachers.

CONCLUSION

Chapter 1 has stressed that problems of student motivation and management are best considered simultaneously rather than as separate and isolated issues. The chapter provided a number of definitions popularly used for both classroom management and student motivation. The concept of discipline also was introduced and defined as what the teacher is engaged in when efforts at management and motivation have not been successful.

The chapter emphasized that teachers need to be well prepared by having well thought out plans for instruction, management, and motivation. Teachers also need to have discipline plans in place and feel comfortable and confident in their use when behavior problems arise. No pilot would leave an airport without a flight plan nor would a coach enter an athletic contest without a game plan. Likewise, no teacher should enter the classroom without having plans to instruct, motivate, manage, and deal with student problem situations should they occur.

Finally, the chapter gave special recognition to the necessity of the teacher being a logical decision maker or reflective practitioner in addressing problems of student motivation and management. The Model for Reflection and Inquiry was introduced to guide the teacher in the decision-making process. Without a logical approach to making decisions, the teacher will not be able to establish and then maintain a well-managed classroom with motivated students. Nor will the teacher be able to effectively solve problems after they have occurred, or possibly even fully understand how problems were solved after conditions have improved.

QUESTIONS/ACTIVITIES FOR REFLECTION

1. If a student consistently fails to complete homework assignments, how might you address the problem as a management concern as well as a motivation concern? What steps would you take or follow in dealing with the problem?
2. Kounin (1970) found effective teachers to be no better than ineffective teachers when responding to student misbehavior after it had occurred. Analyze Kounin's finding; why do you think that he drew this conclusion? Based on your observations of teachers, do you agree? Explain.
3. In Seth's case study, it was stressed that Seth was highly confident; but, his confidence may actually have been overconfidence and then became a problem. As far as being a manager and motivator of students are concerned, what are some of the reasons for and

ways to show confidence? What are some of the pitfalls associated with being or appearing overconfident?

4. The position is taken that, to be an effective manager and motivator, a teacher must be a reflective practitioner. How would you describe a reflective practitioner? Describe a classroom situation illustrating how a teacher who is truly a reflective practitioner might handle a behavior problem associated with students calling out in class when the teacher is teaching a lesson.

5. Develop a list of at least five management rules for the classroom along with related consequences for students when the rules are broken. Identify what classroom purpose each rule serves. In your own classroom, how would you proceed to develop your list of management rules?

REFERENCES

Albert, L. (1996). *Cooperative discipline.* Circle Pines, MN: American Guidance Service, Inc.

Alderman, M. (2004). *Motivation for achievement: Possibilities for teaching and learning* (2nd ed.). Mahwah, NJ: Lawrence Erlbaum.

Association for Supervision and Curriculum Development (ASCD). (2006). The definition of classroom management. Retrieved August 3, 2006, from www.ascd.org/portal/site/ascd/menuitem.

Association for Supervision and Curriculum Development (ASCD). (2007). Poll. Retrieved May 31, 2007, from www.ascd.org/portal/site/ascd/menuitem.

Brophy, J., & Evertson, C. (1976). *Learning from teaching: A developmental perspective.* Boston: Allyn & Bacon.

Brubaker, J., Case, C., & Reagan, T. (1994). *Becoming a reflective educator: How to build a culture of inquiry in the schools.* Thousand Oaks, CA: Corwin Press.

Burden, P. (2003). *Classroom management: Creating a successful learning community* (2nd ed.). New York: John Wiley.

Burden, P., & Byrd D. (2007). *Methods for effective teaching: Promoting K-12 student understanding* (4th ed.). New York: Pearson Education, Inc.

Burden, P., & Cooper, J. (2004). *An educator's guide to classroom management.* New York: Houghton Mifflin.

Charles, C. (2005). *Building classroom discipline* (8th ed.). Boston: Allyn & Bacon.

Clement, M. (1998, April 8). *Beginning teachers' perceptions of their stress, problems, and planned retention in teaching.* Paper presented at the annual meeting of the Midwest Association for Teacher Educators, Urbana, IL.

Coloroso, B. (1994). *Kids are worth it: Giving your child the gift of Inner Discipline.* New York: Morrow.

Coloroso, B. (2000). *Parenting with wit and wisdom in times of chaos and loss.* Toronto: Penguin.

Conway, P., & Clark, G. (2003). The journey inward and outward: A re-examination of Fuller's concerns-based model of teacher development. *Teaching and Teacher Education, 19*, 465-482.

Danforth, S., & Boyle, J. (2000). *Cases in behavior management.* Columbus, OH: Merrill.

Darling-Hammond, L., & Goodwin, A. (1993). Progress toward professionalism in teaching. In G. Cawelti (Ed.), *Challenges and achievements in American education.* Alexandria, VA: Association for Supervision and Curriculum Development.

DiGiulio, R. (2000). *Positive classroom management* (2nd ed.). Thousand Oaks, CA: Corwin Press.

Eggen, P., & Kauchak, D. (2007). *Educational psychology: Windows on classrooms* (7th ed.). Upper Saddle River, NJ: Pearson Prentice-Hall.

Elam, S., & Rose, L. (1995). The 27th annual Phi Delta Kappa/Gallup poll of the public's attitudes toward the public schools. *Phi Delta Kappan, 77*(1), 41-56.

Elam, S., Rose, L., & Gallup, A. (1996). The 28th annual Phi Delta Kappa/Gallup poll of the public's attitudes toward the public schools. *Phi Delta Kappan, 78*(1), 41-59.

Elliott, S., Kratochwill, T., Cook, J., & Travers, J. (2000). *Educational psychology: Effective teaching, effective learning* (3rd ed.). New York: The McGraw Hill Companies, Inc.

Emmer, E., Evertson, C., & Worsham, M. (2006). *Classroom management for middle and high school teachers* (7th ed.). New York: Pearson Education, Inc.

Evertson, C. (1980, May). Effective classroom management at the beginning of the school year. *Elementary School Journal,* 219–231.

Froyen, L., & Iverson, A. (1999). *Schoolwide and classroom management.* Upper Saddle River, NJ: Prentice-Hall.

Gathercoal, F. (1993). *Judicious discipline* (3rd ed.). San Francisco: Caddo Gap.

Glasser, W. (1997, April). A new look at school failure and school success. *Phi Delta Kappan,* 596–602.

Henson, T., & Eller, B. (1999). *Educational psychology for effective teaching.* New York: Wadsworth.

Jones, F. (1987). *Positive classroom discipline.* New York: McGraw-Hill.

Jones, V., & Jones, L. (2007). *Comprehensive classroom management: Creating communities of support and solving problems.* Boston: Pearson Education.

Kher-Durlabhji, N., Lacina-Gifford, L., Jackson, L., Guillory, R., & Yandell, S. (1997, March). *Preservice teachers' knowledge of effective classroom management strategies.* Paper presented at the annual meeting of the American Educational Research Association, Chicago.

Koenig, L. (2000). *Smart discipline for the classroom: Respect and cooperation restored* (3rd ed.). Thousand Oaks, CA: Corwin Press, Inc.

Kounin, J. (1970). *Discipline and group management in classrooms.* New York: Holt, Rinehart & Winston.

Levin, J., & Nolan, J. (2007). *Principles of classroom management: A professional decision-making model.* New York: Pearson Education.

Marzano, R., & Marzano, J. (2003). The key to classroom management. *Educational Leadership, 61*(1), 6–18.

McCaslin, M., & Good, T. (1998, Summer). Moving beyond management as sheer compliance: Helping students to develop goal coordination strategies. *Educational Horizons*, 169–176.

McEwan, B. (2000). *The art of classroom management: Effective practices for building equitable learning communities.* Upper Saddle River, NJ: Prentice-Hall.

Nissman, B. (2006) *Teacher-tested classroom management strategies* (2nd ed.). Upper Saddle River, NJ: Pearson Education.

Peterson, R., & Skiba, R. (2001). Creating school climates that prevent school violence. *The Clearing House, 74*, 155–163.

Rose, L., & Gallup, A. (1998). The 30th annual Phi Delta Kappa/Gallup poll of the public's attitudes toward the public schools. *Phi Delta Kappan, 80*(1), 41–56.

Rose, L., & Gallup, A. (1999). The 31st annual Phi Delta Kappa/Gallup poll of the public's attitudes toward the public schools. *Phi Delta Kappan, 81*(1), 41–56.

Rose, L., & Gallup, A. (2000). The 32nd annual Phi Delta Kappa/Gallup poll of the public's attitudes toward the public schools. *Phi Delta Kappan, 82*(1), 41–58.

Rose L., & Gallup, A. (2003). The 35th annual Phi Delta Kappa/Gallup poll of the public's attitudes toward the public schools. *Phi Delta Kappan, 85*(1), 41–52.

Rose L., & Gallup, A. (2004). The 36th annual Phi Delta Kappa/Gallup poll of the public's attitudes toward the public schools. *Phi Delta Kappan, 86*(1), 41–52.

Rose L., & Gallup, A. (2005). The 37th annual Phi Delta Kappa/Gallup poll of the public's attitudes toward the public schools. *Phi Delta Kappan, 87*(1), 41–54.

Rose L., & Gallup, A. (2006). The 38th annual Phi Delta Kappa/Gallup poll of the public's attitudes toward the public schools. *Phi Delta Kappan, 88*(1), 41–53.

Rose, L., Gallup, A., & Elam, S. (1997). The 29th annual Phi Delta Kappa/Gallup poll of the public's attitudes toward the public schools. *Phi Delta Kappan, 79*(1), 41–56.

Shavelson, R. (1973). What is the basic teaching skill? *Journal of Teacher Education, 24*, 144–151.

Snowman, J., & Biehler, R. (2006). *Psychology applied to teaching* (11th ed.). New York: Houghton Mifflin.

Sternberg, R. (1985). *Beyond IQ: A triarchic theory of human intelligence.* New York: Cambridge University.

Sternberg, R. (1999, Spring). Ability and expertise: It's time to replace the current model of intelligence. *American Educator*, 10–13, 50–51.

Veenman, S. (1984). Perceived problems of beginning teachers. *Review of Educational Research, 54*, 143–178.

Walker, H., Ramsey, E., & Gresham, F. (2004). Heading off disruptive behavior: How early intervention can reduce defiant behavior–and win back teaching time. *American Educator*, Winter, 6, 8–21.

Wilen, W., Ishler, M., Hutchison, J., & Kindsvatter, R. (2000). *Dynamics of effective teaching* (4th ed.). New York: Addison Wesley Longman.

Wolfgang, C. (1999). *Solving discipline problems* (4th ed.). New York: John Wiley.

Wong, H., & Wong, R. (2005). *The first days of school: How to be an effective teacher.* Mountain View, CA: Harry K. Wong.

Wong. H., & Wong, R. (1991). *The first days of school: How to be an effective teacher.* Sunnyvale, CA: Harry K. Wong.

Woolfolk, A. (2007). *Educational psychology* (10th ed.). New York: Pearson Education.

York-Barr, J., Sommers, W.A., Ghere, G.S., & Montie, J. (2005). *Reflective practice to improve schools: An action guide for educators* (2nd ed.). Thousand Oaks, CA: Corwin Press.

Chapter 2

UNDERSTANDING MOTIVATION AND MOTIVATING ENVIRONMENTS

Motivation: an internal state that arouses students to action, directs them to certain behaviors, and assists them in maintaining that arousal and action with regard to behaviors important and appropriate to the learning environment.

Chapter 1 provided an overview of motivation and management as these concepts apply to students and classrooms. It was emphasized that motivation and management are closely related, along with effective teaching, in terms of their relationship to the behaviors that students exhibit in learning environments. Definitions were given for both concepts with the above definition being given for motivation. Three key elements comprise this definition. Motivation is an internal state that:

1. arouses students to action,
2. directs them to certain behaviors, and
3. assists them in maintaining that arousal and action.

Many teachers who understand the meaning of motivation, however, are still unable to motivate students or establish truly motivating environments in their classrooms. Knowing is one thing, and doing is another. The definition provided here represents an important foundation for understanding motivation as it relates to students, and a natural starting point from which to develop the ability needed to motivate students in schooling settings. Teachers have at least three important questions to answer when dealing with challenges of student motivation. First, "What can I do to arouse my students so that they will be engaged in the learning activities that I have planned and further stimulated to learn the subject matter that I am teaching?" Second, "What can I do to help my students become focused on and display the learning behaviors that I desire?" Third, "What can I do to assist my students in maintaining their arousal and action related to the learning activities of the classroom?" The Model for Reflection and Inquiry introduced in Chapter 1 can be helpful in finding answers to these needed areas of understanding.

Part of the answer to these important questions lies in the knowledge that teachers have of their students. "What interests do they bring with them to the classroom?" "What issues do they have as they enter the school each day?" "What are their lives like at their homes?" "How do they really learn best in terms of their learning styles?" "What are their aspirations?" "What have their past records of academic performance been like?" The list of questions and needed answers reflecting knowledge of students can be lengthy. However, questions such as these must be asked, and answered, if teachers hope to be able to establish high levels of student motivation in their classrooms. Beyond their knowledge of their students, it is also critical that teachers have a solid knowledge of motivation itself. "What is motivation?" "What causes it?" "How can it be established and then maintained?" Students choose to do many different things every day in many different situations and for many different reasons. In exploring the concept of motivation in the context of influencing student behavior, it is helpful to break the concept down into its component parts and systematically focus on the *motives* behind the actions that students take. Teachers need to know the reasons underlying their students displaying or not displaying certain behaviors, or becoming or not becoming involved in the learning activities of the classroom, in order to be able to motivate them.

Consider the following comments made by students regarding their learning experiences, and analyze them against what has been presented so far about the concept of motivation. Continue to think about them as important points of reference throughout the rest of the chapter.

Joey (fifth grade):   "That activity was really fun. I really didn't think that we had spent so much time on it, and it's already time to stop."

Sarah (ninth grade):	"I've tried it and tried it and just can't get it. I don't see the point in trying again."
Hannah (seventh grade):	"I thought I understood it, but I guess I didn't. I'm really not very good in that area. I don't like doing this."
Matt (second grade):	"My teacher really spent a lot of time with me today. Maybe she thinks that I can't get it on my own."
Sam (eleventh grade):	"If my friends wouldn't talk so much when I am trying to listen I would understand things better. I don't know why the teacher can't explain things more clearly."

Effective teachers not only understand what motivation is, they also know how to apply this understanding to motivate their students. Serving as a guide to their teaching, and their own personal and professional motivation, they also know what effect motivation has on student learning and behavior. Effective teachers recognize how motivation relates to successful learning for their students as well as how it relates to their own behaviors as individuals charged with the responsibility of guiding this learning. Following are six specific effects that motivation has on students in their learning (Ormrod, 2003). Having an understanding of these effects can assist teachers in establishing their own motivating classroom environments.

1. **Motivation directs behavior toward particular goals:** it helps to determine the specific goals toward which students will work and affects the choices that they make.

2. **Motivation increases effort and energy expended toward these goals:** it helps to determine the extent to which students pursue tasks enthusiastically and wholeheartedly or apathetically and reluctantly.

3. **Motivation increases initiation of, and persistence in, activities:** it helps to determine the level at which students will, on their own, initiate and stay involved in activities.

4. **Motivation enhances cognitive processing:** it influences what and how information is processed; for example, motivated students are more likely to pay attention, try to understand material, and seek help on a task when they need it.

5. **Motivation determines what consequences are reinforcing:** the more motivated students are to achieve in certain areas (e.g., academics, athletics, and social interactions), the more they value the rewards that come from their success in these areas.

6. **Motivation leads to improved performance:** as a result of the aforementioned effects, motivation generally leads to increased performance; students who are motivated to learn tend to be the highest achievers in the school.

Even with all of the studies that have been conducted over the years, myths about motivation do exist. For example, some teachers feel that failure is a good motivator. For most students this definitely is not the case. While it is popularly thought that experience can be a valuable teacher, and that all students can learn from their mistakes, a student who experiences chronic or persistent failure can become trapped in a failure cycle from which he or she may not be able to escape. Some failure can lead to more failure and more and more failure can lead to helplessness. Feeling that success simply is not possible, ultimately, may be the end result (Seligman, 1975). **Learned helplessness** is *the belief held by students that no amount of effort on their part will produce success and that events and outcomes in their lives are beyond their control.*

Learned helplessness in schooling situations occurs when students, usually those who have experienced a great deal of failure, believe that there is nothing that they can do to avoid failure. Upon failing, helpless students typically attribute their failure to their low ability, which they believe is not alterable and not within their control. The following student behaviors are often considered to suggest learned helplessness (Stipek, 2002). The student:

- says "I can't"
- doesn't pay attention to the teacher's instructions
- doesn't ask for help, even when it is needed
- does nothing (e.g., stares out the window)

- guesses or answers randomly without really trying
- doesn't show pride in successes
- appears bored, uninterested
- is unresponsive to the teacher's exhortations to try
- is easily discouraged
- doesn't volunteer answers to the teacher's questions
- maneuvers to get out of or to avoid work (e.g., has to go to the nurse's office)

Learned helplessness is a maladaptive behavior. But, teachers can have a positive impact on students in such situations. Learned helplessness is less common in classrooms where teachers focus on understanding, stimulate creative thinking, and ask students their opinions. Unfortunately, chronic failure leads to more failure unless a better pathway to success is found. Success, even in small amounts, is a more potent motivator for most students than failure, especially those with any pattern of failure in their past.

A second belief is that threats or coercion increase student motivation. Teachers threaten students with detention, retention, low grades, or calling their parents in anticipation that these actions will "get the student's attention" and that improved motivation will be the end result. While the use of such strategies from time to time may result in a short-term positive effect or change in behavior with some students, they generally are not productive in the long term.

Punishment as a motivator is considered to be a part of the later steps of the principle of least intervention. The **principle of least intervention** states that, *when dealing with routine classroom behavior, misbehaviors should be corrected with the simplest, least intrusive intervention that will work* (Slavin, 2000). The main goal in using any intervention is to successfully handle the misbehavior in a manner that avoids unnecessarily disrupting the lesson. The use of punishment, seen as a coercive strategy, is characterized by imposing a penalty with the intention of suppressing undesirable behavior. There are two procedures for achieving this purpose: (1) withholding positive reinforcers or desirable stimuli through techniques such as logical consequences and a behavior modification approach like time-out or loss of privileges, and (2) adding aversive, unpleasant stimuli through actions by which students receive a penalty for their behavior (Burden & Byrd, 2007). Withholding positive reinforcers is considered to be less harmful than adding aversive stimuli. The following factors should be considered when using punishment effectively.

1. Discuss and reward acceptable behaviors.
2. Clearly specify the behaviors that will lead to punishment.
3. Use punishment only when rewards or nonpunitive interventions have not worked, or if the behavior must be decreased quickly because it is dangerous.
4. Administer punishment in a calm, unemotional manner.
5. Deliver a warning before punishment is applied to any behavior.
6. Apply punishment fairly with everyone who exhibits the targeted behavior.
7. Use punishment of sufficient intensity to suppress the unwanted behavior.
8. Select a punishment that is effective, that is not associated with a positive or rewarding experience, and that fits the situation.
9. Avoid extended periods of punishment.

The following practices should be avoided as a part of any effort to change student behavior:

1. Harsh and humiliating reprimands
2. Threats
3. Nagging
4. Forced apologies
5. Sarcastic remarks
6. Group punishment
7. Assigning extra academic work
8. Reducing grades
9. Writing as punishment
10. Physical labor or exercise
11. Corporal punishment

The continued use of a strategy such as punishment may reveal how little some teachers actually know about their students, what interests them, what they enjoy and do not enjoy, and, basically, what motivates them. It also may reflect a lack of understanding of important knowledge about motivation itself. A student who has grown accustomed to receiving low grades, for example, generally will not be motivated by the threat of receiving more low grades. Likewise, a student who has often been made to stay after school for detention or has had his or her parents called by the teacher for misbehavior usually will not see the continuation of such actions on the part of the teacher as motivating. This point will be explored in greater detail later in this chapter.

Actions that teachers take or certain behaviors that teachers exhibit that motivate some students will not motivate others. In the language of motivation, some actions will have *potency* for some students and not for others. **Potency** is *the strength or the power of a reinforcer, reward, praise or criticism, to change behavior.* The most effective teachers are those who have learned what reinforcers work, and with what students, and who have a knowledge of each student's past history of success and failure. Using this knowledge, such teachers select those reinforcers that will have the greatest likelihood of bringing about the desired behavior change.

INTRINSIC AND EXTRINSIC MOTIVATION

In a perfect world, students are eagerly involved in all of the activities planned by the teacher simply because they find enjoyment in learning. Observation verifies, however, that there is no perfect world. And yet, some students do seem to enjoy learning very much and want to experience more and more of it. Others only seem to do what the teacher asks them to do after considering what they will receive if they complete the task or what will happen to them if they do not. These two different observations of learner motivation are often described as representing the concepts of *extrinsic* and *intrinsic* motivation. **Intrinsic motivation** is *motivation to become involved in an activity for its own sake.* **Extrinsic motivation** is *motivation to become involved in an activity as a means to an end.* Intrinsically motivated students become active in their learning because they see the task as important and/or enjoyable. They do not engage in learning activities for concrete rewards or incentives, but because they find the activities themselves rewarding and pleasurable. Extrinsically motivated students, on the other hand, become active in their learning because they understand that they will receive something of value in return if they do what the teacher desires or something that they dislike if they do not. They represent a large part of the student population that wants to know "what's in it for me" when deciding whether to be involved in or not be involved in or complete or not complete a particular learning task. This "what's in it for me" outlook toward life seems to represent a large part of the societal population as well.

Many activities or tasks that characterize school environments are not intrinsically motivating to students, and many students do not find them naturally enjoyable, personally rewarding, or even see the point in them (Brophy, 1983). As a response to this, many teachers approach their challenges of student motivation by relying on extrinsic incentives such as praise, tokens, prizes, and special recognitions (e.g., Student of the Month) to get students to do what they want them to do (Alderman, 2004). Students, in many cases, become accustomed to this reward-giving approach to learning and conditioned to receive rewards as a natural part of the schooling process. They make the association that completing schoolwork on their part produces the giving of rewards on the part of their teachers. Once this cycle begins, and students, in effect, learn to anticipate some type of reward for the completion of their assignments, it becomes a difficult pattern of behavior to break.

It is unrealistic for a teacher to expect to routinely produce what might be considered as ideal motivation in the classroom with each and every lesson taught (Brophy, 1998). Intrinsic motivation does exist, but teachers cannot count on students being intrinsically motivated on every task that they present before them. Working to produce a state of *motivation to learn* is a more realistic and reachable goal. Motivation to learn differs from extrinsic or reinforcement-oriented motivation and intrinsic or pleasure-oriented motivation. **Motivation to learn** is *motivation represented by the quality of a student's cognitive engagement in a learning task or activity.* It is seen as a realistic goal for teachers to develop and then to sustain their students' motivation to learn from academic activities. This will be based, in part, on students finding the academic activities meaningful and worthwhile, along with their ability to be successful with them, and to value the benefits derived from them. The following table provides a comparison of how different factors contribute to motivation to learn (Woolfolk, 2007, p. 395). Motivation to learn is enhanced when the sources of motivation are intrinsic and the goals are personally challenging, the student is focused on the task and has a mastery orientation, attributes successes and failure to controllable causes, and believes ability can be improved.

Contributing Factors to Motivation to Learn

Source of Motivation	Characteristics that Enhance Motivation to Learn	Characteristics that Diminish Motivation to Learn
Type of Goal Set	Intrinsic: Personal factors such as needs, interests, curiosity, enjoyment	Extrinsic: Environmental factors such as rewards, social pressures, punishment
	Learning Goal: Personal satisfaction in meeting challenges and improving; tendency to choose moderately difficult and challenging goals	Performance Goal: Desire for approval of performance in others' eyes; tendency to choose very easy or very difficult goals
Type of Involvement	Task-Involved: Concerned with mastering the task	Ego-Involved: Concerned with self in others' eyes
Achievement Motivation	Motivation to Achieve: Mastery orientation	Motivation to Avoid Failure: Prone to anxiety
Likely Attributions	Successes and failures attributed to controllable effort and ability	Successes and failures attributed to uncontrollable causes
Beliefs About Ability	Incremental View: Belief that ability can be improved through hard work and added knowledge and skills	Entity View: Belief that ability is a stable, uncontrollable trait

A fundamental question for teachers to ask in studying student motivation in the classroom is, "What will arouse students to action, direct them to engage in or exhibit certain behaviors, and assist them in maintaining this arousal and direction?" Motivational theories that address this question can be categorized much like theories of learning: *behaviorist, cognitive,* or *humanist* (Lefrancois, 2000). An understanding of these theories of motivation is beneficial in answering this question. Figure 2.1 provides an overview of how motivation is defined in each theory.

Theories of Motivation

Theory	Definition of Motivation
Behaviorism	Motivation is the result of responses to reinforcement. The effective use of reinforcers, either present internally within the student or externally as influenced by the teacher, is critical to behaviorist approaches to motivation.
Cognitive Theories	Motivation results from students attempting to find order or balance, predictability, and an understanding of the world. Students have a natural motivation to understand their world and bring into balance irregularities that they may experience. These are needs that students have and they are motivated to satisfy them.
Humanism	Motivation results from students attempting to fulfill their full potential as human beings. Individuals have an innate tendency to develop their talents and to grow and enhance themselves. There is no such thing as an unmotivated student.

Figure 2.1. Synopsis of theories of motivation.

BEHAVIORISM AND MOTIVATION

The behaviorist theory of learning emphasizes observable behavior changes that take place as a result of experience. The behaviorist perspective emphasizes external rewards and punishments or consequences as keys in determining a student's motivation (Santrock, 2008). Behaviorism does not focus on what necessarily may have changed in the learner's mind, but on that which can be seen. This view of learning, especially as it relates to motivation, raises a number of interesting and debatable points.

Behaviorism is popularly associated with the giving of reinforcement or the use of reinforcers. A **reinforcer** is *something given or a consequence that adds to the frequency or influences the length of a behavior.* An important question to be answered in the behaviorist theory of motivation would be, "What are the best reinforcers, and when should they be used?" The answer to this question, dealing with the use of reinforcers, is actually quite complex and not without some controversy and criticism (Harter & Jackson, 1992; Kohn, 1992). In spite of this, the giving of reinforcers (e.g., popcorn, soft drinks, watching favorite videos, free time, teacher praise, grades, class positions and responsibilities, etc.), is common in schools today, especially in elementary classrooms.

The concept of punishment was introduced earlier in this chapter as an example of a coercive strategy to modify student behavior and increase motivation. Positive and negative reinforcers are consequences that increase behavior. Some consequences, called punishers, weaken behaviors or decrease the likelihood of them recurring. **Punishment** is *the process of using punishers to decrease behavior.* Punishment frequently is a part of the teacher's discipline process and overall management program. When punishers are used as reinforcers to extinguish a behavior, the teacher must be mindful of both the short term and long term impact of their use. Punishers such as **desists**, *the use of verbal or nonverbal communications of teachers for the purpose of stopping student misconduct or misbehavior* (Kounin, 1970), time out, and detention are commonly used by teachers and can be effective in modifying student behavior. Punishers in the form of physical punishment, embarrassment and humiliation, or the completion of additional class work with the intent of changing student behavior, as noted earlier, are not considered effective and should be avoided.

Teaching activities are some of the most common reinforcers that teachers have available. A helpful guide for choosing the most effective reinforcers is the Premack principle (Santrock, 2008). The **Premack principle**, named after psychologist David Premack, is the *principle that a high-probability or desired activity or behavior can serve as a reinforcer for a low-probability or perhaps less desired activity or behavior.* For example, the Premack principle is being applied when the teacher tells a student, "When you complete your writing assignment, you can play a game on the computer." This approach to motivating students is only effective, however, if playing games on a computer (the high-probability activity) is more desirable for the student than writing (the low-probability activity). The Premack principle can also be used with the entire class. The teacher, for example, might tell the class, "If everyone in the class gets their homework done by Friday, we will take a field trip next week." For the Premack principle to be effective, the low-frequency (less preferred) behavior must happen first. Just as with praise, by making privileges and rewards directly contingent on learning and positive behavior, the teacher can significantly increase both learning and desired behavior. The use of reinforcers, however, has been found to be less effective for middle or high school students and underachieving students in general.

Some reinforcers, as suggested earlier, are more potent or have greater impact than others. A reinforcer that may have potency for one student in one situation may not have such potency for another student, in even a similar or comparable situation. Too, a reinforcer that may be potent for a student at one point may be less potent or not potent at all for the same student at a later point. This could be brought about by inappropriate or overuse of the reinforcer. In spite of their popular use, the following criticisms have been identified with respect to the use of reinforcers.

1. **The use of reinforcers may decrease intrinsic motivation.** Offering reinforcers for engaging in intrinsically motivating tasks can decrease student interest in such tasks. The problem with reinforcers can involve how a behavior is rewarded. Rewarding students for simply completing tasks, rather than for making progress in learning, may ultimately detract from motivation.
2. **The use of reinforcers can narrow the student's focus.** In some cases, reinforcers themselves can become the goals of learning rather than academic content or the beauty of or interest in learning itself. As opposed to adding to the breadth of the learning experience, reinforcers can have the impact of narrowing that experience. The reinforcer can become the reason for the student's motivation to learn, i.e., just so the reward can be received. In such a case, the student would be learning for the reward, not because of it.
3. **The use of reinforcers often creates logistical problems.** Using reinforcers demands time, energy and sometimes even money; additionally, rewards given to some students may cause resentment in other students who do not receive them. This can bring about an inconsistent use of rewards by the teacher with the end result actually being a lower level of student motivation.
4. **The use of rewards ignores student cognitions.** The use of behaviorism as an approach to motivate students is often criticized from the view that it focuses on the application of reinforcers (rewards) and ignores learners' perceptions and beliefs about themselves and about learning. As an example, praise is a common reinforcer and its use seems easily understood. This is far from the case as the use of praise can be misunderstood. Older students may see praise as reward for effort as opposed to an

accomplishment. Such students may interpret praise for performance on easy tasks as a statement that the teacher sees them as having low ability. While intended as a reinforcer, the praise really may be perceived negatively.

As discussed, behaviorist approaches to motivation emphasize extrinsic reinforcers (e.g., reward and praise). These reinforcers are either primary or secondary in nature and both can be used to strengthen or influence behavior. Examples of **primary reinforcers** are *food, water, and safety that meet basic physiological needs.* Examples of **secondary reinforcers** are *praise, grades, and money that may address a student's psychological needs.* The behaviorist theory of motivation rests on the belief that students are motivated through the desire to receive something for their actions. Interestingly enough, this can include love of learning (Henson & Eller, 1999).

COGNITIVE THEORIES OF MOTIVATION

Cognitive theories of motivation are grounded in the belief that individual behavior is influenced by the way people see themselves and their environment (Snowman & Biehler, 2006). According to the cognitive perspective, students' thoughts guide their motivation (Santrock, 2008). Students have a need for order and predictability and an understanding of things around them. When order and understanding are present, they seek to maintain it. When order and understanding are lost, they seek to regain it. Order and understanding represent an important balance for students and, therefore, predictability. Children are naturally motivated to learn when they encounter experiences that are inconsistent with their current understandings (Greeno, Collins, & Resnick, 1996). They seek to establish or perhaps re-establish this consistency when it is absent. They also are naturally motivated to learn when they encounter information that is not yet found in their already-held definitions and ideas of the world. When this type of situation occurs, they seek to acquire an understanding of this information and incorporate it into their individual ways of seeing the world.

The work of Piaget (1952) is applicable to the discussion of motivation and a student's need for order and understanding. Although well known in the study of learning processes, Piaget's concept of equilibrium is important here in that it represents a need that all individuals possess. **Equilibrium** is defined as *a state of balance.* When students experience **disequilibrium**, or *a state of being out-of-balance*, they seek to regain their balance. *The process of searching for order or balance and, in so doing, testing one's understanding against the real world* is referred to as **equilibration**. Certain amounts of disequilibrium actually are felt to be desirable and teachers can carefully create situations of disequilibrium and use them to their teaching advantage to motivate their students. As students encounter out-of-balance situations they are motivated to regain their balance and they grow in their learning through this process as they strive to re-establish a state of equilibrium. Extreme disequilibrium, however, can be counter-productive creating too much frustration and anxiety. When learning activities or teacher actions create out-of-balance situations that are too severe, students may perceive that no amount of effort on their part can bring about a return to balance. Success cannot be achieved. A result of this perception can be the student pulling away from or displaying misconduct toward the learning task, the teacher, or both.

Most teachers have seen students who appear quite motivated as well as those who seem virtually impossible to motivate. A close observation of these two types of students reveals many things. One thing that careful observation can show is how differently the two types of students may really view themselves. Cognitive theories of motivation consider beliefs and expectations as two important personal factors, in particular, the role of expectations in the *expectation X value theory* of motivation (Atkinson, 1964; Feather, 1982). The **expectation X value theory** is the *theory of motivation that suggests that students are motivated to engage in learning tasks to the extent that they expect to succeed on the tasks and the degree to which they value achievement on the tasks or other potential outcomes that may come as a result of task achievement.* The theory takes into account both the behaviorist's concern with the effects or outcomes of behavior and the cognitivist's interest in the impact of individual thinking.

More contemporary motivation theorists have based their research on the early theoretical expectancy X value model developed by Atkinson. Atkinson (1964) identified incentive values in terms of the pride or shame a task was expected to generate. This has been viewed as a narrow conceptualization of values, especially considering that levels of pride and shame are determined, in theory, by an individual's perception of the probability of success or failure (Stipek, 2002). More recent theorists have suggested broader conceptualizations of the value component of expectancy X value theory, i.e., attainment value, utility value and intrinsic value, which are felt to have greater application to classroom practice and student achievement (Eccles, Adler, Futterman, Goff, Kaczala, Meece, & Midgley, 1983).

1. **Attainment value:** Attainment value is determined by how the task or the domain fulfills a person's needs; it concerns the relevance of an activity to a person's actual or ideal self concept. People engage in activities and develop competencies that are consistent with their real and desired concept of themselves.
2. **Utility value:** Utility value focuses on the usefulness of a task as a means to achieve goals that might not be related to the task itself. For example, understanding chemistry and biology would have considerable utility value for students planning to attend medical school.
3. **Intrinsic value:** Intrinsic value is the immediate enjoyment one gets from doing a task. When a task has intrinsic value it is engaged in for its own sake, rather than for some other purpose.

The challenge to the teacher in applying the expectation X value theory is twofold. The teacher must create legitimate learning experiences where students can find success, and the success that they achieve must be on activities that they see as being of value. If students do not necessarily see a task as being of value, it is important that they see value in other outcomes that are associated with successful task attainment. The expectation X value theory of motivation creates a new way of looking at motivation for some teachers in that many believe that student success is the overriding key factor in motivation. In the expectation X value theory, success is necessary but not sufficient in establishing motivation in students. Success, coupled with seeing the value in what is attained, or at least in some other outcome that will be forthcoming, are key to student motivation. Being successful at a task that holds little value will have limited positive motivational impact, at least in the long run.

Self-efficacy

When students are successful on tasks that they value, they develop higher *self-efficacy* (Schunk, 1994). **Self-efficacy** is *one's beliefs about the capability of succeeding on specific tasks.* Students who have high self-efficacy believe in their abilities and see themselves as capable of making genuine progress toward worthwhile goals. Such students are able to sustain their work effort longer as they anticipate that they will be successful at the end of the task. Students who have low self-efficacy see themselves as having limited ability and as likely not being successful when engaging in learning activities. Students with high self-efficacy try hard while holding on to the belief that they can succeed; students with low self-efficacy hardly try. Figure 2.2 provides an analysis of some of the characteristics of students with high and low self-efficacy.

Characteristics of High and Low Self-efficacy Students

Characteristics	High Self-efficacy	Low Self-efficacy
Task Orientation	Accepts challenging tasks	Avoids challenging tasks
Effort	Expends high effort when faced with challenging tasks	Expends low effort when faced with challenging tasks
Persistence	Persists when goals are not initially reached	Gives up when goals are not initially reached
Beliefs	Believes that success will be forthcoming	Focuses on feelings of incompetence
	Controls stress and anxiety when goals are not met	Experiences anxiety and depression when goals are not met
	Believes they are in control of their environment	Believes they are not in control of their environment
Strategy use	Discards unproductive strategies	Continues the use of unproductive strategies
Performance	Performs better than low-efficacy students of equal ability	Performs more poorly than high-efficacy students of equal ability

Figure 2.2. Analysis of students with high and low self-efficacy adapted from Bandura (1993); Schunk (1994); Eggen & Kauchak (2007).

An understanding of self-efficacy is important to an understanding of the potential for the motivation of any student. It is also important to an understanding of the motivational state that a student might be in as related to any given learning task. While having an understanding of self-efficacy is important, being able to recognize a particular student's level of self-efficacy is more important. What is of even greater value is being able to influence students with low self-efficacy to increase their self-efficacy and to influence students with high self-efficacy to either maintain or increase their self-efficacy. The teacher's role is twofold. First, the teacher must diagnose or otherwise gain an understanding of his or her students as to their levels of self-efficacy. Second, the teacher must take appropriate action with this knowledge to motivate his or her students in their learning and, in so doing, increase their levels of self-efficacy. Many struggling students resist academic activities, believing that they lack the ability to succeed, even if they expend great effort (Margolis & McCabe, 2004). A key to reversing this perspective, that is, getting struggling students with low-self efficacy to expend sufficient effort to persist on tasks, to work to overcome difficulties, to take on increasingly challenging tasks, and to develop interest in academics, is for teachers to systematically stress the development of high self-efficacy. Research suggests that teachers can often strengthen struggling learners' self-efficacy by linking new work to recent successes, teaching needed learning strategies, reinforcing effort and persistence, stressing peer modeling, teaching struggling learners to make facilitative attributions, and helping them identify or create personally important goals. Factors identified that influence students' beliefs about their ability to perform include the following (Bandura, 1986).

1. **Past performance:** how a student has done in the past on a particular task influences how he or she will do on a similar task in the future.
2. **Modeling:** being able to see someone else perform a particular task successfully influences the observer to do the same.
3. **Verbal persuasion:** verbal encouragement offers a tangible way for the teacher to communicate to the student the belief that he or she can be successful.
4. **Psychological state:** the teacher must be able to recognize and, if possible, positively influence the student's psychological state; a student who is anxious, tired, fearful, or hungry will experience a lowered level of self-efficacy.

Research on students, in particular at-risk students, has increasingly focused on the concept of resilience. **Resilience** is *the ability to recover quickly from some type of misfortune or adversity; resilience results in a heightened likelihood of success in school and in other aspects of life, despite environmental adversities* (Wang, Haertel, & Walberg, 1995). Students with low self-efficacy are not characterized by having resilience. Students with high self-efficacy, on the other hand, are often considered to be resilient individuals who have developed characteristics and coping skills that help them rise above adverse circumstances. Once students have developed a high sense of self-efficacy, failure on an occasional basis is unlikely to dampen their optimism for the future. When these students encounter small setbacks on the way to achieving success, they learn that sustained effort and perseverance are key ingredients of that success and they persevere. Bandura (1989) identifies that such students have developed resilient self-efficacy. **Resilient self-efficacy** is *the belief that one can perform a task successfully even after experiencing setbacks with the recognition that effort and perseverance are essential for success.*

Just as teachers and schools can have a positive impact on the development of self-efficacy, so too can they have a positive impact on the promotion of resilience. Research has identified the following four school practices that promote resilience (Eggen & Kauchak, 2007, p. 122).

1. **High and Uncompromising Academic Standards:** teachers emphasize mastery of content and do not accept passive attendance and mere completion of assignments.
2. **Strong Personal Bonds:** teachers become the adults who refuse to let students fail, and students feel connected to the schools.
3. **Order and High Structure:** the school and classes are orderly and highly structured; teachers emphasize reasons for rules and consistently enforce rules and procedures.
4. **Participation in After-School Activities:** activities such a clubs and athletics give students additional chances to interact with caring adults and receive reinforcement for achievement.

Regarding teachers themselves, teachers who talk more frequently with students, learn about their families, share their own lives, maintain high expectations, use interactive teaching strategies, and emphasize success and mastery of content, promote student resilience. Such teachers motivate students through personal contacts, instructional support, and attempts to link school to their students' lives. Teachers who are less effective in promoting resilience are more authoritarian and less accessible, distance themselves from their students, and place primary responsibility for learning on them. Lecture is a common teaching strategy and motivation is seen as the students' responsibility. Students often see these teachers as adversaries, to be avoided if possible. Like being an effective teacher in general, promoting resilience lies in the teacher's attitude and commitment to students (Doll, Zucker, & Brehm, 2004; Gschwend & Dembo, 2001).

HUMANISTIC VIEWS OF MOTIVATION

As with the cognitive theories, the intrinsic motivation of students is also important to humanistic views of motivation. Humanists see motivation as an attempt to fulfill the total potential of a human being (Hamachek, 1987). The humanistic perspective stresses students' capacity for personal growth, freedom to choose their destiny, and positive qualities such as being sensitive to others (Santrock, 2008). The humanistic theory of motivation represents a reaction contrary to the belief that reduces human behavior to either a response to the environment or to internal instincts. The humanist view of motivation looks at the entire physical, emotional, interpersonal, and intellectual qualities of an individual as they impact on what that person chooses to do. According to the humanist, there is no such thing as an unmotivated student. All students are motivated. Some students, however, simply may be motivated to do things other than that which the teacher desires for them to do.

The now-classic Hierarchy of Needs theory of Abraham Maslow (1970), called the father of the humanistic movement, is frequently discussed when exploring the question of student motivation as influenced by need. Maslow identified student needs as being in one of two categories: *deficiency needs* and *growth needs*. **Deficiency needs** are *needs at the lower levels of the hierarchy including survival, safety, belonging, and self-esteem.* They are needs that must be fulfilled or met for the student to move to the upper or higher levels. **Growth needs** are *needs at the higher levels of the hierarchy including intellectual achievement, aesthetic* *appreciation*, and *self-actualization*. These needs are never fully satisfied. Growth needs expand and evolve as individuals have experience with them; efforts to satisfy growth needs lead to further development within them. Individuals who are intellectually stimulated, for example, will seek additional intellectual stimulation. Individuals who engage in the pursuit of beauty, through art, music, etc., will seek to continue in this pursuit. Maslow's highest level of the hierarchy is *self-actualization*. **Self-actualization** is identified as *the full development or use of one's potential.* Achieving self-actualization represents an ongoing evolution and is never fully reached.

Applications of Maslow's hierarchy to the work of the classroom teacher are obvious. Students who are hungry and tired will not learn and develop to their fullest potentials as long as these conditions are present. Too, students who do not feel safe and accepted in the learning environment will not be able to reach their fullest potentials in their learning until they do feel safe and accepted. Students who have low self-esteem will not move forward at an optimum rate in terms of either their intellectual achievement or their full understanding of themselves until their self-esteem is strengthened. Figure 2.3 offers a representation of Maslow's hierarchy.

GROWTH NEEDS	**Self-Actualization:** meets and uses one's full potential
	Aesthetic: goodness, beauty, truth, justice, order
	Intellectual (cognitive) achievement: knowledge, understanding, symmetry
DEFICIENCY NEEDS	**Self-esteem:** recognition, respect, approval, feeling of adequacy
	Belongingness and Love: affection, acceptance from family and peers
	Safety: security, absence of physical and emotional threat, psychological safety
	Physiological: food, sleep, drink, shelter, warmth

Figure 2.3. Maslow's Hierarchy of Needs.

While the idea of ordering human needs in a hierarchy may be appealing, not everyone agrees with Maslow's ordering of human motives. As an example, for some students, cognitive needs might be more fundamental than esteem needs. Others might meet their cognitive needs while not having experienced acceptance and belonging. Though thought-provoking, such a hierarchy may not be absolute. An analysis or the appeal of the concept of the hierarchy notwithstanding, the challenge of identifying where any particular student is at any given point in time on the hierarchy would be quite complex.

FACTORS THAT AFFECT STUDENT MOTIVATION

Having a sound theoretical base in understanding the concept of motivation is critical for teachers to be able to motivate students in classroom learning environments. Additional considerations also are important. Factors such as *attribution, locus of control, teacher expectations, goals (performance and learning), anxiety,* and *environment* all affect the teacher's ultimate understanding of, and ability to establish, high levels of student motivation.

Attribution

Attribution is *a cognitive theory that represents a student's view of the causes of outcomes or an event and how this view influences his or her future expectations and behavior* (Alderman, 2004). In looking at why he or she was or was not successful, the student may pose the question, "To what may I attribute my success or failure?" The answer that the student gives to this question has significant bearing on how the student approaches, or may choose to not approach, a learning task. It is suggested that there are two primary reasons that people use to explain their performance: *can* and *try* (Heider, 1958). *Can* speaks to whether a person has the ability to do a task and *try* speaks to how much effort a person puts forth. If a student fails at a task, the student's expectations for future success will differ depending on whether the student attributes the failure to a lack of effort (*try*) or to not having the ability (*can*) to succeed on the task.

One of four reasons is generally given by students as the cause of success or failure in school settings (Weiner, 1990, 1992, 1994a, 1994b):

1. **Ability:** the student might say, "I was successful because I am just good at that," or the student might say, "I was not successful because I just don't have enough ability to be successful."
2. **Effort:** the student might say, "I was successful because I really tried hard," or the student might say, "I know that I could have been successful if I had tried harder and put more time into it."
3. **Task Difficulty:** the student might say, "I was successful because the assignment was really easy," or the student might say, "I was not successful because what the teacher wanted was just too hard."
4. **Luck:** the student might say, "I don't know why I was successful. It must have just been my good luck," or the student might say, "I don't know why I couldn't get it right. It just must not have been my lucky day."

Ability and effort have been found to be the most frequent reasons given by students for their success or failure in schooling settings.

The causes of success or failure have also been classified into three different dimensions:

1. internal versus external,
2. stable versus unstable, and
3. controllable versus uncontrollable.

The internal versus external and controllable versus uncontrollable dimensions, in particular, are especially important to teachers as they explore ways to motivate their students. Teachers need to be able to identify how students see themselves and how they perceive the reasons for their success or lack of success. Knowing this will enable teachers to address the learning needs of their students more completely and, in so doing, better motivate them. The following analysis of the characteristics of attributions offers further perspective on the impact of attributions on student motivation and possible teacher behavior (Eggen & Kauchak, 2007, p. 317).

Though many teachers do not realize it, most students frequently do think about or try to understand and explain the reasons for their failures. When students who are usually successful are unsuccessful, they typically identify internal and controllable reasons (attributions) for their lack of success. Such students may recognize that they did not

Characteristics of Attributions and Dimensions of Motivation

Attribution	Locus (locus of cause)	Stability (of cause)	Control (of learning situations)
Ability	Inside the learner	Stable (cannot change)	Learner out of control
Effort	Inside the learner	Unstable (can change)	Learner in control
Luck	Outside the learner	Unstable (can change)	Learner out of control
Task difficulty	Outside the learner	Stable (cannot change)	Learner out of control

study hard enough or did not understand a particular assignment and had not prepared correctly for what was expected of them. They generally attribute the reason for their lack of success to controllable causes and, because of this, believe that they will be successful the next time they attempt the task. Students who perceive themselves as having sufficient ability and being in control of the situation usually do not pose major motivational problems for teachers.

Students with a history of repeated failure, however, and who attribute their learning difficulties or lack of success on learning tasks to uncontrollable, external forces, generally represent the teacher's greater motivational challenges. These students usually attribute their failure to conditions out of their control. They tend to perceive themselves as helpless, can be depressed and/or anxious about their learning and doubtful of their abilities. They characterize themselves, overall, as more unsuccessful than successful and concentrate more on their own inadequacies. Lack of future effort is a common reaction to failure for such students as they believe that their situation is not likely to change. It is not in their control. They also are less likely to seek help because they do not believe that they can be helped (Ames & Lau, 1982). When students attribute the learning outcomes that they are experiencing to controllable causes, their motivation to learn remains encouraged, regardless of whether they have histories of failure or success. When they attribute the outcomes or results to uncontrollable causes, their motivation to learn tends to lessen (Woolfolk, 2007). Students of this latter type often see themselves as inadequate in learning situations and can represent major problems for teachers.

In addition to student motivation, the study of attribution theory has also provided important observations regarding culture, ethnicity and gender (Alderman, 2004). The following recommendations are of special importance with respect to implications for teachers in these areas:

1. Listen carefully to student expectations and attributions for performance to identify patterns of attributions that might be gender-related or culture-related.
2. Examine your own beliefs about competence for subjects like math and science that have been traditionally gender-typed. If you are an elementary school teacher, do you think of yourself as a math teacher? As a science teacher?
3. Provide feedback that helps both male and female students alike make more realistic estimates of their ability.
4. Become familiar with cultural values for ability and effort. What is the relative value placed on effort and ability?
5. Be prepared to discuss attributional beliefs and their implications with parents.
6. Be especially sensitive to giving feedback that might be seen by students as sympathy and thus be interpreted as their having low ability.

Locus of Control

Locus of control refers to *the degree to which students perceive that both positive and negative events that impact their lives are under their control* (Bernhard & Siegel, 1994). Locus of control, i.e., place of control, is an important aspect of attribution theory and the reasons for or causes of student motivation described earlier. Some students have an **internal locus of control** which is indicated *when students feel that they are responsible for what happens to them.* Others have more of an **external locus of control** which is indicated *when students feel that forces external to or outside themselves control their lives.* Students who hold the view that success comes as a result of skill and not luck or chance believe that they have control over their own destinies. Students who hold the view that success comes as a result of luck or chance and not skill believe that they have little control over their destinies. How students see themselves, as successful or unsuccessful learners, has bearing on whether they, in fact, will be successful or unsuccessful. Knowing how students see themselves will help their teachers be more successful in motivating them to higher levels.

A great deal of research has been done on the concept of locus of control, in particular as it affects students and their learning as well as teachers' attitudes toward students. Some of the findings in this area are relevant to the work that teachers do in motivating their students and are included in Figure 2.4.

Locus of Control and Student Motivation

1. Teachers often look upon students who have an external locus of control more negatively than those who have an internal locus of control; interestingly, students who have an external locus of control frequently look upon their teachers more negatively than do students who have an internal locus of control.
2. Students who have an external locus of control perform better when they receive specific comments with respect to their teachers' expectations.
3. Students with an internal locus of control are more effective than those with an external locus of control in recognizing and using available information.
4. Students with an external locus of control are less successful in competitive situations than are students with an internal locus of control.

Figure 2.4. Locus of control and motivation (from Dacey, 1989).

A student's view regarding what causes him or her to be successful or not successful influences the student's motivation in different situations. If students believe that they are responsible for their own successes, they are referred to as *internals*. If they believe that something or somebody other than themselves is responsible, they are referred to as *externals*. External students often have higher levels of anxiety than internal students as they see themselves as having less power over their surroundings (in this case their classroom and their learning) and what happens to them. Internal students generally have more confidence in themselves, are greater risk-takers, are more curious, and anticipate success rather than failure when they enter into learning activities.

Locus of control, however, can change. When teachers assist their students in gaining greater levels of confidence with respect to their abilities and potentials, the students' sense of having more internal control increases. Their anxiety in learning situations decreases and their performance improves. As students become older and more mature, and as they experience more successes in their learning, their beliefs about the causes of these successes becomes more internal

(Wigfield, 1994). Teachers can enhance this change through the appropriate use of learning activities (e.g., active learning and cooperative learning are much preferred over passive learning and individual and isolated learning), rewards, and approaches to instruction that ensure that students are able to achieve higher levels of success.

Teacher Expectations

Students at times may not be certain as to what teachers expect of them in the completion of particular learning tasks. However, they frequently do understand, or at least think they understand, what their teachers' views are of them in terms of their ability to be successful in completing these tasks. Two concepts important to this dynamic are *teacher expectation* and *teacher efficacy*. **Teacher expectation** refers to *what teachers expect or think students will be able to accomplish.* **Teacher efficacy** refers to *the teacher's belief in his or her ability to be successful in getting students to learn.* Teacher expectations and teacher efficacy are closely related. When teachers have high expectations for their students' learning potentials, they have a greater belief that they will be able to be successful with them. When they have low expectations of their students' abilities, they have greater doubt (lower teacher efficacy) that they can be successful with them. Students themselves have their own views of how their teachers see them as being successful or not successful. This student view has an important relationship to the level of motivation that the student exhibits.

Table 2.1 provides an analysis of attitudes of teachers with high and low efficacy (Alderman, 2004, p. 190). It can be helpful in assisting teachers in preparation for their work in the classroom, in working with students, and in eventual self-reflection after lessons have concluded.

Teacher expectations influence how teachers treat students, tend to perpetuate themselves, and affect student's self-concepts (Ormrod, 2003). Teachers generally treat students in ways consistent with the expectations that they hold for them. This point can become a serious concern when teachers predict or hold the view that certain students are destined to have problems or even fail to learn altogether. When teachers expect students to achieve at higher levels, they typically do. Conversely, when they expect them to not achieve at higher levels, they typically do not (Rosenthal & Jacobson, 1968). This has been

Attitudes of Teachers with High and Low Efficacy

Teacher Attitude	High Efficacy	Low Efficacy
A sense of personal accomplishment	Feel their work with students is important and meaningful, and that they have a positive impact on student learning	Feel frustrated and discouraged about teaching
Positive expectations for student behavior achievement	Expect students to progress and for the most part find that students fulfill their expectations	Expect students to fail, react negatively to their teaching efforts, and to misbehave
Personal responsibility for student learning	Believe it's their responsibility to see their students learn and when students experience failure, look to their own performance for ways they might be more helpful	Place responsibility for learning on students and when students fail, look for explanations in terms of family background, motivation, or attitude
Strategies for achieving objectives	Plan for student learning, set goals for themselves and their students, and identify strategies to achieve them	Lack specific goals for their students, uncertain about what they want their students to achieve, and do not plan strategies according to goals
Positive affect	Feel good about teaching, themselves, and their students	Frustrated with teaching and often express discouragement and negative feelings about their work with students
Sense of control	Confident they can influence student learning	Experience a sense of futility in working with students
Sense of common teacher-student goals	Feel they are involved in a joint venture with students to achieve goals they have in common	Feel they are pitted in a struggle with students with goals and strategies in opposition to theirs
Democratic decision-making	Involve students in decision-making regarding goals and strategies for achieving them	Impose decisions regarding goals and learning strategies on students without involving them in the process

referred to as the **self-fulfilling prophecy** or the *phenomenon that a student's performance is greatly influenced when a teacher holds certain beliefs about the student's ability to perform.* When teachers anticipate or prophesy a higher level of student performance, they will generally get it. When they predict a lower level of student performance, this is also what is usually found. As a correlate to this, a student's level of motivation responds to or is influenced by what the student perceives as being the prophecy held by the teacher. A student's behavior in both motivation and learning responds to what the student perceives as being the belief held by his or her teacher. The following behaviors may indicate differential teacher treatment of high and low achieving students (Good & Brophy, 2003, p. 77).

1. Waiting less time for lows to answer a question (before giving the answer or calling on someone else).
2. Giving lows answers or calling on someone else rather than trying to improve their responses by giving clues or repeating or rephrasing questions.
3. Inappropriate reinforcement: rewarding inappropriate behavior or incorrect answers by lows.
4. Criticizing lows more often for failure.
5. Praising lows less often for success.
6. Failing to give feedback in the public response of lows.
7. Generally paying less attention to lows or interacting with them less frequently.
8. Calling on lows less often to respond to questions, or asking them only easier, non-analytic questions.
9. Seating lows farther away from the teacher.
10. Demanding less from lows (e.g., teach less, gratuitous praise, excessive offers of help).
11. Interacting with lows more privately than publicly, and monitoring and structuring their activities more closely.
12. Differential administration or grading of tests or assignments, in which highs but not lows are given the benefit of the doubt in borderline cases.
13. Less friendly interactions with lows, including less smiling and fewer other nonverbal indicators of support.
14. Briefer and less informative feedback to questions of lows.
15. Less eye contact and other nonverbal communication of attention and responsiveness (forward lean, positive head nodding) in interaction with lows.

16. Less use of effective but time-consuming instructional methods with lows when time is limited.
17. Less acceptance and use of lows' ideas.
18. Exposing lows to an impoverished curriculum (overly limited and repetitive content, emphasis on factual recitation rather than on lesson-extending discussion, emphasis on drill and practice tasks rather than application and higher-level thinking tasks).

The relationship between expectation and performance is now a part of the supporting argument on a national scale (e.g., No Child Left Behind legislation) that teachers should have overall higher expectations for their students. When teachers expect more, they typically will receive more. As with the population as a whole, teachers are likely to maintain their expectations about their students once they are developed. This can be positive or negative for the student depending on how he or she is viewed by the teacher. Positive views more normally result in higher levels of performance while negative views more often result in lower levels of performance. Some teachers, for example, underestimate the capabilities of students from minority and low-income backgrounds and maintain these expectations (Garcia, 1994; Knapp & Woolverton, 1995). This outlook can be devastating in terms of the impact on the achievement levels of such students. Again, when teachers expect less, they get less.

A key part of these perspectives on understanding that also must be acknowledged is how students view themselves as influenced by how they perceive their teachers view them. If students identify that their teachers see them as capable of only low achievement, they too often will perceive themselves of being capable only of low achievement. And, their individual self-concepts will respond in a like manner. In the end, the level of motivation of such students is frequently lower as it has been negatively influenced by what their teachers believe about and expect of them. On the other hand, if students feel as though their teachers have confidence in them as learners, and that they can succeed on the learning tasks that are assigned, this influences the students to be better motivated and to persevere on tasks. In turn, this has a positive influence on their achievement. The following six-step process describes the effect of the self-fulfilling prophecy (Good & Brophy, 2003).

1. Early in the year, the teacher forms differential expectations for student behavior and achievement.
2. Consistent with these differential expectations, the teacher behaves differently toward different students.
3. This treatment tells students something about how they are expected to behave in the classroom and perform on academic tasks.
4. If the teacher's treatment is consistent over time, and if students do not actively resist or change it, it will likely affect their self-concepts, achievement, motivation, levels of aspiration, classroom conduct, and interactions with the teacher.
5. These effects generally will complement and reinforce the teacher's expectations, so that students will come to conform to these expectations more than they might have otherwise.
6. Ultimately, this will affect student achievement and other outcome measures. High-expectation students will be led to achieve at or near their potential, but low-expectation students will not gain as much as they could have gained if taught differently.

Each child is different. And though all teachers know this, they often overlook the differences and focus on the similarities. While young people may share a common blood type or ethnic background, speak a common language or share a particular religious upbringing, despite these similarities, each human being is unique. Both teachers and students, at times, can feel isolated. With so many children being at risk, and sometimes not due to only socioeconomic circumstances, perhaps in some ways the entire culture in one way or another is at risk as well. For students and parents not socialized in the ways of education, it is easy not to realize that something is amiss. The raw power of education is so strong that many children and their families often feel left out and inadequate (Strother, 1991). These feelings manifest themselves in a number of different ways. Some students are silent and sullen, some make lots of noise, some become the class clown, some turn to violence, some get high on drugs, and some are just absent a lot. All of these are ways that they use to defend themselves against the feeling of not belonging. Sadly, they also are all ways of failing.

As noted, teacher efficacy, the belief held by the teacher as to his or her capability of being successful with students, can have a profound influence on student motivation. When teachers believe students are capable of only low levels of performance, this has already influenced and in some ways predetermined the way they approach their teaching activities with them. Students who are felt to be more capable are challenged more, taught with greater energy and vigor, involved in more dynamic lessons and activities, and receive a richer set of learning experiences than those who are not seen in this way. However, teachers are encouraged to treat all students like the best students (Bottoms, 2007). By completing a rich and challenging program of study, students are better prepared throughout their schooling experiences and to pursue their career goals beyond high school. While some argue that making schools, in particular high schools, more rigorous may prompt at-risk students to drop out before graduating, this is not the case. The High Schools That Work program reports that, as rigor and relevance are added to the curriculum, more students believe that their studies are worthwhile and linked to their future success (Bottoms, 2007). Students are more thoroughly prepared not just in academic and technical knowledge and skills, but also in such intangible assets as time-management skills, relationship-building skills, and the ability to work hard and to achieve their goals. The following table provides an analysis of teachers' attitudes toward students and communications of differential expectations (Good & Brophy, 2003, p. 79).

Goals–Learning and Performance

The type of goals that teachers set influences the amount of motivation that students have to reach them. Goals that are moderately difficult, specific, and likely to be reached in the near future enhance motivation and persistence (Pintroch & Schunk, 2002). Specific goals provide a clear standard for judging performance and moderate difficulty provides a challenge, but not an unreasonable one. When goals are too complex, vague and/or confusing, too challenging, or seem to have no importance, students are more likely not to pursue them. Likewise, when goals are perceived as being too simplistic, they are not seen as being interesting or important either. While they may be achieved, the achievement has little meaning.

There are four main goal orientations: mastery (learning), performance (looking good), work-avoidance, and social (Pintrich & Schunk, 2002). Goal orientations are patterns of beliefs about goals related to

Teacher Communications and Differential Expectations

Characteristics	Students Believed to Be More Capable Have:	Students Believed to Be Less Capable Have:
Task environment (curriculum, procedures, task definition, pacing, quality of environment)	More opportunity to perform publicly on meaningful tasks	Less opportunity to perform publicly, especially on meaningful tasks (supplying alternate endings to a story vs. learning to pronounce a word correctly)
	More opportunity to think	Less opportunity to think (since much work is aimed at practice)
Grouping practices	More assignments that deal with comprehension, understanding (in higher ability groups)	Less choice on curriculum assignments—more work on drill-like assignments
Locus of responsibility for learning	More autonomy, more choice in assignments, fewer interruptions	Less autonomy, frequent teacher monitoring of work, frequent interruptions
Feedback and evaluation practices	More opportunity for self-evaluation	Less opportunity for self-evaluation
Motivational strategies	More honest/contingent feedback	Less honest/more gratuitous/less contingent feedback
Quality of teacher relationships	More respect for the learner as an individual with unique interests and needs	Less respect for the learner as an individual with unique interests and needs

achievement in school and include the reasons students pursue goals along with the standards used to evaluate progress toward them. The most common distinction in research on students' goals is between mastery goals, also called task or learning goals, and performance goals, also called ability and ego goals.

One might wonder how a teacher's goals or desired outcomes can have a specific impact on a student's motivation. What teachers establish as their desired instructional outcomes or goals for students, in fact, has the potential to send an important message and to have a significant effect on a student's level of motivation. Teachers communicate in many ways what they value and what they want their students to value. One way they do this is in their selection of the goals that they would like for their students to pursue and attain. A **goal** is *that which an individual is striving to achieve or accomplish* (Locke & Latham, 1990). Teachers should remember that they frequently if not typically identify goals for their students that their students do not identify for themselves. In terms of best instructional practice, and best student motivation in the classroom, teachers' goals are of limited value when students are not focused and dedicated in striving to achieve or accomplish them. How can teachers create higher levels of student motivation so that students will strive to achieve their goals? The answer to this question, at least in part, lies in the kinds of goals that teachers select for their instruction (i.e., learning versus performance goals) and in how they select them. This is especially true to the degree that students accept these goals as their own and see them as being achievable and of value.

Goals most closely related to students and their academic achievement can be divided into two categories or types: *performance (ability, ego) goals* and *learning (mastery, task) goals*. **Performance goals** are *goals that emphasize the demonstration of high ability and the avoidance of failure*. **Learning goals** are *goals that emphasize the challenge of learning and the mastery of a task*. The point of a learning goal for the student is to improve and learn, no matter how many mistakes may be made. In performance goals, the focus for the student is on looking smart or informed and displaying accomplishments without failure. The teacher's primary responsibility, however, is or should be to get students to learn, not perform. The following table provides an analysis of characteristics of performance and learning goal orientations toward academic tasks (Alderman, 2004, p. 89).

Goals that are specific, seen by students as being of at least moderate difficulty, which can be attained in a reasonable period of time, and as having value, tend to enhance student motivation and persistence (Stipek, 2002). Specific goals provide greater clarity as to the teacher's expectations and standards for evaluating student performance. This quality, coupled with reasonableness of difficulty and time involved, contributes to increased levels of student motivation (Pintrich & Schunk, 2002). Students' beliefs about their abilities to be

Characteristics of Student Behaviors and Learning and Performance Goals

Characteristics	Learning/Mastery	Performance/Ego
Value of learning	Has intrinsic value for learning in itself. The goal is to increase learning.	Learning is not an end in itself. The focus is on looking smart and not looking dumb.
Effort/ability	Effort and ability are related; effort enhances ability.	Ability is capacity; effort means lack of capacity.
Error/failure	A strategy was not effective.	Provokes fear of low ability.
Attribution	Uses effort/strategy attributions most frequently, ability least frequently.	Uses ability attributions most frequently.
Feedback	Used to judge progress and as self-corrective information.	Used to compare performance with another's.
Persistence	High persistence in difficult tasks.	Low persistence in face of difficulty.
Challenge	Seeks challenge.	Avoids risk taking and challenge.

successful, i.e., self-efficacy, also have impact on their engaging or not engaging in learning tasks and their levels of persistence to stay with them once engaged. Because learning goals focus on mastery of information without great concern for or overemphasis on mistakes, they contribute to increased levels of student motivation. Performance goals, on the other hand, where the focus is on performing, looking good, and not being seen as failing, contribute more to decreased levels of motivation.

The following table provides a helpful comparison between the characteristics of learning and performance goals (Stipek, 2002, p. 162). The learner or learning-focused classroom presented in Chapter 1, as opposed to the performer or performance-focused classroom, is recommended for its positive relationship to student motivation as related to goals established and student achievement.

Characteristics of Learning and Performance Goals

Characteristics	Learning Goals	Performance Goals
Success defined as:	Improvement, progress, mastery, innovation, creativity	High grades, high performance compared to others, winning, recognition
Value placed on:	Effort, persistence, attempting difficult tasks	Avoiding failure, succeeding with low effort
Reason for effort:	Intrinsic and personal meaning of activity, learning, mastery	Demonstrating ability and one's own worth
Evaluation criteria:	Absolute criteria (standard) evidence of progress	Norms, social comparisons, another individual
Errors viewed as:	Part of the learning process, informational	Failure, evidence of lack of ability or worth
Competence viewed as:	Increasing through effort, "incremental"	Inherited, fixed, and "entity"

Anxiety

Who reading these pages has never had an anxious moment or felt worry or concern? **Anxiety** has been defined as *a feeling of apprehension, worry, tension, or nervousness* (Lefrancois, 2000) and as *a general uneasiness with a sense of foreboding and feeling of tension* (Hansen, 1977). Though some may feel that being anxious from time to time is not such a bad thing, research on the effects of anxiety on student achievement has consistently identified a negative relationship between anxiety and achievement (Covington & Omelich, 1987). Anxiety has both cognitive and affective components. From the cognitive side, one sees worry and negative thoughts, such as thinking about how bad it would be to fail and worrying that this is going to happen. From the affective side, one can experience physiological and emotional reactions such as sweaty palms, upset stomach, racing heartbeat, or fear (Woolfolk, 2007). Anxiety can interfere with learning and test performance at three levels: focusing attention, understanding what is being taught, and the ability to show or in some way demonstrate what one understands. Anxiety can be a reason for a student to lose focus, become irritable or act out, withdraw and not try, be physically ill, or perform poorly in school with the resulting poor performance only serving to increase the student's anxiety.

The concept of equilibrium was introduced earlier in this chapter with reference to the human desire to achieve balance in life. If not too extreme, mild or even moderate out-of-balance situations, or situations of disequilibrium, can represent situations that motivate students to do things in an effort to get back into balance. Some situations of anxiety, however, can be so great that students are not able to discover the balance that they need. Anxiety in a small amount (i.e., a situation of mild disequilibrium) can help to improve performance by motivating students to positive action. This is referred to as **facilitating anxiety** or *anxiety in such a small amount that it actually helps to improve performance.* Too much anxiety, however, can have the opposite effect of being not motivational and interfering with student performance in a way that diminishes the performance. This anxiety is referred to as **debilitating anxiety** or *anxiety so extreme that it gets in the way of successful performance.*

This point reinforces the importance of teachers understanding their students and their various learning and personal needs and characteristics. What may seem to create an anxious moment for one student may not for another. And, something that would be thought to not be anxiety producing to an internalizing student with a history of success might be quite debilitating to another who has a history of failure. Students frequently become anxious before taking a test that they perceive as being difficult. Most people get nervous when they have to give a prepared speech in front of others. This type of condition is referred to as **state anxiety** or *temporary feelings of anxiety brought about by certain situations.* For students, such anxiety is typically the result of a sense of fear, concern, or threat, especially when they feel that their performance will not be seen as positive (Deci & Ryan, 1992). Some students, though, appear to be anxious even where there is no particular cause or state to link their anxiety to, such as in working on less complex assignments or assignments that do not appear as though they should bring about any reason for fear of failure. **Trait anxiety** is *when students are anxious in circumstances that should not be seen as threatening.* Students characterized by trait anxiety by far are the more difficult for teachers to motivate. Considerable evidence indicates that students who report high anxiety in achievement situations perform poorly compared to students who report relatively low anxiety (Stipek, 2002).

Figure 2.5 identifies seven common situations under which students may experience anxiety, even, for some, debilitating anxiety (Ormrod, 2003). Being aware of and having the opportunity to prepare for these circumstances represents a chance for the teacher to be proactive in working to decrease student anxiety and, therefore, increase student motivation.

High anxiety brought about by intense motivational situations can have a significant negative effect on student performance. Moderate motivation is a more desirable condition for increasing student success on learning complex tasks. Ideal motivation decreases in intensity with increasing task difficulty. As tasks become more challenging and complex, the level of student motivation, likely also driven by the student's level of confidence to be successful, tends to diminish. Increasing intensity improves performance, but only to a certain level. From that point where the performance is no longer improving, continued intensity results in a lessening of the level of motivation along with the quality of the performance. This point illustrates that an understanding of the individual level of student confidence to complete a given task, as this pertains to motivation and performance, is important knowledge for the teacher to have.

Environment

Maslow's Hierarchy of Needs introduced earlier offers an important perspective to the discussion of the impact of environment on student motivation. Environments where students feel safe, both physically and emotionally, where they are desired and cared for, and where they "fit in" or belong, contribute significantly to higher motivational levels. Popular phrases found in educational literature today refer to the preferred classroom environment or climate as needing to be inviting, warm, student-centered, safe and secure, learner-oriented, nurturing, participatory, etc. While phrases such as these may only represent trendy language to some, they say a great deal with respect to student motivation. Perhaps the phrases would mean more if one were to think of a classroom environment that reflected the opposite of these characteristics.

Students and Anxiety-Producing Situations

Type of Situation	Definition
Physical Appearance	Students are often concerned about their appearance. They might see themselves as too thin, too heavy, too tall, or too short. Teachers must not take these concerns lightly as they can have significant impact on some students and their motivation and performance.
New Situations	Students frequently experience uneasiness when encountering new individuals and situations such as teachers, peers, classes, and schools.
Judgment/Evaluation by Others	Most students experience worry over being judged by others. This includes being evaluated by teachers on assignments and activities as well as being accepted by classmates and friends.
Tests	Test anxiety is often not taken seriously enough by teachers. Comments such as "Just relax," "Don't worry," or "You will get it if you study harder next time," generally have little positive impact on students who are truly anxious or experiencing debilitating anxiety in testing situations.
Excessive Classroom Demands	What may not seem excessive to teachers may seem extremely excessive to some students, especially students with high levels of anxiety. Students normally feel anxious when confronted with expectations that they feel are beyond their ability to respond to successfully.
The future	Though some current research suggests that young people have more positive than negative outlooks for the future, this does not mean all young people. Concern over the future, especially for students at the middle and secondary levels, can be significant and effect their motivation and performance in the classroom.
Situations Where Self Is Threatened	Fear of failure anywhere can be powerful and debilitating. Fear of failure in public can be especially so. Many students experience levels of anxiety that are virtually paralyzing in terms of effecting their motivation and performance when the concern includes a dimension of public criticism.

Figure 2.5. Sources of anxiety in students from Ormrod (2003).

The concept of *membership* is important when discussing motivation and the learning environment. When students are assigned to a teacher and a class, they become physical members of the class. But, do they also become psychological members? This is a critical question. **Psychological membership** in the classroom is *the degree to which students feel personally accepted, respected, included and supported* (Goodenow, 1993). The greater the level to which this is achieved, the greater will be the level of student motivation. When students feel a sense of belonging in the classroom through this feeling of positive psychological membership, they are more likely to adopt those goals held to be valuable there. When students do not feel as though they belong or have psychological membership, goals will be perceived simply as the teacher's goals, not really applying or relevant to them and not be readily adopted by them. The social and psychological bonding that comes when students feel that they are true members of the classroom group influences the level or degree to which motivation will occur and academic engagement and learning will take place.

One of the most thoroughly researched theories of motivation is self-determination theory (Brophy, 2004; Pintrich & Schunk, 2002). Self-determination theory identifies a continuum that moves through stages of extrinsic motivation and ends in intrinsic motivation. While primarily a cognitive motivation theory, it also incorporates aspects of humanistic views of motivation. **Self-determination** is *the process of deciding how to act on one's environment.* In self-determination theory, having choices and making decisions are intrinsically motivating. People aren't content if all of their needs are satisfied without their having had opportunities to make decisions. The theory identifies that individuals have three innate psychological needs: *competence, autonomy,* and *relatedness.* These three needs are all linked to the student's adjustment to, membership in, and eventual success in the instructional environment. They are defined as:

Competence: *the ability to function effectively in the environment.*

Autonomy: *independence and the ability to alter the environment when necessary.*

Relatedness: *the feeling of being connected to others in one's social environment and feeling worthy of love and respect.*

Relatedness is similar to Maslow's (1970) need for belonging, identified as the third level in the Hierarchy of Needs.

Higher levels of motivation, as influenced by membership, are seen when student needs are met for belonging/social connectedness, autonomy/self-direction and competence (Battistich, Solomon, Kim, Watson, & Schaps, 1995). An environment perceived by students as being caring represents the type of environment where higher levels of student motivation can be both achieved and maintained. Three characteristics (Alderman, 2004) considered essential for providing such an environment are:

1. a classroom structured for autonomy and responsibility,
2. social support through cooperative learning activities, and
3. teacher support.

Just as teachers send messages to students, so, too, do school and classroom environments. These messages come from the classroom context, the structure of the classroom and messages conveyed by teachers, and influence whether a student is involved in more of a learning goal or performance goal teaching orientation (Alderman, 2004). Classroom dimensions or cues that convey messages about the purpose of achievement include teacher expectations for learning, the type of evaluations used, how students are grouped, and the extent to which students have opportunities for making decisions. All of these factors influence how students see themselves in the classroom. Context factors for classrooms that contribute to a learning goal environment are identified in Figure 2.6.

Student motivation is higher where students have a sense of freedom and responsibility, have opportunities to work with others in support of their own learning and the learning of others, and see their teachers as providing ongoing and enduring support. Even when they are not always successful, students in caring environments perceive their teachers as "being there for them" and this contributes to their ability to persevere and maintain their motivation.

CONCLUSION

Chapter 2 introduced the concept of motivation as it applies to student learning and the role of the classroom teacher. Three important

Classroom Context Factors and Student Motivation

Classroom Structure or Message	Example
Opportunities to develop an increased sense of competence	Made sure that students not only had a basic understanding of the content, but also developed competencies in other areas.
Opportunities for self-directed learning	Helped students evaluate their own work; transferred responsibility to students as they gained competence.
Emphasis on expectations and intrinsic value of learning	Emphasized the value of interest, the application of what students are learning, and expected that all students would learn.
Opportunities for cooperation and collaboration	Group work with emphasis on working together effectively and on helping each other.
Ability/effort messages`	Recognized progress; allowed students to retake tests for improvement.

Figure 2.6. From: Alderman, M. (2004). *Motivation for achievement: Possibilities for teaching and learning* (2nd ed.). p. 91,

theories of motivation–behaviorist, cognitive, and humanist–were introduced and discussed. Critical questions of what affects student motivation including attribution, locus of control, teacher expectations, goals, anxiety, and environment were also raised and explored.

The need for teachers to be informed, reflective educators with respect to achieving student motivation cannot be overemphasized. Teachers in classrooms throughout the country can define the term motivation and can even identify it when it occurs. Many of these same teachers, however, are not able to take what knowledge they have about motivation and apply it consistently and effectively in their classrooms. It is often said that teachers should teach for transfer of learning in that they should assist their students to not only have the ability to "know and do" in the classroom but to be able to apply this knowledge and ability to novel situations. As with the students themselves, teachers must also be able to transfer what they know about student motivation to their teaching and the active environments of their classrooms. They must be able to effectively apply what they know about motivation as this knowledge relates to student learning in order to energize their teaching and engage their students in their learning activities. Motivated students are happier, feel better about themselves, and learn more. These three outcomes are each desirable and attainable providing that teachers understand and can apply what is known about motivating students in learning environments.

QUESTIONS/ACTIVITIES FOR REFLECTION

1. Describe how you might motivate a student who has average ability but who does not regularly work up to his potential. The student comes from a home where neither parent is educated beyond the sixth grade and little English is spoken; Spanish is the dominant language spoken in the home. The student's parents, however, are very supportive and want their child to learn and do well in school.

2. What are some problems found in classrooms taught by teachers who lack high teacher efficacy? How can teachers come to a point where their teacher efficacy is low?

3. Why might poor performance on a test motivate some students but not others to work harder in school? Is there any type of student that might be positively motivated by poor test results? Explain.

4. A father wanted his son to excel in baseball and practiced with him from the time he was five years old. He attended all youth league games and even served as a volunteer coach on his son's teams. Although the son progressed well and seemed to be headed toward high school stardom, he refused to play baseball when he reached high school. What do you think might be some possible explanations for this dramatic change in direction? How do you think that this situation applies to the role of the teacher in the classroom?

5. If a student seems to be a victim of learned helplessness, how can the teacher address the student's need to be a successful learner and not lower his or her classroom teaching standards at the same

time? Is it possible to successfully address this problem in the traditional American education system today? Explain.

REFERENCES

Alderman, M. (2004). *Motivation for achievement: Possibilities for teaching and learning* (2nd ed.). Mahwah, NJ: Lawrence Erlbaum.

Atkinson, J. (1964). *An introduction to motivation.* Princeton, NJ: Van Nostrand.

Ames, R., & Lau, S. (1982). An attributional analysis of student help-seeking in academic settings. *Journal of Educational Psychology, 84*, 261–271.

Bandura, A. (1986). *Social foundations of thought and action: A social cognitive theory.* Upper Saddle River, NJ: Prentice-Hall.

Bandura, A. (1989). Human agency in social cognitive theory. *American Psychologist, 44*, 1175–1184,

Bandura, A. (1993). Perceived self-efficacy in cognitive development and functioning. *Educational Psychologist, 28*(2), 117–148.

Battistich, V., Solomon, D., Kim, D., Watson, M., & Schaps, E. (1995). Schools as communities, poverty levels of student populations, and student attitudes, motives, and performances: A multilevel analysis. *American Educational Research Journal, 32*(2), 627–658.

Bernhard, J., & Siegel, L. (1994). Increasing internal locus of controls for a disadvantaged group: A computer intervention. *Computers in the Schools,* 11(1), 59–77.

Bottoms, G. (2007). Treat all students like the "best" students. *Educational Leadership, 64,* 30–37.

Brophy, J. (1983). Conceptualizing student motivation. *Educational Psychologist, 18,* 200–215.

Brophy, J. (1998). *Motivating students to learn.* New York: McGraw-Hill.

Brophy, J. (2004). *Motivating students to learn* (2nd ed.). Boston: McGraw-Hill.

Burden, P., & Byrd, D. (2007). *Methods for effective teaching: Promoting K-12 student understanding* (4th ed.). New York: Pearson Education.

Covington, M., & Omelich, C. (1987). "I knew it cold before the exam": A test of the anxiety-blockage hypothesis. *Journal of Educational Psychology, 79*, 393–400.

Dacey, J. (1989). *Fundamentals of creativity.* Lexington, MA: D.C. Heath/Lexington Books.

Deci, E., & Ryan, R. (1992). The initiation and regulation of intrinsically motivated learning and achievement. In A.K. Boggiano & T.S. Pittman (Eds.), *Achievement and motivation: A social-developmental perspective.* Cambridge, England: Cambridge University Press.

Doll, B., Zucker, S., & Brehm, K. (2004). *Resilient classrooms: Creating healthy environments for learning.* New York: Guilford Press.

Eccles, J., Adler, T., Futterman, R., Goff, S., Kaczala, C., Meece, J., & Midgley, C. (1983). Expectancies, values, and academic behavior. In J.T. Spence (Ed.), *Achievement and achievement motives: Psychological and sociological approaches* (pp. 75–146). San Francisco: Freeman.

Eggen, P., & Kauchak, D. (2007). *Educational psychology: Windows on classrooms* (7th ed.). New York: Pearson Education.

Feather, N. (Ed.). (1982). *Expectations and actions.* Hillsdale, NJ: Erlbaum.

Garcia, E. (1994). *Understanding and meeting the challenge of student cultural diversity.* Boston: Houghton-Mifflin.

Good, T., & Brophy, J. (2003). *Looking in classrooms* (9th ed.). New York: Pearson Education.

Goodenow, C. (1993). The psychological sense of school membership among adolescents: Scale development and educational correlates. *Psychology in the Schools, 30,* 79-90.

Greeno, J., Collins, A., & Resnick, L. (1996). Cognition and learning. In D. Berliner & R. Calfee (Eds.), *Handbook of educational psychology* (pp. 15–46). New York: Macmillan.

Gschwend, L., & Dembo, M. (2001, April). *How do high-efficacy teachers persist in low-achieving, culturally diverse schools?* Paper presented at the annual meeting of the American Educational Research Association, Seattle.

Hamachek, D. (1987). Humanistic psychology: Theory, postulates, and implications for educational processes. In J. Glover & R. Ronning (Eds.), *Historical foundations of educational psychology* (pp. 159–182). New York: Plenum Press.

Hansen, R. (1977). Anxiety. In S. Ball (Ed.), *Motivation in education.* New York: Academic Press.

Harter, S., & Jackson, B. (1992). Trait versus nontrait conceptualizations of intrinsic/extrinsic motivational orientation. Special issues: Perspectives on intrinsic motivation. *Motivation and Emotion, 16,* 209–230.

Heider, F. (1958). *The psychology of interpersonal relationships.* New York: Wiley.

Henson, K., & Eller, B. (1999). *Educational psychology for effective teaching.* Belmont, CA: Wadsworth/Thompson Learning.

Knapp, M., & Woolverton, S. (1995). Social class and schooling. In J.A. Banks & C.A.M. Banks (Eds.), *Handbook of research on multicultural education.* New York: Macmillan.

Kohn, A. (1992). *No contest: The case against competition.* Boston, MA: Houghton-Mifflin.

Kounin, J. (1970). *Discipline and group management in classrooms.* New York: Holt, Rinehart & Winston.

Lefrancois, G. (2000). *Psychology for teaching* (10th ed.). Belmont, CA: Wadsworth/Thompson Learning.

Locke, E., & Latham, G. (1990). *A theory of goal setting and task performance.* Englewood Cliffs, NJ: Prentice-Hall.

Margolis, H., & McCabe, P. (2004). Self-efficacy: A key to improving the motivation of struggling learners. *The Clearing House,* July/August, 241–249.

Maslow, A. (1970). *Motivation and personality* (2nd ed.). New York: Harper & Row.

Ormrod, J. (2003). *Educational psychology: Developing learners* (4th ed.). Upper Saddle River, NJ: Merrill Prentice-Hall.

Piaget, J. (1952). *Origins of intelligence.* New York: International Universities Press.

Pintrich, P., & Schunk, D. (2002). *Motivation in education: Theory, research, and application* (2nd ed.). Upper Saddle River, NJ: Merrill/Prentice Hall.

Rosenthal, R., & Jacobson, L. (1968). *Pygmalion in the classroom: Teacher expectation and pupils' intellectual development.* New York: Holt, Rinehart & Winston.

Santrock, J. (2008). *Educational psychology* (3rd ed.). New York: McGraw-Hill.

Schunk, D. (1994, April). *Goal and self-evaluative influences during children's mathematical skill acquisition.* Paper presented at the annual meeting of the American Educational Research Association, New Orleans.

Seligman, M. (1975). *Helplessness.* San Francisco: Freeman.

Slavin, R. (2000). *Educational psychology: Theory and practice* (6th ed.). Boston: Allyn & Bacon.

Snowman, J., & Biehler, R. (2006). *Psychology applied to teaching* (11th ed.). Boston, MA: Houghton Mifflin Company.

Stipek, D. (2002). *Motivation to learn: Integrating theory and practice* (4th ed.). Boston: Allyn & Bacon.

Strother, D. (Ed.). (1991). *Learning to fail: Case studies of students at risk.* Bloomington, IN: Phi Delta Kappa.

Wang, M., Hertel, G., & Walberg, H. (1995, April). *Educational resilience: An emerging construct.* Paper presented at the annual meeting of the American Educational Research Association, San Francisco.

Weiner, B. (1990). History of motivational research in education. *Journal of Educational Psychology, 82,* 612–622.

Weiner, B. (1992). *Human motivation: Metaphors, theories, and research.* Newbury Park, CA: Sage.

Weiner, B. (1994a). Ability versus effort revisited: The moral determinants of achievement evaluation and achievement as a moral system. *Educational Psychologist, 29,* 163–172.

Weiner, B. (1994b). Integrating social and personal theories of achievement striving. *Review of Educational Research, 64,* 557–573.

Wigfield, A. (1994). Expectancy-value theory of achievement motivation. A developmental perspective. *Educational Psychology, 6,* 49–78.

Woolfolk, A. (2007). *Educational psychology* (10th ed.). New York: Pearson Education.

Chapter 3

CREATING A MANAGED ENVIRONMENT: MODELS AND THEORIES OF MANAGEMENT

MANAGEMENT

The fundamental theme of this book is one that acknowledges the important relationship that exists between motivating students to learn and managing student behavior in the classroom. Effective classroom management, as well as motivation, is essential as it relates to student learning. In the context of promoting learning in the classroom, management has been defined as follows:

Management: *a system of organization that addresses all elements of the classroom (i.e., students, space, time, materials, and behavioral rules and procedures) in order to reach optimum levels of instruction and learning.*

Three key elements comprise this definition. Management is characterized by:

1. a specific system of organization,
2. a focus on many elements of the classroom to include physical as well as personal elements, and
3. the purpose of reaching optimum levels of instruction and learning.

The major purpose of Chapter 3 is to provide an overview of some of the most important and influential models that have been developed to manage student behavior in classroom environments. A recent poll conducted by the Association for Supervision and Curriculum Development (2007) asked the question, "Which element of effective classroom management is the most challenging to implement?" In order of the difficulty of the challenge, the top five answers to this question were: (1) fostering student responsibility, (2) establishing schoolwide policies, (3) monitoring the classroom and addressing problems, (4) forming teacher-student relationships, and (5) setting behavior expectations and consequences. The models discussed in this chapter will help greatly to focus on the implementation of strategies to deal with the most frequent answers to this question. Some of these models rely less on the motivation of students in their learning than might be thought of as appropriate given the primary foundation of this text. However, a lack of understanding of these basic models in terms of their underlying themes will limit readers of this book as they endeavor to construct what will eventually be their own best models for classroom management for their own individual classrooms. To be effective, teachers must be well grounded in best practice information that relates to student motivation, classroom management, and instruction. A gap in knowledge in any of these three areas will lessen the potential for optimum student learning in the classroom.

MANAGEMENT MODELS AND THEORIES

A number of important management models have been developed over the years and used by educators, wholly or in part, to create positive learning environments and to manage student behavior. A central thread running through most of these models is the emphasis on creating environments that are conducive to *preventing* student misbehavior, not simply *reacting* to misbehavior once it occurs. Nevertheless, even with the best prevention measures, times will occur when students disobey their teachers or violate stated school rules. When this takes place, teachers must be able to respond effectively to such situations in order to maintain a desirable, safe, and productive learning environment. As noted in Chapter 1, teachers must have a discipline plan and know how to use it when problems arise. Although it is important for the teacher to know how to respond to student misbehavior so that the misconduct is ended, knowing how to establish a classroom environment that is preventive in nature is considered an even more significant teaching skill (Good & Brophy, 2007). Little learning is likely to occur in a classroom where students feel unsafe or where teachers and students face constant distractions and interruptions (Borman & Levine, 1997; Lezotte, 1997).

An initial step in learning how to establish a well-managed classroom is to study and develop an understanding of models and approaches designed for this purpose. Following this study and gaining this understanding, the next important step is to adopt a model, or features of one or more models, to a particular classroom situation. Because it is difficult to see that any one model can satisfy all circumstances, most teachers develop an eclectic, self-stylized approach to classroom management that borrows from the best ideas presented by one or more models or recommended behaviors. The approach that is then developed is one that is compatible with the teacher's own teaching style and philosophy of education.

Some management models actually are best used when the entire faculty and administration of a school participates in their implementation. However, since many teachers discover theories and procedures they would like to implement in their own individual classrooms, when other teachers and administrators in their schools may not be participating in their use, a personalized approach to management generally has more appeal and can be more effective. The major ideas found in ten different management models, and the theorists who are associated with their development, are presented here along with an emphasis on their most important characteristics as applied to classroom practice. Figure 3.1 provides an overview of the models that will be considered and the theorists who are credited for their development.

Jacob Kounin's Theories

Jacob Kounin's theories have had great impact on the way many educators view the learning environment (Eggen & Kauchak, 2007). An interesting characteristic of Kounin's theories is that they tend to focus on constructs more often associated with a sociological study of small groups. Many of the other management theories that have been developed are grounded in what are more traditionally thought of as psychological constructs (Hunt, Touzel, & Wiseman, 1999). Central to the work of Kounin is the position that the classroom should be looked upon as a small community where interactions with any member of the community may affect the rest of its members. In order for the

Theorists	Focus of Management Models
1. Jacob Kounin	The focus is on teachers learning behaviors that will allow them to become better leaders in the classroom.
2. Rudolph Dreikurs	The focus is on analyzing behavior problems to determine their source of origin and responding to them.
3. William Glasser	The focus is on empowering students to become better group members.
4. Hiam Ginott	The focus is on improving communication in order to avoid alienating students inhumanely.
5. Fred Jones	The focus is on keeping students engaged in academically appropriate activities.
6. Thomas Gordon	The focus is on teachers using counseling techniques to improve communication with their students.
7. Lee & Marlene Canter	The focus is on teachers asserting their right to teach and their students' right to learn.
8. B.F. Skinner	The focus is on shaping student behavior with positive reinforcement.
9. David & Roger Johnson	The focus is on students resolving their own conflicts.
10. Alfie Kohn	The focus is on students becoming intrinsically motivated to value good behavior.

Figure 3.1. Management theorists and management models.

classroom community to function well and reach its goals (i.e., in order for high levels of academic progress to be realized), the teacher must be able to exhibit the characteristics of a successful group leader.

Five factors characterize the classrooms of teachers who adopt the ideas described by Kounin (1970).

1. Student boredom is avoided.
2. Transitions between tasks and momentum within tasks flow smoothly.
3. All students remain alert and focused.
4. Teachers are aware of what is taking place in all parts of the classroom.

5. Teachers understand that interaction with any one student may have an effect on the total group.

It is recommended that teachers use a variety of different methods and materials to maintain high levels of student interest and participation in order to avoid student boredom. When students are aware that they are making progress toward their learning goals, and are involved in a variety of interesting and meaningful activities, they are much less likely to become involved in misconduct behaviors and pose management problems for their teachers. It is also important that smooth transitions exist between learning activities and that *momentum* within lessons moves consistently toward closure. When instruction is characterized by such *thrust*, or positive momentum, the classroom group tends to function better and individual students are more likely to stay on task. Educational research suggests that there is a greater value in the teacher establishing a quicker paced as compared to a slower paced delivery of instruction (Hunt et al., 1999).

Keeping students alert and focused on assigned activities also lessens the probability of classroom disturbances. Most misconduct occurs during "down times" or idle times when students are not on task, often because they either do not understand what they are supposed to do or how to do it. Kounin referred to this as maintaining **group focus** or *on-task behavior where all students in the classroom attend to the teacher or activities that the teacher has assigned at the same time.* Teachers who are able to create functional, effective learning environments have what Kounin called *withitness.* **Withitness** occurs *when a teacher displays the ability to have an ongoing awareness of events throughout the entire classroom, not just one area of the setting.* This awareness, sometimes referred to as "eyes in the back of the head," allows teachers to pre-empt many disturbances and distractions before they become serious problems.

When teachers reinforce students or correct their misbehaviors, these interactions will have an effect on other students in the classroom creating what Kounin identified as the *ripple effect.* The **ripple effect** is *the effect on other students in the classroom when the teacher reinforces or corrects particular students for their behavior.* It is critical that teachers recognize the impact that their actions may have on all students in the classroom when they correct the behavior of only one or two. Kounin believed that there is a positive effect on all students in the entire class when one student's misconduct is handled firmly and fairly. The ripple effect also can have a positive impact when one student is praised or encouraged in front of classmates as the entire class has the opportunity to observe and learn which behaviors are desired and rewarded (Borman & Levine, 1997). Conversely, a negative ripple effect can occur if the teacher handles a management problem inappropriately, thus sending the wrong or undesired message to students about unacceptable behavior.

Rudolf Dreikurs' Theories

Rudolf Dreikurs' theoretical position was founded on his experience with psychoanalytic psychology (Dreikurs, 1968; Dreikurs & Cassell, 1972). Dreikurs expanded on the concepts of Alfred Adler and provided a control methodology that allowed teachers to avoid punishment (Burden, 2003), believing that students often misbehave because they desire recognition from the teacher and/or classmates. It was also Dreikurs' belief that students develop certain defense mechanisms that are designed to protect their self-esteem. He theorized that student misbehavior is goal directed, perhaps to get recognition or to otherwise protect self-esteem. Goals that misdirect student behavior, listed from least to most severe, are (1) *attention-seeking*, (2) *power-seeking*, (3) *revenge-seeking*, and (4) *overtly displaying inadequacy in order to receive special treatment.*

Attention-seeking is *a student behavior problem often exhibited by tattling and showing off, class-clowning, or in some other way drawing focus to one's self.* **Power-seeking** is *a student behavior problem where the student seeks to control the teacher instead of being directed by the teacher.* Students who seek revenge do things to hurt other students, either physically or emotionally. **Revenge-seeking** is *a student behavior problem where a student may do something to cause other students to be punished to "get back at them."* It was Dreikurs' belief that students who pretend they lack the ability to do assigned work, *overtly displaying inadequacy in order to receive special treatment,* are exhibiting the most serious misconduct. Students may exhibit different behaviors to reach any of these four goals and teachers should work to create learning environments with distinct characteristics designed to prevent these problem situations before they occur. Some of these distinct characteristics of the desired learning environment are:

1. students are not reinforced when they exhibit behaviors leading to undesirable goals,
2. when students exhibit undesirable behavior, they receive preannounced logical consequences that will be unpleasant to them,
3. students should be involved in helping the teacher set logical consequences for misconduct,
4. teachers should not merely treat symptoms when dealing with misconduct but seek to determine the motivation behind the student's action(s),
5. students should feel a responsibility to influence their peers' conduct,
6. students must understand that, ultimately, they are responsible for their own behavior, and
7. students should be encouraged to develop self-respect while learning to respect others.

In order to fully utilize Dreikurs' theories, teachers must be able to analyze their students' misbehaviors, focusing on the cause(s) of the behaviors, in order to determine the goals motivating the misconduct. They must also develop and be able to use the necessary interpersonal guidance skills needed to help them understand and change their students' misdirected behaviors in the future (Hunt et al., 1999). The Cooperative Discipline model, introduced in Chapter 1, is basically an extension of the work of Adler and Dreikurs (Albert, 1996).

William Glasser's Theories

William Glasser's theoretical model is known as Reality Therapy, more recently referred to as Choice Theory, and has been used and discussed for decades (Glasser, 1965, 1969). Over the years, Glasser has refined his theories and his work is widely endorsed by many educators today (Glasser, 1992, 1993). Glasser drew on the work of Dreikurs in developing his theories (Zabel & Zabel, 1996) and believes that students often display misbehavior or apathy because they feel powerless in the adult world. Central to Glasser's concept of an effective learning environment is the strong belief that students must play an active role in the decision making process.

An important tenet of Glasser's theory is that, when dealing with specific misconduct, the teacher should help students become aware of and responsible for the consequences of their own behaviors. One way that this can be done is by developing individual student behavior contracts that result in the use of logical consequences when student misbehavior occurs. The behavior contract should be designed to clearly identify (1) the expectations that the teacher has for the student, (2) the consequences that have been identified if the behavior is exhibited or if it is not exhibited, and (3) a system for recording or monitoring the student's behavior over time. In this approach, the teacher uses behavior modification techniques to reinforce positive behavior and end unwanted conduct. If the reinforcements through behavior modification do not bring about the desired results, the student is removed from the group through a series of steps beginning with simple isolation and moving to in-school suspension (ISS), out-of-school suspension (OSS), and, finally, expulsion (Bennett, 1997). Research indicates that positive effects can be expected when Glasser's theories are applied correctly (Good & Brophy, 1986).

Glasser's approach to management includes the use of **class meetings** as *a process to involve students in the establishing of guidelines for acceptable behavior and as a forum for collaborative problem solving.* When rules and regulations must be adjusted or unique situations arise, the class meets to discuss and make decisions about the situation. Class meetings are regularly recurring events that are used to enable students to be an ongoing part of the decision making process in the classroom and help prevent possible behavior problems, not just react to unwanted problem occurrences. When students believe their interests and ideas are considered important and are valued, they become stakeholders in the group. They then are more likely to assume needed responsibility and ownership for their behaviors (Zabel & Zabel, 1996).

Glasser believes that the learning environment should feature at least five distinct characteristics:

1. the teacher functioning as a democratic leader,
2. students taking part in the decision making process,
3. students having an opportunity for cooperative or team activities,
4. students being part of the group being seen as a privilege and source of satisfaction and enjoyment, and
5. the classroom as a place where guidelines are established and problems are solved through collaborative *class meetings.*

Glasser has long been recognized as a leader in the field of classroom management and student motivation. Like Dreikurs, he recognizes that students taking responsibility for their own behavior and helping in the establishment of the guidelines for acceptable conduct are critical elements in establishing and maintaining a well-managed learning environment. Glasser has more recently moved to a position that identifies that school managers are responsible for creating many of the management problems that take place in schools today. Glasser feels that, too often, schools accept low standards for student work which leads to many management problems that could and should have otherwise been avoided (Glasser, 2000).

Hiam Ginott's Theories

Hiam Ginott (1965, 1969, & 1971) was a very popular child psychologist whose books, weekly syndicated newspaper column, and television appearances (he was a regular guest on the "Today Show") influenced many parents and teachers in terms of how they interacted with children and teenagers. Ginott stressed the importance of what he called *sane messages*. **Sane messages** are *messages that focus on the undesired behavior of a student, not on the student as a person.* They never represent an attack on a student on a personal level. When teachers use sane messages, they lessen the chance of alienating students while, at the same time, provide an important model for the type of behavior students themselves should demonstrate. Since positive modeling should be a significantly important aspect of any teacher's approach to classroom management, Ginott stressed that teachers need to endeavor to maintain self-discipline, thus serving as models for their students of disciplined individuals.

Ginott felt that a system of effective management evolved over time through what he called "a series of little victories." In order to achieve these "little victories," teachers should:

1. avoid labeling students,
2. avoid using sarcasm,
3. avoid praising personalities instead of behaviors,
4. send *sane messages,*
5. model desired behaviors,
6. accept student apologies, and
7. help students build their self-esteem.

Ginott encouraged teachers to create learning environments where students can realize a genuine feeling of satisfaction. He believed that students are much more satisfied in classrooms where team or cooperative learning activities are utilized. Teachers should make a conscious effort to encourage or invite this type of cooperation, thus giving students an opportunity to make choices and behave independently. Rather than try to boss and force students to comply through positions of power, teachers should give students the opportunity to decide on their own which alternative to take. For example, "Do we want to work together quietly on the floor or do we want to get back in our desks? It is up to you," is a better way to address students than, "Be quiet or I will make you get in your desks." When teachers avoid ordering, bossing, and commanding, students are much more willing to cooperate and less likely to become negative and hostile.

Ginott believed that teachers should be compassionate, understanding models who communicate to students in such a way as to confirm positive expectations. A teacher who demonstrates polite, respectful behavior toward students creates an atmosphere where students learn to communicate their own feelings in a similarly acceptable fashion. This is best accomplished when teachers are aware of students' feelings and communicate with them through the use of sane messages.

Fred Jones' Theories

Fred Jones (2000) supports the theory of Positive Discipline which states that most classroom management problems occur because students are not on task. It is Jones' position that the majority of classroom management problems occur when students are not focused and not using their time constructively. Students exhibit unwanted behaviors because they are allowed to be idle or waste time, not because they are naturally unruly, defiant, or aggressive. If teachers can control the learning environment in order that "down time" is minimized, management problems will be greatly reduced (Borman & Levine, 1997; Burden, 2003). Specifically, Jones believes that the teacher's ability to plan and develop a positive learning environment is the key to effective management (Manning & Bucher, 2007).

In order to provide an environment where time is not wasted and where students are productive, teachers must:

1. learn to send messages to students through clear nonverbal communication,
2. develop reward systems for students who are on task,
3. arrange the physical environment to facilitate communication, and
4. use teaching methods that keep all students focused and on task.

When the teacher does not have to interrupt the lesson to address unwanted behavior problems, the flow of the lesson is maintained and instructional time is not wasted. Facial expressions, gestures, and movement toward students (an element of what is sometimes called proximity control) can stop unwanted behavior problems without interrupting the teacher's lesson. The overuse of corrective verbiage should be avoided. Students whose behavior is task-oriented should be rewarded, and this reward should then become an incentive for the entire class. A student who finishes his or her work appropriately and in a timely manner, for example, might be allowed to spend extra time on favorite activities.

The physical environment of the classroom should be arranged in such a way that the teacher can efficiently help students who are having difficulty. Jones recognizes that students are sometimes seated in seating arrangements that make it difficult for teachers to easily get to them or near them without interrupting the flow of instruction. Considering this, desks arranged in semi-circles, for example, may be preferable to desks in straight rows.

Additionally, students often waste time for the following reasons:

1. they cannot do what has been assigned to them,
2. they do not understand what is expected of an assignment,
3. they finish their work and have nothing else to do, and
4. they see the task as boring, too difficult or unchallenging.

Teachers must provide activities for their students that are interesting, challenging, and that keep them moving toward a desired and meaningful goal. Jones recommends that teachers use models, charts, and examples and illustrations to provide clear directions to students. He further emphasizes that the majority of the students in the class should not be kept waiting for extended periods of time while the teacher is explaining or re-explaining something to one or only a few individuals. This type of situation creates unnecessary idle time for the majority of the class. Jones' theory stresses the importance of the teacher's role in managing the classroom to prevent student behavior problems from occurring. The environment that is structured to foster consistent student time on task behavior limits wasted time and minimizes student misconduct. Effective teaching practices are clearly a key part of Jones' model.

Thomas Gordon's Theories

Thomas Gordon (1974) developed the highly popular Teacher Effectiveness Training (TET) model for classroom management that is based on a Gestalt psychology point of view similar to the position taken by Carl Rogers (Rogers & Freiberg, 1994). Gordon emphasizes the necessity of effective communication between teacher and student if productive relationships are to exist (Woolfolk, 2007) and condemns the use of both rewards and punishment (Manning & Bucher, 2007). Through the use of the TET model, the teacher is encouraged to utilize certain counseling behaviors in order to create an effective, well-managed learning environment. In this approach:

1. teachers should diagnose problems to determine problem ownership,
2. teachers should not send accusatory messages when correcting student behavior,
3. teachers should practice active listening when communicating with students, and
4. students are encouraged to resolve their own conflicts through a no-lose process.

Diagnosis of problem ownership is a key aspect of the successful functioning of TET. When unacceptable student behavior occurs, teachers should first determine if the problem that is being experienced is actually theirs or their students. Student-owned problems may be associated with fears or anxiety. Teacher-owned problems, on the other hand, often involve student misconduct that frustrates the teacher because it interrupts the flow of instruction. The owner of the problem needs to be the one who initially talks or moves ahead to solve the problem. If the problem belongs to the student, the teacher needs to use appropriate questioning and listening techniques to counsel the student through the problem or otherwise guide the student to a positive resolution to the problem. If the problem belongs to the teacher, a clear, nonaccusatory message should be sent by the teacher to the student creating the frustration letting the student know the impact that his or her behavior is having on what the teacher is trying to accomplish in the classroom.

When the teacher owns the problem, Gordon recommends that the teacher send what he calls an *I message* to the student. The *I message* (as opposed to a *You message*) explains how a specific behavior affects the teacher without making an accusatory assault on the person or persons who exhibited the unwanted behavior. The **I message** is *a three-part communication that (1) delineates the undesired behavior, (2) describes the effect the behavior has on the teacher, and (3) lets the student know how the teacher feels when such behavior occurs. I messages* focus on behaviors, not students. For example, the teacher might say to a misbehaving student, "When you talk out loud when I am teaching I am unable to finish the activity that I have underway. This frustrates me and makes it difficult for me to complete the lesson that I had planned." This approach does not criticize the student personally, but makes it clear that the student's behavior, talking out loud during the lesson, creates problems for the teacher as well as the learning of the other students. A *You message*, such as, "You are really creating problems for me today with your constant talking and I am tired of it," comes across as being more directed at the student personally than to the student's behavior. The **You message** is generally seen as *a statement to the student interpreted as a personal attack or put down of the student.* Such a message is counter productive in terms of helping to develop the desired positive atmosphere in the classroom.

Active listening, an important aspect of TET, is *a specific approach to listening where the teacher gives full attention to both the emotional as well as intellectual content of what the student is saying* (Sokolove, Garrett, Sadker, & Sadker, 1990). Active listening is especially important when the student owns the problem and needs to talk about emotions and feelings. The teacher's aim in using active listening is to show students that the teacher takes their problems seriously, wants to hear what they have to say, and is willing to help them arrive at their own solutions. Through this process teachers are encouraged to:

1. maintain eye contact with the student who is talking,
2. paraphrase what was said by the student back to the student to give assurance that the message is both understood and important to the teacher, and
3. project an open, nonjudgmental demeanor communicating to the student that what is being said by the student is genuinely important.

Gordon encourages students, where possible, to resolve their own conflicts through a process he calls the *no-lose approach.* The **no-lose approach** is *an approach to helping students resolve their own conflicts or problems in such a way that all students involved feel positive about the resolution and no one is considered a loser.* In using this approach, students first define their problem. Next, each student suggests a possible solution to the conflict. The concerned parties then work together to establish a solution through consensus building that is satisfactory to all involved. The solution is then implemented on a trial basis. If it is found to be unsatisfactory, another solution is similarly developed and tried. This process, recommended as following the steps of the Model for Reflection and Inquiry introduced in Chapter 1, is designed to teach students how to solve their own conflicts in a logical and reasoned way without the need for teacher intervention. Gordon's model is based on effective communication among students and teachers. When students feel their teachers listen to them when they share their feelings, they are more likely to trust their teachers and respond more openly to them (Woolfolk, 2007). Some do feel that Gordon's theory is less effective with serious problems that need immediate responses (Manning & Bucher, 2007).

Lee and Marlene Canter's Theories

Lee and Marlene Canter developed a model for classroom management known as *Assertive Discipline.* **Assertive Discipline** is *a management model based upon the fundamental position that teachers have the right to teach while students have the right to learn, and no one has the right to disrupt the learning environment* (Canter & Canter, 1976, 1992). Assertive Discipline encourages teachers to make their expectations clear to their students and to follow through with established consequences for those students who choose to break established rules.

Clarity and consistency must be evident if Assertive Discipline is to be successful. Important features of the model include:

1. students must face the consequences for their own misconduct,
2. teachers are neither hostile nor passive when dealing with misconduct,
3. teachers do not debate or argue about the fairness of rules with students, and
4. teachers rely heavily on the use of proper nonverbal communication and behavior monitoring strategies when managing specific student misconduct.

In a well-managed classroom, students understand what is expected of them and the consequences for violating or not fulfilling these expectations. The Canters stress that teachers must communicate their expectations to students firmly and clearly and then follow these communications with appropriate actions responding in ways that increase student compliance.

Effective teachers are firm but not hostile to students and always avoid making attacks on a student's character. Such comments as, "You are acting immaturely!" or "You should be ashamed of yourself!" are ineffective and alienating. Comments such as, "You might get away with that when you are home, but you will not do it at school!" actually can be seen as attacking the character of the student's parents and also should be avoided. The passive teacher ignores misbehavior and fails to assert needed leadership in the classroom while the hostile teacher alienates students with a "me against you" attitude. Teachers must appropriately assert themselves and become firm managers of student behavior. This firm approach to management, however, must never conflict with the best interests of the students for whom they are responsible.

The Assertive Discipline model stresses the importance of avoiding arguments with students, especially arguments in public. Because everyone should know and be clear about the rules of the classroom, teachers should avoid nagging, fussing, and debating the rules with a misbehaving student. The overuse of such verbiage is a waste of valuable instructional time and will only serve to lessen the teacher's stature in the eyes of the students and weaken the teacher's position.

In order to avoid superfluous talking while correcting student misbehaviors, teachers are advised to learn to use appropriate nonverbal communications. Eye contact, gestures, touches, and proximity are all effective means to help teachers assert that they are serious and in charge. Gestures, as the Canters instruct, can give added impact to verbal messages along with factors such as tone of voice and facial expression. Such nonverbal communications will help the total communication of the teacher be clearer to the student and minimize the necessity for the teacher to repeat directions and use longer, and, at times, protracted verbal interactions. The use of appropriate nonverbal communication, and the use of a specific recordkeeping system that monitors the frequency of a student's misbehavior that leads to increased levels of consequences, are key to the Canter model.

The public's concern, along with the fact that many teachers fail in the profession as a result of not being able to manage the behavior of their students, has led advocates of Assertive Discipline to believe that effective teaching is dependent upon the teacher's ability to exhibit the firmness needed to control behavior in the learning environment. Some educators, however, have questioned the use of Assertive Discipline. Render, Padilla, and Krank (1989) report that they could find little research supporting the effectiveness of Assertive Discipline that had been conducted by researchers other than the Canters and their associates. While there is evidence that Assertive Discipline may work in severe cases with highly disruptive students, there is no evidence to recommend or support the approach for schoolwide or districtwide adoption. Curwin and Mendler (1988) and Covaleski (1992) voice concerns that go beyond whether or not Assertive Discipline does or does not work to control student behavior. These educators note a concern that models of management such as Assertive Discipline do little to teach students self-control or bolster their self-worth or value systems. The Canters and their associates have answered their critics with logical arguments related to the research base for Assertive Discipline (McCormack, 1989) and the issues surrounding the model's impact on students (Canter, 1988). As Manning and Bucher (2007) point out, while there are a number of people who have been critical of Assertive Discipline, thousands of teachers have tried it and found that it works for them. It is clear that teachers should thoroughly examine as many theories and models of management as possible to determine what may be best for them to use in their own individual classrooms to bring the greatest benefit to their students and themselves.

B. F. Skinner's Theories

B.F. Skinner's theories have been widely applied to behavior management and his work goes beyond what one might consider as representing only theories for behavior management in the classroom. The application of operant conditioning principles in everyday (i.e., not laboratory) settings has been common practice since the late 1950s (Kauffman, 1989). **Operant conditioning** is *a form of learning where an observable response changes in frequency or duration as a result of a consequence; the response increases in frequency as a result of its being followed by reinforcement.* Originally called Behavior Modification, the techniques were typically used with the severely retarded, the autistic, and the emotionally disturbed. As positive outcomes were documented, the techniques were used more broadly with nondisabled populations (Zirpoli & Melloy, 2004). Since the late 1980s, Behavior Modification has been replaced by Applied Behavior Analysis because Behavior Modification, to many, has taken on a negative connotation (Alberto & Troutman, 2005; Woolfolk, 2007).

Early in the twentieth century, E.L. Thorndike (1905, 1911) established that people repeat behaviors that bring pleasant feelings and that the more a behavior is repeated the better one's performance becomes. These findings lay the foundation for today's Applied Behavior Analysis. **Applied Behavior Analysis** is *an approach to management that focuses on the positive, rewarding appropriate behaviors, as opposed to concentrating on the negative, punishing unwanted or inappropriate behaviors* (McCaslin & Good, 1992).

Teachers who manage their classrooms using Applied Behavior Analysis exhibit characteristics derived from behaviorist principles. Examples of these principles are:

1. students receive positive reinforcements after exhibiting desired behaviors,
2. teachers do not punish students who exhibit unwanted behaviors, and
3. teachers shape students' behaviors to become more desirable over time.

The concept is simple. Students are reinforced (i.e., given positive reinforcement or rewards) when they behave in a fashion the teacher desires. Based on behaviorist theory, the student who receives a reward will repeat the desired behavior because the reward brings pleasure. If the teacher wants a student to stay seated, for example, the student will be rewarded in some way for being seated. Applied Behavior Analysis has been referred to as a remunerative strategy because students receive a payoff or some type of remuneration for doing what the teacher wants done.

Not only does the model emphasize reinforcing or rewarding good behavior, teachers practicing Applied Behavior Analysis are advised to avoid the use of punishments. The positive aspect of this approach is that teachers focus on the students who are behaving in an acceptable manner, not the ones who are not. Teachers are encouraged to spend more time rewarding and praising their students, not punishing or giving them verbal retributions for misdeeds. Many behaviorists, though, have warned against a "praise good behavior while ignoring bad behavior" philosophy (Pfiffner, Rosen, & O'Leary, 1985). In some cases, especially those of a more serious nature, disruptive behavior will persist and may even escalate if ignored. Teachers are advised to channel students to positive behavior and then reinforce this conduct. Obviously, no teacher can be positive and complimentary all of the time. In general, however, it is strongly recommended that emphasis be placed on what students are doing correctly as opposed to what they may be doing incorrectly.

Shaping behavior is an important aspect of Applied Behavior Analysis. **Shaping** refers to *the practice of gradually changing a student's unwanted actions to more acceptable behavior over time through the use of reinforcements.* There are several ways by which this shaping can take place, varying from an informal approach where the teacher simply waits for a student to exhibit desired behavior and then rewards it, to a more structured system where the teacher elicits desired behavior through the use of tangible rewards. In order to shape an individual student's behavior, the teacher must first carefully measure the degree to which the behavior occurs (i.e., establish baseline data) and then analyze the environment to determine what precedes the behavior and what may be reinforcing the behavior after it occurs. Following this careful analysis, a schedule can be developed to intervene by offering appropriate reinforcers when desired behaviors occur in order to change the unwanted behavior to more acceptable conduct. Finally, the changed behavior must be measured to determine if the new behavior is greatly different from the previous baseline behavior.

The unwanted behavior of a student could be the student's failing to complete any of the teacher's assigned homework. Using Applied Behavior Analysis, the teacher would first observe the student for some period of time (e.g., one week) in order to determine the degree to which the student failed to complete the work that had been assigned. Following the completion of the observation, the teacher then would institute a reward system to motivate the student to complete the homework assignments (e.g., some tangible reinforcer could be given each time the student satisfactorily completed a set amount of work). After a period of time (perhaps two-to-three weeks), the teacher would then measure the student's level of homework completion again to determine if progress had been made. The teacher should maintain assessment over time and make modifications in the reinforcement schedule as needed.

The use of behaviorist principles to shape student behavior is a somewhat controversial topic (Kohn, 1993). Although supported by many (Alberto & Troutman, 2005; Zirpoli & Melloy, 2004), questions have been raised about its use (Travers, 1977). It has been noted that ethical questions regarding its use may exist in that some students may be reinforced for actions that might be viewed as negative by others (Woolfolk, 2007). The question has also been raised as to whether or not the wrong message is being sent when some students receive rewards for doing what they are normally expected to do anyway, while other students exhibit the same behavior without being rewarded. Though evidence suggests that behavior can be changed through the use of Applied Behavior Analysis, questions remain concerning which students benefit most from such techniques and the impact the techniques have on the entire class (Hunt, Touzel, & Wiseman, 1999). As with most highly systematic models for classroom management, Applied Behavior Analysis techniques can only be used successfully with maximum benefit after professional training has been received.

David and Roger Johnson's Theories

David and Roger Johnson and their associates developed the *Conflict Resolution* model to student behavior management where students receive formal training so that they might be able to better deal with their own problems (Johnson & Johnson, 1995; Johnson & Johnson, 2005; Stevahn, Johnson, Johnson, Green, & Laginski, 1997).

Conflict Resolution is *a management model used in school settings where students are trained to use creative problem solving in such a way as to increase the probability that students involved in a conflict can get what they want in terms of a problem solution.* This is not unlike Gordon's no-lose approach. To use Conflict Resolution, students complete a designed training program in order to learn how to negotiate and engage in peer mediation with their classmates when conflicts arise. The goal of Conflict Resolution is to involve students in the decision making process to develop a workable solution to a problem that will allow all parties involved in the conflict to feel satisfied about the resolution that has been developed. The program is most commonly used on a schoolwide basis where students take part in specialized training before using the approach to assure that their negotiations and problem solving actions can be successful and conducted in a consistent and appropriate manner. The traditional role of the teacher is somewhat minimized in Conflict Resolution in that the model emphasizes the role of students in the management of their own conflicts.

Many claims have been made supporting this integrative approach to mediation of conflicts as a model which helps decrease management problems in schools (Tolson, McDonald, & Moriarty, 1992). Johnson and Johnson (1995), however, believe that much more research needs to be done on the process. For example, it has been argued that the model requires specialized training that must take place in ways that are not cost effective and that take students away from their academic studies (Webster, 1993). Johnson and Johnson (2004) report that, in schools where students were trained in conflict resolution and peer mediation, there were fewer management problems, both in classrooms and on school grounds. And, students continued to use their conflict resolution strategies at home as well as at school. The approach is believed to be cost effective and can provide positive results when students receive proper training.

Conflicts among students have become all too common in school environments across the nation. Some of these conflicts have been manifested in violent acts where students and teachers have experienced serious injury or loss of life for little or no understandable reason. Although these extreme acts of violence account for a very small percentage of the total number of student conflicts that actually take place in schools, they are extensively covered by the media and are widely publicized. Many school conflicts result in arguments and verbal taunting and some even culminate in physical fights; too many end when one or more students has been seriously injured. As a result of the serious and frequent nature of these problems, many educators suggest that students themselves should be involved in and learn how to find solutions to their own conflicts in a constructive manner. Conflict Resolution has promise as a model that educators can use to ease management problems on a schoolwide basis. Further research, especially in middle and high schools, is needed to determine how it can best be instituted.

Alfie Kohn's Theories

Alfie Kohn, unlike some of the other theorists that have been presented, has discussed and written on a wide variety of topics in education. Many who are familiar with his work may not associate him as much with behavior management as with other current topics of interest in the profession. Kohn is considered one of the leading opponents of the national movement toward a greater emphasis on test scores; his *The Case Against Standardized Testing* (Kohn, 2000) is a short but powerful argument that the testing movement is hurting, not helping education. His *No Contest: The Case Against Competition* (Kohn, 1992) is seen as an important critique of the impact of competition on American life.

Kohn (1993) takes the position that rewards and punishments represent "opposite sides of the same coin" and both should be avoided. Kohn describes himself as a person who has long been an opponent of the principles of behaviorism which he believes are flawed and lead to many educational problems. Some of the problems directly affect the way teachers motivate and manage students. His position holds that rewards (often referred to by Kohn as "bribes") and punishments can change behaviors, but that the change will be short-lived because rewards and punishments function only to change specific behaviors in specific situations. Rewards and punishments do not function to change value systems and individual character. While they may be used to produce temporary compliance, they tend not to help bring about long-term, worthwhile goals such as increased student self-reliance, creative thinking, or self-confidence. The essence of Kohn's theory is that, for long-term positive change to occur, students must internalize prosocial values and become a part of a caring community. Students must exhibit prosocial behavior. **Prosocial behavior** is *behavior directed toward promoting the well-being of someone else.* This is as opposed to **antisocial behavior,** or *behavior directed toward bringing about a negative consequence for someone or something.* Rewards and punishments merely train students much the way animals are trained. As opposed to being trained like animals, students must be enculturated into a learning community where they can think about and act on basic human values such as kindness, fairness, and personal responsibility. Central to the functioning of this community are the teachers' abilities to communicate with students while allowing students to communicate with them and each other (Powell, McLaughlin, Savage, & Zehm, 2001). Kidron and Fleischman (2007) have identified that prosocial behavior means positive actions that benefit others, prompted by empathy, moral values, and a sense of personal responsibility rather than a desire for personal gain. Research suggests that the following schoolwide approaches can promote prosocial behavior in schools: (1) train teachers to integrate values instruction into classroom management, (2) foster a caring community throughout the school, and (3) use positive discipline practices.

When one sets out to not only change observable behavior, but to transform a student's core being, the task seems almost Herculean in nature. Kohn (1993) has provided a set of guidelines for teachers to follow that can serve as a framework for developing what he sees as the proper learning environment. The following elements are included in the formation of this framework.

1. Collaboration
2. Choice
3. Caring
4. Modeling
5. Explaining
6. Attributing Positive Motives
7. Offering Opportunities to Care
8. Emphasizing Perspective Taking

Collaboration: As children mature they should be brought into the decision making process more and more and be given input into deciding what is and is not acceptable. Mutual problem solving is at the heart of this type of collaboration. Teacher and student should plan together how best a problem can be faced and prevented in the future.

Kohn suggests that students will often make restitution and prevent future problems when they do not fear punishment for their mistakes.

Choice: Children should be given the opportunity to participate in meaningful decision making concerning what will happen to them as a result of unacceptable behavior. Students need to have real autonomy to make choices after giving their input.

Caring: Children will care for other people more if they feel other people care for them. A caring, supportive environment is at the heart of Kohn's theory.

Modeling: Adults teach by example. If students are to be intrinsically motivated to do good deeds and care for one another, they need to have teachers who are well respected to model desired conduct (e.g., listen respectfully, care for students, and treat all students honestly and fairly).

Explaining: It is not enough to model desired traits. Explanations of what is desired and why certain things should or should not be done must be given in language that is understood by the students. Such clear explaining behavior leads to reasoning with students instead of demanding simple obedience. Explanations are not lectures but are explorations of why things should be done in certain ways.

Attributing Positive Motives: A basic belief that children are born good and not bad and a desire to accept a reasonable excuse for undesired activity are at the core of providing the type of learning environment that students need. Teachers who believe that students are basically good, and attribute to them the best possible motive for behavior consistent with the facts, are more likely to help students develop good values.

Offering Opportunities to Care: Teachers who want caring students must give their students opportunities to demonstrate caring behaviors. Students who tutor other students, care for pets, and help classmates solve problems, for example, will more readily become caring individuals themselves.

Emphasizing Perspective Taking: If a goal is to produce students who perform good deeds from a desire to do good and to help others, as opposed to seeking rewards, teachers must help students view the world from the eyes of those who are less fortunate or in some way weaker. Students must empathize or perform what is called "perspective taking." "How does it feel to be called names?" "How does it feel to be bullied?" "How does it feel to be laughed at by others?" These are questions students might reflect on in order to appreciate the effect negative behavior can have on others. Failure to take on or at least understand other people's points of view accounts for much of the behavior seen as troublesome in schools today.

Beyond this framework for developing the proper learning environment which focuses on the teacher as a stimulus for creating a positive classroom atmosphere, Kohn (1993) notes that entire schools can be organized to help students develop prosocial behaviors. Activities should be adopted across the entire school that will assist educators in developing the type of caring environment that children need and deserve.

Class Meetings: Kohn believes that students at all ages benefit from opportunities to take time to plan together, make decisions, solve problems, and reflect on the happenings of the day. These types of activities have the potential to create a feeling of community in the school and classroom and provide an opportunity to take on the perspectives of other students. This approach is consistent with the theories of other educators such as William Glasser.

Unity-building Activities: Activities designed to build a feeling of community and a belonging to the group or team are important. Such activities help students communicate better and develop understanding and empathy for one another. Some groups or teams create logos, develop newsletters, put on plays, participate in intramural activities, and arrange for many other unity-building activities that strengthen the ability of students to communicate with and understand their fellow students.

Schoolwide Programs: Schoolwide community service programs serve to develop a feeling of community within and among students. Programs that foster older students mentoring or tutoring younger students have great value when trying to develop feelings of caring.

Prosocial Literature: The stories teachers use in their classrooms serve a similar function as modeling. A school wide literature program, for example, can stress the use of materials that emphasize desired values such as fairness, kindness, tolerance, and honesty.

Kohn's theory of behavior emphasizes the education of students to value goodness and respect for others. Students must want and desire to be good. It is not enough to just avoid negative behavior or to act acceptably. Students do not look for rewards or seek to avoid punishment, but, to learn to become good human beings. While it is hard to argue with this theory, the question seems to be one of utility. Can teachers show the patience that is needed for such a long, slow process of personal development to take place? Kohn would ask if teachers can afford not to show such patience.

SELECTING MANAGEMENT MODELS

The information presented in the first part of this chapter has provided an overview of key theories and models for managing students in school and classroom settings. Teachers are asked to analyze this information to determine which theory or collection of theories would be best suited to their individual personalities and classrooms. Before making the decision to adopt any management model, it is suggested that teachers undertake more in-depth study to include, when possible, site visitations to where different programs or models are being successfully utilized.

Curwin and Mendler (1988) provide a list of helpful questions to ask to guide teachers in their analysis of theories and models of classroom management. Figure 3.2 provides a list of these questions. The remainder of the chapter offers a brief analysis of each theory and model that has been presented as related to each question.

---

1. What happens to students who break rules? Punishments or consequences?
2. Is it realistically possible to reinforce the program consistently?
3. What do students learn as a result of the program?
4. Are the principles of behavior as visible and as important as the rules?
5. Do students have a say in what happens to them?
6. Do teachers have discretion in implementing consequences?
7. Is adequate time given for professional development of teachers and administrators? Is the training completed in only a day or two? Is there continuous follow-up and administrative support?
8. Does the plan account for the special relationship between teaching and discipline style, or does it focus exclusively on student behavior? Does it encourage teachers to examine their own potential contributions to discipline problems?
9. Is the dignity of the students preserved? Are students protected from embarrassment?
10. Is the program consistent with the stated goals of the school?

Figure 3.2. Guidelines to help teachers select management models (Curwin & Mendler, 1988).

1. *What happens to students who break rules?*

Kounin: The teacher handles the misconduct firmly in order to positively impact the entire class.

Dreikurs: Students receive logical consequences that they perceive as being unpleasant.

Glasser: Behavior contracts make students aware of and responsible for the consequences of their misconduct. If a student's behavior cannot be modified, the student is removed from the group.

Ginott: Students are given the choice of conducting themselves correctly or losing certain freedoms. The teacher's focus is on the behavior, not the person.

Jones: Emphasis is placed on keeping students on task to prevent misconduct.

Gordon: The teacher sends an *I message* to the student that identifies the infraction, why it is unacceptable, and how it effects the teacher's work or makes the teacher feel.

Canter and Canter: Students are given consequences when rules are broken.

Skinner: The focus is placed on channeling students in the correct direction in order that positive reinforcements can be given for good conduct. As a result, the misdirected student is shaped into a student behaving acceptably. Serious misconduct is not ignored.

Johnson and Johnson: Emphasis is directed toward student-to-student conflict. Students should resolve these conflicts in ways that all parties see as acceptable.

Kohn: The teacher talks to the student about the misbehavior and tries to induce the student to reflect on ways to improve the situation. The teacher is certain to seek input from the student concerning what should happen while avoiding the use of rewards and punishments.

2. Is it realistically possible to reinforce the program consistently?

Kounin: The model focuses on individual teacher behavior in the classroom. When the suggested behaviors become part of the teacher's everyday conduct, consistency should be maintained.

Dreikurs: Yes. The model focuses on individual teacher behavior. Consistency will come as teachers master the behavior.

Glasser: Yes. However, consistency becomes a bit more difficult; with In-School Suspension (ISS), for example, teachers and administrators must work with all teachers. High levels of coordination are needed to maintain consistency.

Ginott: Yes. The model focuses on the interaction between a teacher and a group of students. There will be the challenge to make certain that *sane messages* are provided equitably to all students.

Jones: Yes. Nonverbal communication, reward systems, and time on task are emphasized. The challenge is to maintain the same level of effectiveness with students of varying ability and motivation.

Gordon: Yes. Like Ginott's theory, Teacher Effectiveness Training (TET) is based on interaction between teacher and student. As students increase in number and diversity, consistency will be a greater challenge and concern.

Canter and Canter: Yes. When teachers learn the procedures involved, they will be able to consistently reinforce the program.

Skinner: The behaviorist principles guiding Applied Behavior Analysis are designed to provide consistency in the reinforcement of the program.

Johnson and Johnson: The model relies on the support of trainers, counselors, administrators, and teachers in order to produce the desired results and focuses on the peer mediation skills of individual students. Consistently reinforcing such a program is a challenge. Further evidence is needed to answer this question.

Kohn: Yes. As was true with Ginott and Gordon, effectiveness of this model is based on the teacher's ability to communicate with students. Some students are more likely to respond to this type of reasoning than others.

3. What do students learn as a result of the use of the program?

Kounin: Students learn to stay on task and remain focused. An emphasis on reducing student boredom may lead to learning to enjoy school more.

Dreikurs: Students learn to feel responsible for their own behavior as well as the behaviors of classmates. Students develop more self-respect as well as more respect for others.

Glasser: Students learn to feel more empowered to make decisions, control their own environment and improve their ability to work and communicate in groups.

Ginott: Through cooperative activities students learn self-respect, self-esteem, and to develop greater satisfaction with themselves.

Jones: Students learn the importance of staying on task and making academic progress.

Gordon: Students learn to better communicate their own feelings, relate to the feelings of others, and resolve problems.

Canter and Canter: Students learn that there are consequences for interfering with the rights of others and that it is not necessary for teachers to debate and defend their positions of authority.

Skinner: This is an important point for debate. Critics of behaviorist principles often maintain that students learn to think they should be rewarded for doing what they should be doing as a matter of fact. Behaviorists feel students learn whatever adults want them to learn by shaping the students' behaviors. Some critics fear that student creativity is hampered.

Johnson and Johnson: Students learn to resolve conflicts in mutually satisfying ways that are fair to all concerned parties.

Kohn: Students learn to develop and use their critical thinking skills as they reflect on their own behavior as it relates to specific situations. Perhaps, most importantly, students learn to be caring, responsible, empathetic human beings who value good conduct.

4. Are the principles of behavior as visible and as important as the rules?

Kounin: Yes. The principles of good leadership by the teacher and appropriate conduct by students are not lost to any rigid set of rules and procedures.

Dreikurs: The answer is yes as in the case of Kounin's theories.

Glasser: The principles of behavior are explained clearly. The rules for conduct and consequences for misconduct are evident; if the teacher understands Glasser's theory, the principles for behavior at the theory's foundation should not be lost.

Ginott: Although Ginott dedicated much time to explaining the rules (i.e., the *do's* and *don'ts*) for teacher and student behavior, he also carefully explained the principles guiding these rules.

Jones: The basic principle guiding this theory is that most problems occur because students are allowed to waste time. This principle does not get lost in the discussion of rules and procedures.

Gordon: Although TET was developed on the principles of Gestaltist psychology similar to those of Carl Rogers, teacher techniques and student rules often seem to dominate when educators discuss the model.

Canter and Canter: Teachers often focus on the rules for behavior and techniques of administering Assertive Discipline instead of the principles upon which it is based.

Skinner: The principles of operant conditioning go hand in hand with techniques and rules for behavior. The principles upon which the system is based are not lost.

Johnson and Johnson: The principle that students should learn to resolve their own conflicts in an amiable fashion is reinforced in the process.

Kohn: The principle that students should become caring, empathetic people is central. There is no reliance on a long list of rules.

5. Do students have a say in what happens to them?

Kounin: The emphasis is on teacher behaviors. A concern about student input is not paramount.

Dreikurs: Yes. Dreikurs suggests that students should take part in setting logical consequences for their misconduct.

Glasser: The teacher utilizes class meetings to ensure student input concerning the setting of logical consequences. Students are encouraged to develop their own plans for correcting behavior throughout the process.

Ginott: An emphasis is placed on students making choices, not on forced compliance. The teacher is asked to remain sensitive to students' feelings.

Jones: The emphasis is on the prevention of problems. Student input into what will happen when rules are broken is not a major concern.

Gordon: Much emphasis is placed on student input as teachers are encouraged to use active listening techniques.

Canter and Canter: The theory is based on the need for students to comply to established, nondebatable rules.

Skinner: Students have little control over what happens to them as their behavior is shaped. This has been an issue with the critics of behaviorism.

Johnson and Johnson: Conflict Resolution stresses the importance of training students so that they determine what happens to them when conflicts arise.

Kohn: In order for Kohn's theory to be actualized, students must always be involved in deciding what happens to them.

6. Do teachers have discretion in implementing consequences?

Kounin: Yes. Teachers are encouraged to be leaders and decision-makers.

Dreikurs: Yes. Teachers provide logical consequences to students who exhibit misconduct. However, teachers use their own discretion in determining, along with students, the actual consequences.

Glasser: Teachers can use their discretion to a point. When student misconduct reaches a level where isolation is necessary, consequences are prescribed.

Ginott: Teachers are asked not to order, boss, or force students to comply. Teachers are given guidelines by these directions and do not lose their freedom in making judgments concerning the implementation of consequences for misbehavior.

Jones: Teachers should limit verbal corrections while using nonverbal expressions and gestures to communicate with students. The emphasis is on avoiding problems by keeping students active and engaged. Consequences for misbehavior are not a central issue. Teachers have freedom to make judgments as needed.

Gordon: TET is a structured, systematic program emphasizing clear communication between teacher and student. The structure does limit teacher discretion in the use of consequences.

Canter and Canter: Teachers have discretion to set consequences for misconduct. After the consequences are set, teachers are expected to consistently adhere to the system.

Skinner: Although consequences are sometimes used, especially when misbehavior is severe, the model specifically emphasizes rewarding good behaviors. Teachers have freedom to set rewards and consequences as judged appropriate.

Johnson and Johnson: Conflict Resolution does not focus on teachers setting consequences for misconduct. Students resolve problems without teacher intervention.

Kohn: Teachers have discretion since the emphasis is on individual problem solving and growth, not on consequences. Punishments (consequences) and rewards are to be replaced by reasoning, reflection, and support.

7. Is adequate time given for professional development of teachers and administrators? Is there continuous follow-up and administrative support?

These questions must be answered in the context of a specific school environment. The successful use of any model requires adequate training and administrative support over an extended period of time if maximum results are to be realized. Some models, for example TET, Reality Therapy or Choice Theory, Conflict Resolution, and Applied Behavior Analysis, require extensive and long-term specialized training and support.

8. Does the plan account for the special relationship between teaching and discipline style, or does it focus exclusively on student behavior? Does it encourage teachers to examine their own potential contributions to discipline problems?

Kounin: The relationship between teaching style and management style is apparent in the discussion of concepts such as *withitness, thrust,* and *ripple effect.*

Dreikurs: The plan allows teachers to make their personal contribution to solving problems as they analyze student behavior and react accordingly. The relationship between teaching style and discipline style is not as obvious.

Glasser: The group and cooperative activities link the management and teaching styles of teachers. Teachers have a great potential to contribute in leading class meetings.

Ginott: Sending *sane messages*, modeling desired behaviors, and eliminating sarcasm toward and labeling of students are all avenues to link teaching and discipline styles.

Jones: The theory is built upon the relationship between teaching and discipline styles. Methods of instruction to be used to diminish discipline problems by keeping students on task are emphasized.

Gordon: *Active listening* techniques can be used in management and instruction; yet, the focus more so is on management styles. Teachers using TET should feel they are making an important contribution to the solution of problems.

Canter and Canter: Management of student behavior is the main focus. The model is also designed to empower teachers in order to help them realize their potential to contribute to the successful management of discipline problems.

Skinner: The behaviorist principles of Applied Behavior Analysis can be used for instructional practices in a method similar to the ones used to manage behavior; however, there is a definite focus on isolated behaviors as opposed to an interaction of management and instructional style.

Johnson and Johnson: Conflict Resolution focuses on student behavior, not the relationship between teaching and discipline styles. The potential contribution that teachers make is limited.

Kohn: The theory focuses on the special relationship between teaching style and discipline style. In the tradition of the early

Progressive Educators, reflection in a democratic classroom permeates Kohn's ideal for managing and teaching students.

9. Is the dignity of the students preserved? Are students protected from embarrassment?

Kounin: Yes. The importance of maintaining student interest and participation is stressed. Any incident that embarrasses a student would have a definite negative *ripple effect* on the entire class.

Dreikurs: Students must develop self-respect in order to adjust to the environment of the classroom. Any action that negatively impacts the student's self-image is inappropriate.

Glasser: The teacher is a democratic leader who involves students in group discussion and decision making processes. The type of relationship encouraged between teacher and student could not exist if students were not treated with dignity.

Ginott: Central to the theory is the position that teachers avoid sarcasm and labeling when interacting with students. Teachers should treat students with dignity in order to foster growth in their self-esteem.

Jones: Yes. Students are rewarded for productivity. There is nothing to suggest that students should be treated in an undignified fashion.

Gordon: Teachers are encouraged to avoid being accusatory and to treat students with dignity.

Canter and Canter: Yes. It is important to remember that, although teachers should avoid passive behaviors, Assertive Discipline opposes teacher hostility. When being assertive, teachers must guard against crossing the line that would result in students being treated in an embarrassing, undignified manner.

Skinner: The behaviorist focus is on rewarding desired behavior; the purpose is to encourage students to behave well in order that they can be rewarded. Although Behaviorism is often discussed vis-à-vis Humanism, this in no way implies that behaviorists are inhumane in their treatment of students.

Johnson and Johnson: Yes. Conflict Resolution is designed to empower students to solve their own problems in ways that are fair to all parties concerned.

Kohn: Fundamental to this model is the belief that no student's self-worth should ever be compromised. The teacher models a caring, empathetic attitude so students will learn to treat each other with dignity.

10. Is the program consistent with the stated goals of the school?

This question can only be answered in the context of a specific school environment. It can be said, however, that it is important to match the school's goals and philosophies with any management model to be used by the faculty in order to ensure maximum consistency and support from administrators and parents. For example, if the school has the goal of increasing time spent on academic activities, Kounin's and Jones' theories may be more of a match with the school's needs than would be the theories of Johnson and Johnson and Kohn.

CONCLUSION

Chapter 3 has provided an overview of ten popular models for classroom management and identified the theorists associated with their development. An extensive amount of material (e.g., books, journal articles, tapes, training kits, etc.) can be found on each of the models and theories that has been discussed. Teachers should review this information, find ideas that appeal to their personal style and philosophy, and do further research prior to making a final decision about what would work best for them. It is recognized that other theories exist and that new theories will evolve as the knowledge base in this area continues to grow and as societal changes take place.

Questions developed to assist teachers in the selection of management models were used as a way to systematically analyze and examine the models and guide decisions about their use in particular settings. The last section of the chapter provided preliminary answers to each question from the perspective of each of the ten models presented. Teachers are encouraged to answer each of these questions in greater detail for themselves based on further analysis of the models and a comparison to their own educational settings.

Without a theoretical basis or underpinning to guide their actions, teachers run the risk of becoming inconsistent in their behaviors and, perhaps worse, making managerial decisions without understanding the full ramifications and implications for the students involved. The information presented in this chapter can serve as a starting point to the development of this needed theoretical foundation.

QUESTIONS/ACTIVITIES FOR REFLECTION

1. Why should a teacher be aware of such a large number of models or theories for management when he or she is not likely to use most of them? What are important points to consider in adopting any model or part of a model for classroom use?
2. Take the side of a teacher who does not agree with the principles upon which Applied Behavior Analysis are based and develop an argument against its use. Now, take the opposite point of view and argue for the use of Applied Behavior Analysis.
3. Create a scenario illustrating how a teacher might apply Alphie Kohn's principles of management to a classroom management problem dealing with student cheating.
4. Of all of the models discussed, which one do you think is the most sound? Explain why you chose this one. Which one do you think is the least sound? Why?
5. In what way or ways is the theory of William Glasser (Reality Therapy/Choice Theory and the use of *class meetings*) more or less applicable to teachers who teach in the upper grades (grades 7-12) as opposed to the lower grades (grades PreK-6)?

REFERENCES

Albert, L. (1996). *Cooperative discipline.* Circle Pines, MN: American Guidance Service, Inc.

Alberto, P., & Troutman, A. (2005). *Applied behavior analysis for teachers: Influencing student performance* (7th ed.). Columbus, OH: Merrill.

Association for Supervision and Curriculum Development (ASCD). (2007). Poll. Retrieved May 31, 2007, from www.ascd.org/portal/site/ascd/menuitem.

Bennett, B. (1997). Middle level discipline and young adolescents: Making the connection. In J.L. Irvin (Ed.), *What current research says to the middle level practitioner.* Columbus, OH: National Middle School Association.

Borman, S., & Levine, J. (1997). *A practical guide to elementary instruction: From plan to delivery.* Boston: Allyn & Bacon.

Burden, P. (2003). *Classroom management: Creating a successful learning community* (2nd ed.). New York: Wiley.

Canter, L., & Canter, M. (1992). *Lee Canter's assertive discipline: Positive behavior management for today's classroom.* Santa Monica, CA: Canter.

Canter, L., & Canter, M. (1976). *Assertive discipline: A take-charge approach for today's educator.* Seal Beach, CA: Canter.

Canter, L. (1988). Let the educator beware: A response to Curwin and Mendler. *Educational Leadership, 46*(2), 71–73.

Covaleski, J. (1992). Discipline and morality: Beyond rules and consequences. *The Educational Forum, 56*(2), 56–60.

Curwin, R., & Mendler, A. (1988). Packaged discipline programs: Let the buyer beware. *Educational Leadership, 46*(2), 68–71.

Dreikurs, R. (1968). *Psychology in the classroom* (2nd ed.). New York: Harper & Row.

Dreikurs, R., & Cassell, P. (1972). *Discipline without tears.* New York: Hawthorn Books.

Eggen, P., & Kauchak, D. (2007). *Educational psychology: Windows on classrooms* (7th ed.). Upper Saddle River, NJ: Pearson Education.

Ginott, H. (1965). *Between parent and child.* New York: Avon.

Ginott, H. (1969). *Between parent and teenager.* New York: Macmillan.

Ginott, H. (1971). *Teacher and child.* New York: Macmillan.

Glasser, W. (1965). *Reality therapy: A new approach to psychiatry.* New York: Harper & Row.

Glasser, W. (1969). *Schools without failure.* New York: Harper & Row.

Glasser, W. (1992). *The quality school: Managing students without coercion* (2nd ed.). New York: Harper-Perennial.

Glasser, W. (1993). *The quality school teacher.* New York: Harper-Perennial.

Glasser, W. (2000). *Every student can succeed.* Chatsworth, CA: Black Forest Press.

Good, T., & Brophy, J. (1986). *Educational psychology: A realistic approach* (3rd ed.). New York: Holt, Rhinehart, & Winston.

Good, T., & Brophy, J. (2007). *Looking in classrooms* (10th ed.). New York: Allyn & Bacon.

Gordon, T. (1974). *Teacher effectiveness training.* New York: Wyden.

Hunt, G., Touzel, T., & Wiseman, D. (1999). *Effective teaching: Preparation and implementation* (3rd ed.). Springfield, IL: Charles C Thomas.

Johnson, D., & Johnson, R. (2005). *Joining together: Group theory and group skills* (9th ed.). Boston: Allyn & Bacon.

Johnson, D., & Johnson, R. (1995). *Teaching students to be peacemakers* (3rd ed.). Edina, MN: Interaction.

Johnson, D., & Johnson, R. (2004). The three Cs of promoting social and emotional learning. In J. Zins, R. Weissberg, M. Wang, & H. Walberg (Eds.), *Building academic success on social and emotional learning* (pp. 40–58). New York: Teachers College Press.

Jones, F. (2000). *Positive classroom discipline* (3rd ed.). New York: McGraw-Hill.

Kauffman, J. (1989). *Characteristics of behavior disorders of children and youth* (4th ed.). Upper Saddle River, NJ: Merrill/Prentice Hall.

Kidron, Y., & Fleischman, S. (2007). Research matters: Promoting adolescents' prosocial behavior. *Educational Leadership,* Retrieved May 31, 2007, from www.ascd.org/portal/site/ascd/template.

Kohn, A. (1992). *No contest: The case against competition* (Rev. ed.). Boston: Houghton Mifflin.

Kohn, A. (1993). *Punished by rewards: The trouble with gold stars, incentive plans, A's, praise, and other bribes.* New York: Houghton Mifflin.

Kohn, A. (2000). *The case against standardized testing: Raising the scores, ruining the schools.* Portsmouth, NH: Heinemann.

Kounin, J. (1970). *Discipline and group management in classrooms.* New York: Holt, Rhinehart, & Winston.

Lezotte, L.W. (1997). *Learning for all.* Okemos, MI: Effective Schools Products.

McCaslin, M., & Good, T. (1992). Compliant cognition: The misalliance of management and instructional goals in current school reform. *Educational Research, 21*(3), 4–17.

McCormack, S. (1989). Response to Render, Padilla and Krank: But practitioners say it works! *Educational Leadership, 46*(6), 77–79.

Manning, L. & Bucher, K. (2007). *Classroom management: Models, applications, and cases* (2nd ed.). Upper Saddle River, NJ: Pearson Education, Inc.

Pfiffner, L., Rosen, L., & O'Leary, S. (1985). The efficacy of an all-positive approach to classroom management. *Journal of Applied Behavior Analysis, 18,* 257–261.

Powell, R., McLaughlin, H., Savage, T., & Zehm, S. (2001). *Classroom management: Perspectives on the social curriculum.* Upper Saddle River, NJ: Merrill/Prentice Hall.

Render, G., Padilla, J., & Krank, H. (1989). What research really shows about assertive discipline. *Educational Leadership, 46*(6), 72–75.

Rogers, C., & Freiberg, H. (1994). *Freedom to learn* (3rd ed.). Columbus, OH: Charles E. Merrill.

Sokolove, S., Garrett, S., Sadker, M., & Sadker, D. (1990). Interpersonal communication skills. In J. Cooper (Ed.), *Classroom teaching skills.* Lexington, MA: D.C. Heath.

Stevahn, L., Johnson, D., Johnson, R., Green, K., & Laginski, M. (1997). Effects on high school students of conflict resolution training integrated into English literature. *The Journal of Social Psychology, 137*(3), 302–313.

Thorndike, E.L. (1905). *The elements of psychology.* New York: Seiler.

Thorndike, E.L. (1911). *Animal intelligence: Experimental studies.* New York: Macmillan.

Tolson, E., McDonald, S., & Moriarty, A. (1992). Peer mediation among high school students: A test of effectiveness. *Social Work in Education, 14,* 86–93.

Travers, R. (1977). *Essentials of learning.* New York: Macmillan Publishing.

Webster, D. (1993). The unconvincing case for school-based conflict resolution programs for adolescents. *Health Affairs,* Winter, 127–141.

Woolfolk, A. (2007). *Educational psychology* (10th ed.). Needham Heights, MA: Allyn & Bacon.

Zabel, R., & Zabel, M. (1996). *Classroom management in context: Orchestrating positive learning environments.* Boston: Houghton Mifflin.

Zirpoli, T., & Melloy, K. (2004). *Behavior management: Applications for teachers and parents* (4th ed.). Upper Saddle River, NJ: Merrill/Prentice-Hall.

Chapter 4

BEST PRACTICE IN TEACHING FOR BEST PRACTICE IN STUDENT MOTIVATION AND CLASSROOM MANAGEMENT

No study of motivation and management in the classroom would be complete without addressing the topic of best practice in teaching. The relationship between best practice in teaching and best practice in motivation and management is well documented. Where motivation and management problems arise, problems in teaching practice generally will also be found. Educational research reinforces the fact that higher levels of student motivation and fewer instances of student management problems are evident where teachers use effective teaching practices. Lieberman (2007) recommends a strategy for improving low student performance as beginning with exploring the answers to three basic questions. These are: "Who are our students?", "What do we want them to learn?", and, "What do we want them to do when they don't learn it?" This straightforward approach to seeking answers to these core questions that pertain to student learning reinforces the need for the continued and deliberate study of motivation, management, and instructional practice.

Regardless of the classroom management or student motivation technique used, no approach will be effective for long if the teacher is not also using effective teaching practices (Tauber, 1999). Classroom management models and their accompanying theories and recommended strategies that go with them cannot serve as substitutes for good teaching. In many ways, effective teaching itself represents a preventive discipline measure in that, when teaching is effective, students are involved and interested in their learning to the degree that they are not inclined to cause problems (Glasser, 1990). But, as identified here, merely understanding effective teaching is not sufficient. It is the

127

teacher's ability to understand and implement sound practices in student motivation and classroom management, coupled with similarly sound practices in teaching, that pulls the entire learning experience together and make the most optimum levels of learning possible for students and comparable levels of teaching possible for teachers.

It is easy to sometimes forget or underestimate the ongoing challenges found in the typical classroom and not fully recognize the power of their ultimate impact on both teachers and students. William Chandler Bagley of the University of Illinois wrote in 1907 that, "Absolute fearlessness is the first essential for the teacher on whom rests the responsibility for governing an elementary or secondary school. This fearlessness is not alone or chiefly the expression of physical courage, although this must not be lacking. It is rather an expression of moral courage . . . standing firm in one's convictions even though the community may not approve . . . it is this sort of courage that is the rarest and, at the same time, the most essential" (Curwin & Mendler, 1999, 1). Courage will always be an important part of the learning process and, for many, the greatest challenge is in the courage to establish, manage, and teach in the type of classroom environment that will produce the best learning for all students involved. The following statement of a high school senior reflects the power of this environment:

Silent Defiance

I'm the one who watched,
as you laughed;
I'm the one who listened patiently,
while you talked unceasingly;
I'm the one who sat silent,
as your shouts grew louder;
I'm the one who always came,
while your chair sat empty;
I'm the one whose dreams were hidden,
as yours were fulfilled;
I'm the one who cared,
while you butchered knowledge;
I'm the one who reasoned,
as you discussed;
I'm the one who will remember
when all of you will forget.

(by Heather Osborn, high school senior, from
Curwin and Mendler, 1999, pp. 1–2)

Recognizing that effective student motivation and classroom management rest on a solid foundation of effective teaching, an overview of best teaching practices that have been identified through educational research is presented here. The relationship between quality teaching, quality student motivation, and quality classroom management will be evident in this analysis.

In establishing the overall framework for this text, Chapter 1 introduced the Model for Reflection and Inquiry and it was identified that, to be effective, teachers must be good reflective practitioners. Three case studies of beginning teachers who had experienced problems of motivation and management in their classrooms were also presented. Of the three teachers featured in these case studies, Tameka (in the case study *Tameka's Planning and Analysis*) was the only teacher of the three who really embraced and dealt directly as a reflective practitioner with the problems that she encountered. Tameka systematically reflected on the events of her difficult day and how these events contributed to her problems in student motivation and classroom management. With her reflections being presented as an example of the use of the Model for Reflection and Inquiry, Tameka's behaviors were consistent with those of a reflective educator. She identified the problems that she had encountered, reviewed specific events of the day related to them, analyzed the events with respect to their impact on her classroom management and ability to motivate her students, and, based on this information, made decisions as to how she should move forward in making adjustments for the next day. Tameka was engaged in guided problem solving and reflective thinking. And, of special importance, Tameka accepted the responsibility for her student motivation and classroom management difficulties and did not lay blame for her problems on the "type" of students she was working with, their parents, her administrative support, or anything else. While her problems involved others, the problems were hers to solve.

Tameka's situation and the process of reflection that she went through needs to be considered as they relate to the information on best practice in teaching that is developed throughout the remainder of this chapter. A formal model such as the Model for Reflection and Inquiry can be used to bring logical reasoning to problems associated with student behavior and help combat what is often the emotionally charged environment that accompanies challenges of student motivation and dealing with student behavior problems. It can also guide the development of well-grounded decision making with respect to identifying solutions to these problems. Such an approach will systematically lead to higher quality in instruction, motivation, and management in the classroom.

The search for best practice in teaching, and, therefore, in student motivation and classroom management, must always be ongoing and at times may seem to be an intellectually exhausting endeavor. A mistake made by some teachers occurs when they believe that what needs to be known about best teaching practices is already understood. Full understanding in this area, in fact, will never be reached as the knowledge base related to best practice in teaching continues to develop and expand. The application of this knowledge base should always be situational or contextual in its use, resulting in the need to not only know "what works" in teaching but also to know when, where, and with whom it works best. Regarding reflective practice and best practice in teaching, Henson and Eller (1999, p. 10) note:

> Effective teachers are always looking for better ways to teach . . . are willing to explore different approaches. . . . This is why curiosity, experimentation, and risk-taking are so important to teachers. Throughout their careers, successful teachers improve their ability to reflect on their behavior and use their reflective judgment to improve their teaching.

Educational research has identified and continues to reinforce certain teacher characteristics related to effective teaching resulting in higher student achievement. These characteristics are often referred to as best practices in teaching.

ESTABLISHING A FOUNDATION FOR BEST TEACHING PRACTICE

Much of what is known about best practice in teaching includes information related to classroom planning and organization, goal setting and communication, teacher instructional strategies, time management, teacher-to-student interactions, relationships with students, and classroom management rules and procedures. As a starting point to the investigation of effective teaching practices and teacher characteristics, consider the following teacher characteristics and behaviors (Armstrong, Henson, & Savage, 1997).

Planning and Organization

Effective teachers play a central, dominant role in the classroom but involve students in planning and organization. Effective teachers accept their important responsibility in classroom leadership, but also that students who are personally invested in their own learning will develop a greater sense of ownership for their learning and achieve at higher levels.

High Goals and Communication

Effective teachers set high goals and communicate these goals to their students. It is important that teacher expectations be high though realistic; it is critical that teachers make their goals for their students clear, not only in terms of the learning experiences that will be undertaken, but also in terms of how students will be evaluated.

Instruction: Entire Class, Small Group, Independent

Effective teachers work mostly with the entire class and less often with small groups, sometimes providing independent work for students. Teachers who are able to coordinate the learning of all students at the same time through large group instructional experiences will develop a greater sense of community in the classroom and allow students to more clearly perceive their own progress, but also the work and activities of others at the same time.

Pace and Participation

Effective teachers maintain a brisk lesson pace, requiring public and overt student participation. Lessons that are seen by students as moving too slow, essentially only dragging along, allow for greater opportunities for students to drift away and become disengaged from the teacher; students who move forward with the lesson at a quicker pace, and who are overtly involved in the instruction, typically learn at higher levels and enjoy their learning more.

Criticism

Effective teachers use little criticism, shape student responses so that they are correct, hold students responsible for their work, and attend to students equitably. Treating students fairly, providing uplifting rather than negative comments, and letting students know that they have responsibilities as learners, just as the teacher has responsibilities as a teacher, result in a more wholesome and positive learning environment; students who feel safe in the learning environment, and who are meaningfully involved in it, are more successful in their work.

Clear Rules for Behavior

Effective teachers set and maintain clear rules for students' academic and social behavior. Though perhaps not thought to be the case by some, students do desire and need clear boundaries in the classroom; students work better in environments that are well-defined in terms of the *do's* and *don'ts*, the *right's* and *wrong's*, than they do in settings where there is ambiguity and inconsistency as to what is acceptable and not acceptable behavior.

Four specific teacher characteristics related to teaching effectiveness can be broken down into the broad categories of *lesson clarity, instructional variety, task orientation and engagement,* and *student success rate* (Borich, 1992).

Lesson Clarity

Lesson clarity refers to how well students understand the lessons of their teachers. It is not just important that teachers believe that they are clear; what is really more important is whether or not their students truly understand them. Teachers who are vague, use vocabulary that students do not understand, or who are generally not well organized in their work typically are not considered as being clear in their teaching. When students do not understand the various communications of their teachers, there is little reason to think that they will be able to perform at the highest levels of their potentials. Students need to understand what their teachers are saying and expect of them in order to benefit the most from their learning experiences.

Instructional Variety

Instructional variety refers to the general teaching repertoire of the teacher. For example, "Does the teacher use a number of different teaching strategies or only a very few?", "Does the teacher utilize many different resources in his or her teaching or use the same resources over and over?" Having variety in instruction contributes to the perceived "energy" of the teacher and offers students different stimuli during lesson activities to which they may respond. Using different instructional approaches makes the teacher appear more interesting and exciting to students, piques students' natural curiosity to learn, and varies the stimuli in the classroom. Most students learn best through their encounters with a variety of different stimuli. The teacher with variability in the use of instructional techniques is able to offer students a greater number of connecting points as lessons are delivered. Consequently, the teacher who is skilled in using a number of different types of strategies is more effective than the teacher who is limited to only a few approaches.

Task Orientation and Engagement

Time on task is a powerful concept when analyzing the teaching-learning process. When one considers that there are only a limited number of hours in the day in which students are in school, and that a good portion of the typical school day is given over to noninstructional activities (e.g., moving from class to class, recess in the lower grades, lunch, traveling to and from the restroom), the question of time available for learning becomes even more critical. Having a high level of meaningful and successful time on task communicates to students that the teacher is well prepared and "in charge." It also communicates in clear terms where the teacher's instruction is headed and what students will be expected to know or be able to do when the end of the instructional period is reached. Students who are on task are much less likely to present behavioral problems for their teachers.

Effective teachers use their time wisely. Jones' theory of management was presented in Chapter 3 with the foundation of the theory identifying that problems of student management are frequently brought about by poor or inappropriate use of time in the classroom. Wasted or idle time lead to problems in management that should and could have been avoided. Time in schools and classrooms is often broken down into the following four dimensions.

1. **Allocated Time:** the amount of time a particular teacher or school designates to an identified course, topic or activity,
2. **Instructional Time:** the portion of Allocated Time that is actually devoted to learning activities,
3. **Engaged Time:** sometimes referred to as time-on-task, Engaged Time is the portion of Instructional Time that students actually spend directly involved in learning activities, and
4. **Academic Learning Time:** Academic Learning Time takes all other forms of time into account and is characterized by students not only paying attention during instructional activities, but also interacting successfully with the content that is being taught; it is that portion of the classroom time where students are successfully engaged in meaningful learning experiences.

Teachers who have greater levels of **Academic Learning Time**, *time when students are actively and successfully involved in the lesson's activities,* have students who learn at higher levels.

Given the multifaceted nature of any school, many events take place on a regular basis that compete for time which otherwise could be available for instruction. Instructional time is lost through different disruptions, interruptions, late starts, and less than smooth transitions. Out of a typical school year only thirty to forty percent of the time is given over to quality Academic Learning Time (Karweit, 1989; Weinstein & Mignano; 1993). Research supports that, the greater the amount of Academic Learning Time found in the classroom, the greater the level of student achievement. The best use of time in the classroom is determined, to a large extent, by the degree to which the teacher is fully planned for instruction. The better planned the teacher is for instruction that is relevant to the interests and needs of the students in the classroom, and responsive to their learning styles and abilities, the greater will be the levels of student achievement that can be reached.

Student Success Rate

Not only is wise use of time an important characteristic of effective teachers, effective teachers also have higher rates of student success in their teaching. **Student success rate** is defined *as the rate at which students understand and correctly complete their work.* Students should not be involved in just "doing things" in the classroom. What they do should be meaningful, learning-related as to what the teacher has planned for instruction, and result in successful achievement and productivity. Teachers need to know the abilities and interests of their students and plan their instruction accordingly based on this knowledge. Instruction in which few students can be successful falls far short of what needs to be accomplished in the classroom. This type of situation serves no one well. Success breeds success, and students who are successful one day will be better able to see themselves as being successful on another day. (See the discussion of Attribution Theory, Locus of Control, and Teacher Expectations in Chapter 2 as related to reasons given for student success.) Likewise, students who experience little or no success have far greater difficulty in seeing themselves as being successful and, in the end, in actually being successful. If teachers desire for their students to be successful in their learning, they must plan, teach, and evaluate in ways that ensure success for them.

A prevailing though problematic characteristic of the American society is one that focuses on identifying quick solutions or quick fixes to problems. The American society has even been referred to as a "fast food" or "microwave" society. It is no wonder that in such an environment that many teachers take this same outlook into their classrooms with respect to finding quick solutions to the problems that they encounter there. The fact is, there are no quick solutions or quick fixes to difficult and complex problems of student learning, motivation, and classroom management. The solutions that work best, in fact, may be just as readily found discussed in the research related to best practice in teaching as in studies of motivation and management.

EARLY RESEARCH ON BEST TEACHING PRACTICE

As motivation relates to management and management relates to motivation, so does best practice in teaching relate to both of these concepts together. One of the most significant and thorough reviews of the research in the area of teacher effectiveness was conducted over thirty-five years ago (Rosenshine & Furst, 1971). It is still considered important reading in the field today. Although considerable research has been conducted more recently, the early work of Rosenshine and Furst serves as a sound beginning point for the study of effective teaching behaviors related to student achievement. The effective teaching characteristics identified by Armstrong et al. (1997) and Borich (1992) may be looked upon, to some degree, as an expansion and further refinement of characteristics identified through this earlier research.

Of particular importance to the work of Rosenshine and Furst is the understanding given to the meaning of effective teaching. While teachers are expected to accomplish many things in their work, perhaps the most important accomplishment is guiding students to achieve at higher levels. Defining effective teaching as teaching that results in higher levels of student achievement is not to discount the importance of students developing positive feelings about themselves and the world around them, and toward learning itself. It does recognize, though, that the primary purpose of the teacher is to guide and advance students in their learning. In their early research, Rosenshine and Furst report a total of eleven teacher behaviors or variables (i.e., teaching practices) related to student achievement; they are presented here in the order of the degree to which they are so related.

1. Clarity
2. Variability
3. Enthusiasm
4. Task-Oriented and/or Business-Like Behavior
5. Student Opportunity to Learn Criterion Material
6. Use of Student Ideas and General Indirectness
7. Criticism
8. Use of Structuring Comments
9. Types of Questions
10. Probing Behaviors
11. Level of Difficulty of Instruction

Clarity

Teachers who have the ability to explain concepts clearly and who are able to answer student questions so that their students understand the answers given to them are characterized by clarity in their instruction. When teachers are clear in their communications, their students feel more secure in their learning. They are better able to comprehend what is expected of them and, as a result of this, perform at higher academic levels.

Variability

Variability, also referred to as instructional variety (Borich, 1992), is represented by the teacher's diversity of information-sending techniques or strategies used during the presentation of lessons. Teachers who have variability in their teaching utilize multiple strategies to get the main ideas of their lessons across to their students. Effective teachers have the ability to utilize expository lesson delivery as well as organize students for cooperative learning activities as appropriate to the purpose of the lesson. They are capable of exhibiting many different strategies in teaching and do so regularly. Through this variety, especially when strategies are matched to student learning styles, students remain more interested in the learning activities that their teachers have planned for them and learn more as a result.

Enthusiasm

Enthusiasm has been identified as the estimation of the amount of vigor and power displayed by the teacher. It also has been associated with the teacher's level of excitement, energy, involvement, and even interest regarding both the subject matter and teaching itself. Although an abstract concept, students definitely have their own ideas about the enthusiasm of their teachers. Students feel they know when teachers are enjoying their work and are excited about being in the classroom and when they are not. Students draw from the enthusiasm shown by their teachers, or at least from what they perceive as their teachers' enthusiasm, and respond accordingly. Teacher enthusiasm is related to the concept of *teacher efficacy* discussed earlier in Chapter 2 as a part of the teacher's attitude toward teaching and student learning. Teachers who exhibit enthusiasm communicate that they are confident in what they are doing, not only in their own abilities, but also in the abilities of their students.

Task-Oriented and/or Business-Like Behavior

Task-oriented teachers project that they know what they expect concerning student performance and the lessons that they teach and how to attain the student performance that they desire. They are seen by their students as being in charge, knowing what they are doing, organized, and focused on what needs to be accomplished. Being task-oriented and business-like does not mean being impersonal, aloof, cold, or distant when working with students. It does, however, communicate that the teacher knows that something important needs to be done and that the teacher and students, together, will be successful in completing the task that has been or is to be undertaken.

Student Opportunity to Learn Criterion Material

Teachers who are criterion-focused in their teaching communicate to students their expected instructional outcomes prior to beginning their instruction and then teach specifically toward the students' successful attainment of these desired outcomes. What is desired is not kept secret; there is no mystery. Students know what is expected of them and how they will be evaluated (the criteria used) as to their level of success in achieving the identified learning outcomes. This security of direction and understanding of the evaluation process is important to students as they engage in the teacher's planned learning activities. It also is important to the teacher in that it offers the teacher additional focus and direction with respect to addressing stated learning objectives.

Use of Student Ideas and General Indirectness

The use of student ideas by teachers during instruction and, in so doing, communicating to students that their ideas and input are important enhances student achievement. The use of student ideas is a good way to personalize the instruction and is an important part of *indirect teaching*. Students have higher levels of meaningful participation and interest in their learning when their ideas are regularly incorporated into the learning process. And, they have greater academic success as they perceive their teachers as valuing both them as individuals as well as their ideas.

Criticism

A negative relationship exists between the use of teacher criticism and student achievement. This point was identified earlier by Armstrong et al. (1997). Teachers who are characterized by using criticism in their teaching, often seen by students as an attempt to justify their authority, typically have students who achieve less in most subject areas. Teachers who use frequent criticism are perceived by their students as being less prepared for their work and less sure of themselves. The use of criticism can create a threatening environment for students, push students away, and detract from the learning process resulting in lower student achievement.

Use of Structuring Comments

The teacher's use of structuring comments or statements in communicating with students, i.e., alerting students to the more important instructional events which are to follow in the lesson, or important points to be made, is highly recommended and supported by educational research. The use of structuring comments is appropriate at the start of lessons and at the start of different sections of lessons. Such comments help students focus on and attend to what will be taking place during the instruction that follows. The use of structuring comments also projects to students that the teacher is well planned and has a clear understanding of where the learning activity is headed. All of this, in turn, correlates to higher levels of student achievement.

Types of Questions

Effective teachers are skilled at asking both higher and lower level questions of cognition; the use of both types is related to student achievement. The classic system of question categorization identified by Gallagher and Aschner (1963) is helpful in understanding levels and types of questions. This system places questions into four categories: *cognitive memory, convergent, divergent,* and *evaluative.* It serves as a guide for teachers as to the different levels of cognition of questions that they may choose to use in their teaching and the intellectual processing on the part of students that they invoke. The use of different types of questions helps to maintain student interest and projects a greater variability in teaching. The following explanation of the basic characteristics of the questions used in this system will help in the further analysis of this important teacher behavior (Hunt et al., 1999).

Cognitive Memory Questions: questions that ask students to recall previously learned and memorized information; single-word answers are often used in answering questions; answers tend to sound alike and are predictable; even though more lengthy answers may be provided, they do not require creative thought and are classified clearly as right or wrong; behaviors such as recalling, recognizing, and reporting are typically involved.

Examples of Cognitive Memory Questions:

1. Who painted the Mona Lisa?
2. What is the city with the largest population in Indiana?
3. In what year was the Declaration of Independence signed?

Convergent Questions: questions that ask students to put facts or concepts together in order to obtain the single correct answer; answers to convergent questions are more complex than answers to cognitive memory questions but are still classified as either right or wrong; questions may require students to make comparisons, explain facts or concepts, state or describe relationships, or solve problems using learned procedures.

Examples of Convergent Questions:

1. What is the relationship between crude oil and plastic?
2. How are amphibians and reptiles alike?
3. How are present methods of communication different from those used in the 1800s?

Divergent Questions: questions that ask students to engage in divergence of thought and produce responses that are original; student thinking is much more creative at this level of questioning; questions may require students to predict, hypothesize, or infer; expressions such as "what if" are common to questions in this category.

Examples of Divergent Questions:

1. What do you think our society will be like in terms of technology in one hundred years?

2. If you were in charge of our town, what is the first thing you would do? Why?
3. What might happen to our voting system if all voting was done electronically?

Evaluative Questions: questions that ask students to make judgments or evaluations based on logically derived evidence; evidence is derived from the use of the levels of thought identified in the previous three question categories; students must defend or explain their judgments based on criteria that they designate or which have been established by others.

Examples of Evaluative Questions:

1. Do you believe that people are more inquisitive today than in the past? Why do you think this?
2. Who do you think is the best candidate in the presidential election? Why?
3. Where do you think would be the most exciting place to go on a winter vacation? Why?

Probing Behaviors

Probing behaviors occur when the teacher requests students to go deeper into their thinking or to elaborate on comments made or positions taken. The use of probing behaviors, typically through the use of probing questions, communicates to students that the teacher is interested in knowing more about their ideas. Probing behaviors cause students to review their ideas and explore them more deeply. They also help the teacher in creating a classroom atmosphere that includes student ideas and general indirectness that was described earlier. Since, by its very purpose, probing for student ideas does not involve looking at what students say as being either right or wrong, probing behaviors offer natural and excellent opportunities for teachers to praise students for their thinking. To be effective, probing behaviors need to be carried out in a way that is seen by students as being nonthreatening and nonjudgmental.

Level of Difficulty of Instruction

Teachers who have created learning environments where students feel appropriately challenged, but not overchallenged, have established environments where students achieve at higher levels. Teachers should offer instruction that is neither too hard nor too easy for students. Much has been said in recent years about the importance of increasing academic rigor in schools and holding students to higher standards. While important, this should not be done at the expense of students who are simply unable to reach the higher standards that may be established. If students perceive that the difficulty of instruction offered by the teacher is beyond their ability, they may either withdraw from the instruction or act out against it. It is important for teachers, in knowing the abilities and interests of their students, to establish levels of instruction which are out of the immediate reach of their students (therefore not too easy), but which are reachable with effort and teacher assistance (therefore appropriately challenging). In terms of fully knowing their students and utilizing this knowledge in planning and delivering their instruction, it is helpful for teachers to apply the concept of the *zone of proximal development* to their teaching. The **zone of proximal development** is defined as *a range of tasks that a student cannot yet do alone but can accomplish when assisted by a more skilled partner* (Eggen & Kauchak, 2007). To continually challenge students in appropriate ways, it is important for learning tasks to be presented at the outer reaches of this range or zone. Presenting tasks that are simply too complex and thought to be unreasonable will cause student interest in the tasks to diminish as students will see the tasks as being too difficult for them to be successful. Working toward them will appear to be not worth their effort for this reason and whatever interest they may have will wane. Likewise, if the teacher too regularly presents tasks at the lower end of this range or zone, students also will lose interest because the tasks will be viewed as not challenging enough, too simplistic and unimportant.

MORE CURRENT RESEARCH ON BEST TEACHING PRACTICE

Additional research on best teaching practices has been conducted since the work of Rosenshine and Furst in the early 1970s. Such factors as teacher knowledge, clarity and organization, and warmth and enthusiasm have each been consistently identified over the years as characteristics of effective teachers (Woolfolk, 2007). Although more current research has expanded the knowledge base related to best practice in teaching, it has not contradicted earlier findings. The following essential teaching characteristics or skills are also correlated with student achievement (Eggen & Kauchak, 2007).

1. Attitudes
2. Organization
3. Communication
4. Focus
5. Feedback and Praise
6. Questioning
7. Review and Closure

Attitudes

The consideration of teacher attitude goes beyond seeing the teacher as merely having a "good" or "bad" attitude. Were it this simple, the influence of attitude on teaching and learning would have been much more completely understood long before now. Teachers have studied attitude, researchers have studied attitude, and students have responded to teacher attitude since the beginning of formal education. Teachers have a responsibility for the attitudes of their students, both positive and negative. Where students have negative attitudes toward themselves or their learning, teachers need to identify the causes of these negative attitudes so that they may help them become more positive in order for their learning to advance. An important aspect of this process relates to teachers and their own attitudes.

As presented earlier, teachers who hold the belief that they and their schools can have a positive effect on their students and their learning are said to have high *teacher efficacy* (Bruning, Schraw, & Ronning, 1995). Classrooms and schools with such teachers have increased student achievement. Teachers with high efficacy work well with low-achieving students and use praise rather than criticism to motivate and reward them. Such teachers use their time effectively and are more accepting of the unique, individual qualities of their students. High-efficacy teachers do not give up on students and more readily change their strategies and adopt and adapt instructional materials as needed to meet their students' needs (Pool, Okeafor, & Sloan, 1989). Low-efficacy teachers are more critical of their students and persevere less when seeking solutions to their students' learning and motivational problems. Such teachers do not hold strong beliefs that they really can make a difference in the lives of their students (Kagan, 1992). Teachers with low efficacy tend to stratify their classes more by student ability, or what they perceive to be student ability, while giving more effort, attention, and affection to their students felt to have higher ability (Ashton & Webb, 1986). Low-efficacy teachers also perceive their students' behaviors, particularly those of their low-achieving students, in terms of potential threats to the orderliness of their classrooms. Teachers with high efficacy are not as likely to feel threatened by the misbehavior or potential misbehavior of their students.

Organization

Being well organized does not mean being overly restrictive. Students can tell if a teacher is organized or not. Teachers who are organized, or at least perceived by their students as being organized, have higher achieving students than those who do not have or do not project this quality.

Organization involves management of the classroom in terms of its physical elements and rules and procedures as well as academic concerns with respect to the teaching process. **Management organization** in the classroom refers to *the general organizational structure and procedures that the teacher has developed to keep the classroom running smoothly.* Organized teachers have their teaching materials ready when it is time to begin their lessons, start on time, have established learning routines (e.g., certain ways of taking roll and collecting papers to minimize the time these activities take and making transitions from one activity to another quickly and smoothly), and engage their students throughout the entire instructional period. Established routines in the classroom enable teachers and their students to know what to anticipate as the teacher's instruction moves forward. Effective management organization allows for classroom time to be used more productively. Although the ability to be spontaneous as the situation dictates is important, teachers who have well-established routines and procedures bring a positive predictability to their teaching, giving their students a greater sense of order, balance and direction. This order and balance, i.e., equilibrium, in the environment, and the direction that results from it, contribute to higher levels of student learning. **Academic organization** in the classroom is reflected by *the teacher's means of ordering and arranging information for instruction so that students will be better able to understand the information communicated.* Effective teachers have specific organization schemes to assist students in ordering and arranging information. Being well organized academically does not mean teachers lack spontaneity or the ability to teach to the moment. Rather, academic organization refers to the teacher being well prepared to carry out instruction in a way that assists the students as they learn and remember what is being taught. The use of diagrams, outlines, hierarchies, schematics, and technology can be significant in not only helping teachers in presenting organized lessons, but also in assisting students in making better organization of and use of the information being presented. The teacher's ability to be clear in communications with students is, in many ways, related to the teacher's ability to be academically organized. Good teacher organization is founded upon the routines, procedures, and rules the teacher has developed for both student motivation and classroom management that effectively organize and use time wisely, thus enabling the classroom to run in an efficient and effective manner.

Communication

As previously noted, there is a strong, positive correlation between language clarity and student achievement, reinforcing the importance of teachers being clear in the use of their verbal communication (Cruickshank, 1985: Snyder, Bushur, Hoeksema, Olson, Clark, & Snyder, 1991). Four aspects of language clarity have been identified related to best practice in teaching:

1. **Precise Terminology:** the teacher eliminates or restricts the use of vague and ambiguous words and phrases, e.g., perhaps, maybe, usually, might, and so on, from explanations and responses to students' questions, presentations, and interactions with students;
2. **Connected Discourse:** the teacher's presentation is thematically well connected and leads to a goal, going point by point; the ab-

sence of this type of discourse results in communication that may seem rambling to the student, being disjointed and not appropriately linked; if the lesson isn't clear, is presented in a poor order of events, or if incidental information is included without indicating how it relates to the topic, classroom discourse becomes disconnected;

3. **Transition Signals:** transition signals assist in blending one topic area with the next that follows; without such signals the teacher may be seen as merely, and abruptly, moving or jumping from topic to topic or point to point; essentially, the signals are verbal statements indicating that one idea is ending and another is beginning; since all students are not at the same place cognitively, a transition signal alerts the students that the lesson is making a conceptual shift, i.e., moving to a new topic, and allows them to prepare for it; and

4. **Emphasis:** emphasis denotes the teacher specifically identifying information that is to be remembered; phrases such as, "This is important," and "Be sure to remember this," are examples of the use of emphasis; if something is of special importance, tell the students; emphasis consists of verbal and vocal cues that help students take focus on important information in a lesson; repeating a point or asking a question about an important point previously considered can also be an effective form of emphasis.

Students cannot be expected to learn at their maximum potentials when their teachers are not clear. Though a teacher may comment that a particular student does not pay attention and does not understand something, this is really more the teacher's problem than the student's. It is the teacher who must be expert in communication and reaching students with the language used in the classroom. Teacher clarity was first on the list of effective teaching behaviors or teacher characteristics identified in the early research in this area (Rosenshine & Furst, 1971).

Focus

Focus is an important aspect of the teacher's ability to communicate and attend to ideas in the classroom. Focus represents bringing student attention to the lesson at the very beginning of the instructional experience, and then maintaining this attention throughout the remainder of the lesson. This has also been identified as establishing an *anticipatory set* (Hunter, 1984). **Anticipatory set** is *the mental or attitudinal foundation established by the teacher for the students at the beginning of the instructional experience that helps students to understand what they may anticipate in the instruction which will follow.* When students are focused at the beginning of the lesson, they are better connected to the body of the lesson being presented. Teachers who have good introductory focus are able to, more easily, gain and maintain student attention and provide a stronger connection for the students with the material being taught as the lesson progresses. Focus serves to motivate students, increase their curiosity, and make the lesson seem more interesting. Teachers often can gain student attention successfully through the use of certain visual or auditory sensory techniques such as pictures, models, songs, concrete objects, riddles, the overhead projector, the chalkboard, the Internet and computer technology. The importance of using such techniques, classically referred to as **advance organizers**, or *the use of introductory statements or activities to frame new content as a part of the lesson focus,* was developed in detail by Ausubel (1978). The use of focus techniques brings students more into the overall mainstream of the lesson than into any specific part of it. This helps students avoid difficulties in understanding the main intent of the teacher's instruction, but also assists them in attending to the important individual components that make it up.

Feedback and Praise

Few individuals function well in environments characterized by ambiguity and uncertainty. Students certainly do not as such environments bring about unnecessary stress and pressure. Teachers who regularly provide feedback to their students regarding the accuracy or appropriateness of their responses and their work have higher achieving students. The most effective feedback provides constructive information, praise, and encouragement as appropriate and is immediate and specific. Pertinent individual feedback that is aimed at constructively correcting errors made during learning positively affects student performance and attitude (Elawar & Corno, 1985). Such feedback not only results in increased achievement, but also in increased motivation. It contributes to a greater sense of balance and self-regulation as students are able to monitor their own progress. It also helps students create associations that result in more meaningful learning and advancement toward stated goals.

Feedback generally comes in one of two forms: written or oral. Providing written feedback poses a challenge for some teachers as it is more time consuming. Because of its time-consuming nature, many teachers often provide only sketchy written feedback for their students or information that is not terribly constructive in quality. Although it may take more time, written feedback that is specific to the nature of the students' performance is an important part of effective teaching and is positively related to student achievement. Specific written feedback helps students to focus on their weaknesses and correct these through their own efforts. The time spent in giving more detailed feedback should, eventually, result in savings in instructional time. It should also result in improvements in student attitudes that will have a positive impact on classroom climate. It is suggested that teachers might regularly ask themselves specific questions when they review their students' work: (1) What is the key error if there is one? (2) What is the probable reason for the error? (3) How can I guide the student to avoid the error in the future? (4) What did the student do well that could be noted? Using questions such as these as guides to responding to student work in written form will result in benefits not only to student learning, but also to the learning environment as a whole (Elawar & Corno, 1985). In the future, as teachers use more and more electronic instruction, the ability to use written feedback will be especially important. Oral feedback is more easily given as it can be used in ongoing discussions and question-and-answer periods. The constructive value of oral feedback also is critical to enhancing student achievement. Quick, one word responses, or responses that merely inform the student that he or she is correct or not correct are not as effective as more elaborate responses. More elaborate or extended responses let the student know that he or she was correct or incorrect but also why this was the case.

Praise is one of the most common and adaptable forms of teacher feedback. Some interesting and not especially positive patterns in teacher use of praise have been identified through educational research (Brophy, 1981).

- Praise is not used nearly as often as most teachers believe, being used less than five times per class.

- Praise for good behavior is actually quite rare and occurs only once every two or more hours in the elementary grades and less than that as students get older.
- Praise is influenced by the type of student such as on the quality of the responses that students give. High-achieving, well-behaved, and attentive students receive greater amounts of praise than do low-achieving and inattentive students.
- Praise is often given by teachers based on the responses that they expect to receive as much as it is on the answers that the students actually give.

Alderman (2004, p. 254) provides a helpful analysis of the difference between effective and ineffective use of praise in Figure 4.1.

Considering the potential positive impact of the use of praise in the classroom, in particular in the areas of student motivation, management, and learning, it is recommended that teachers should praise:

1. genuinely,
2. immediately,
3. accomplishments that students may not be aware of,
4. strategically with different types of students,
5. the effort as well as the answer,
6. specifically, and
7. judiciously.

Understanding the elements of the effective use of praise is important to the teaching process as they impact the student's motivation to stay or become involved in the teacher's lesson.

Additionally, teachers are advised to use variety as well as frequency in their approaches to praising their students. Some teachers fall into a routine pattern of using the same praise words over and over again, such as "good" or "well done." In that praise is a very special type of reinforcer, its potency is enhanced when it avoids being too routine. In an effort to add variety to their approaches used to praise, and keep themselves and their praise exciting and more interesting, it is recommended that teachers utilize as much variety as possible in their praising vocabulary. For example, words and phrases such as "terrific," "very good job," "outstanding," "excellent," and "wonderful," will make the teachers' praise efforts much more interesting and

Characteristics of Effective and Ineffective Use of Praise

Effective Praise	Ineffective Praise
Is delivered contingently	Is delivered randomly or unsystematically
Specifies the particulars of the accomplishment	Is restricted to global, positive reactions
Shows spontaneity, variety, and other signs of credibility; suggests clear attention to the student's accomplishment	Shows a bland uniformity, which suggests a conditioned response made with minimal attention
Rewards attainment of specified performance criteria (that can include effort criteria)	Rewards mere participation, without consideration of performance processes or outcomes
Provides information to students about their competence or the value of their accomplishments	Provides no information at all or gives students information about their status
Orients students toward better appreciation of their own task-related behavior and thinking about problem solving	Orients students toward comparing themselves with others and thinking about competing
Uses students' own prior accomplishments as the context for describing present accomplishments	Uses the accomplishments of peers as the context for describing students' present accomplishments
Is given in recognition of noteworthy effort or success at difficult (for this student) tasks	Is given without regard to the effort expended or with meaning of the accomplishment (for this student)
Attributes success to effort and ability, implying that similar successes can be expected in the future	Attributes success to ability alone or to external factors such as luck or easy task
Fosters endogenous attributions (students believe that they expend effort on the task because they enjoy the task and/or want to develop task-relevant skills)	Foster exogenous attributions (students believe that they expend effort on the task for external reasons--please the teacher, win a competition or reward, etc.)
Focuses students' attention on their own task-relevant behavior	Focuses students' attention on the teacher as an external authority figure who is manipulating them
Fosters appreciation of and desirable attributions about task-relevant behavior after the process is completed	Intrudes into the ongoing process, distracting attention from task-relevant behavior

Figure 4.1. From "Teacher praise: A functional analysis," by Brophy, 1981, *Review of Educational Research, 51*, 5–32.

positively received by the students. In the end, the teacher's praise will be more motivational as it will be seen as being more dynamic by the students.

Questioning

Research on teacher questioning strategies has increased considerably over the last twenty years. Questioning is considered by many to be the most important tool that teachers have for helping students build understanding. While it is important that teachers have well-developed questioning skills, such skills do not develop naturally. The development of good questioning skills comes only through specific question-asking applications that are consistently analyzed in terms of whether or not the questions, and the way they were asked, elicited the desired outcomes. Research continues to reinforce the relationship between the quality of a teacher's questioning skills and student achievement.

Though some might think that certain questions are preferred over others, such as low cognitive over high cognitive or vice versa, this is not the case. Different types of questions serve different learning and teaching purposes. The teacher should select questions as they relate to the learning outcomes desired. If the objective of the lesson is to focus on the development of certain basic skills or remembered information, low-cognitive questions are of greater value. If the purpose is to place students in situations where they will be expected to analyze or evaluate information, or share their personal ideas, high-cognitive questions should be used (Bloom, Englehart, Furst, Hill, & Krathwohl, 1956; Good & Brophy, 2000). Both high- and low-cognitive questions correlate positively with student achievement. Frequency, equitable distribution, prompting and wait-time are considered to be characteristics of effective questioning strategies (Eggen & Kauchak, 2007; O'Flahavan, Hartman, & Pearson, 1988; Tobin, 1987).

1. **Frequency:** generally, the more questions the better; greater numbers of questions allow for more students to be involved in the dynamics of a lesson and more opportunities for the teacher to monitor the students' and the lesson's progress; questioning increases the opportunity for student involvement and contributes to improved achievement;

2. **Equitable Distribution:** teachers should strive for a pattern of questioning in which all students are called on as equally as possible; more questioning with equal distribution across the class increases the opportunity for providing more feedback and helps students stay motivated and connected to the lesson; this reduces the likelihood that students will drift away from the instruction and become involved in misconduct behaviors;

3. **Prompting:** the technique of prompting is one of helping students respond to questions by providing cues after an incorrect or incomplete answer or silence; an additional question or statement the teacher uses to elicit an appropriate student response after a student answers incorrectly is considered prompting; prompting is not appropriate if the question calls for remembering specific factual information, but is of value when studying conceptual, procedural knowledge and when using cognitive processes beyond remembering; and

4. **Wait-time:** wait-time is the period of silence before or after a student is asked a question and when the teacher speaks again; the use of wait-time increases student learning by giving students time to think; in most classrooms, regardless of grade or ability level, wait-times are very short, frequently less than one second (Rowe, 1986); research suggests that increasing wait-time to at least three seconds will positively impact student learning; wait-time should be implemented strategically, for example, if students are practicing basic skills such as multiplication facts, quick answers are desirable and wait-times should be short, and, if a student appears too uneasy, the teacher may wish to intervene earlier.

Review and Closure

Clear *review* and *closure* consistently serve as aids to learning and enhancing academic achievement. **Review** is *when the teacher summarizes important points from previous work in helping students to link what has been learned to what will be taught in the future; review can occur at different points of the lesson, either close to the beginning, midpoint during the body of the lesson, or at the end.* When review is used effectively, teachers are able to guide students beyond a focus on only the specific information presented in the lesson into more substantive conceptual understandings (Dempster, 1991). **Closure** is *a type of review that occurs at the end of* *the instructional period that enables the student to end the lesson with a better understanding of the topic and a place to build on in the future.* This can be accomplished through a number of techniques such as the use of questions, short written assignments, or classroom discussion. The use of each technique normally provides the teacher with valuable information related to identifying the most important place, or perhaps way, to begin the next lesson. An effective use of closure is to ask students to state in their own words important points of information covered in the lesson. This enables students to end the lesson with a better understanding of the lesson's content. It also serves to inform the teacher. If teachers are uncertain as to what level of understanding their students have at the end of one lesson, they will not be well prepared to begin the next lesson that follows. They may know what they taught, but this does not mean that they know what their students understand.

In a detailed study of teacher behaviors, Marzano (2003) identifies nine specific instructional strategies and related teacher behaviors that affect student achievement. These strategies represent useful suggestions for teachers, but not necessarily guidance as to how to specifically plan for effective instruction.

1. **Identifying similarities and differences:** assigning in-class and homework tasks that invoke comparison and classification; assigning in-class and homework tasks that invoke metaphors and analogies.
2. **Summarizing and note taking:** asking students to generate verbal summaries and/or written summaries; asking students to take notes; asking students to revise their notes, correcting errors and adding information.
3. **Reinforcing effort and providing recognition:** recognizing and celebrating progress toward learning goals throughout a unit; recognizing and reinforcing the importance of effort; recognizing and celebrating progress toward learning goals at the end of a unit.
4. **Homework and practice:** providing specific feedback on all assigned homework; assigning homework for the purpose of students practicing skills and procedures that have been the focus of instruction.
5. **Using nonlinguistic representations:** asking students to generate mental images representing content; asking students to draw

pictures of pictographs representing content; asking students to construct graphic organizers representing content; asking students to act out content; asking students to make physical models of content.

6. **Cooperative learning:** organizing students in cooperative groups when appropriate; organizing students in ability groups when appropriate.

7. **Setting objectives and providing feedback:** setting specific learning goals at the beginning of a unit; asking students to set their own learning goals at the beginning of a unit; providing feedback on learning goals throughout the unit; asking students to keep track of their progress on learning goals; providing summative feedback at the end of a unit; asking students to assess themselves at the end of a unit.

8. **Generating and testing hypotheses:** engaging students in projects that involve generating and testing hypotheses through tasks such as problem solving tasks, decision-making tasks, investigation tasks, experimental inquiry tasks, systems analysis tasks, and invention tasks.

9. **Using questions, cues, and advance organizers:** prior to presenting new content, asking questions that help students recall what they might already know about the content; prior to presenting new content, providing students with direct links with what they have studied previously; prior to presenting new content, providing ways for students to organize or think about the content.

Even having in-depth skills and knowledge of instructional strategies, however, will produce only limited results if the teacher does not also know when as well as how to use them. Marzano (2007) identifies that knowing and understanding skills may be identified as the science of teaching where knowing when to use certain skills, and with whom, may be considered the art. He suggests a comprehensive model, i.e., framework, for ensuring quality teaching that balances the need for research-based information with the importance of understanding the strengths and weaknesses of individual students. The model is presented in the form of ten teaching and instructional design questions.

1. What will I do to establish and communicate learning goals, track student progress, and celebrate success?

2. What will I do to help students effectively interact with new knowledge?
3. What will I do to help students practice and deepen their understanding of new knowledge?
4. What will I do to help students generate and test hypotheses about new knowledge?
5. What will I do to engage students?
6. What will I do to establish or maintain classroom rules and procedures?
7. What will I do to recognize and acknowledge adherence and lack of adherence to classroom rules and procedures?
8. What will I do to establish and maintain effective relationships with students?
9. What will I do to communicate high expectations for all students?
10. What will I do to develop effective lessons organized into a cohesive unit?

In addition to the work already cited, Rosenshine and his colleagues identified six specific teaching functions or basic teaching skills and processes building on the research on effective teaching (Rosenshine, 1988; Rosenshine & Stevens, 1986; Woolfolk, 2007, p. 488).

1. **Review and check the previous day's work.** Reteach if students do not have an acceptable grasp of the material.
2. **Present new material.** Make the purpose of the lesson clear, teaching in incremental steps, and provide examples and nonexamples.
3. **Provide guided practice.** Give practice problems, question students, and listen for misunderstandings. Reteach as needed.
4. **Give feedback and correctives.** This needs to be regularly done and based on the answers that students give. Reteach as needed.
5. **Provide independent practice.** Give students the opportunity to apply the new learning on their own in various settings such as homework, seatwork and cooperative groups. The success rate during independent practice should be about 95 percent. Based on the prior teaching, students should practice until the skills become overlearned and automatic and where they are confident with their understanding.

6. **Review weekly and monthly.** This will help consolidate learning and should be done regularly; this can be done through reviews of homework and tests. Reteach as needed.

The six teaching functions or skills identified here are not necessarily sequential, i.e., to be followed in a particular order. Nevertheless, they are recognized as elements of effective instruction and should be used as needed and appropriate to organize lessons and content, present material, check for understanding, and guide new teaching and reteaching as these activities enhance student learning.

The last ten to fifteen years has produced a special focus on teaching practices as related to student learning styles, brain research, and teaching and learning standards. The teaching practices identified by Tiletson (2005) can be important to teachers when paired with the best research linked to their implementation. The practices reinforce earlier research and are based on research in the field along with actual classroom experiences of teachers. Most teachers today are especially interested in guidance that is as real-world oriented and as practical as it can be. The following teaching practices are believed to meet these criteria.

1. Create an enriched and emotionally supportive environment.
2. Use a variety of teaching strategies that address different learning styles.
3. Use strategies that help students make connections from prior learning and experiences to new learning and across disciplines.
4. Teach for long-term memory as a primary goal.
5. Integrate higher-level thinking skills into learning activities.
6. Use collaborative learning as an integral part of the classroom.
7. Bridge the gap between all learners, regardless of race, socio-economic status, sex, or creed.
8. Evaluate learning through a variety for authentic assessments.
9. Promote real-world applications of learning.
10. Provide a seamless integration of technology for high-quality instruction.

Burden and Byrd (2007) suggest that, when examining effective teachers and building on the research reported, the most essential teacher characteristics may be placed into the three organizing categories of *knowledge, skills,* and *dispositions.*

Knowledge: To be effective, teachers must know the subjects that they teach. Although, this in and of itself is not sufficient to ensure effective teaching. Teachers must also have at least three other types of knowledge.

1. **Professional Knowledge:** Teachers must have knowledge about teaching in general; this includes knowledge about learning, diversity, technology, schooling and education, and the profession of teaching as a whole.
2. **Pedagogical Knowledge:** Teachers must have knowledge that includes the general concepts, theories, methods, and research about effective teaching, no matter the content area.
3. **Pedagogical Content Knowledge:** Teachers must have knowledge of teaching methods and approaches that are specific to the particular subject, or the application of certain strategies in a special way, that they teach. This includes an understanding of the content in order to teach it in a variety of ways, drawing on the cultural backgrounds and prior knowledge and experiences of the students.

Skills: Teachers must have the necessary skills to use their knowledge effectively in making decisions about basic teaching functions such as planning for, implementing, and assessing instruction to ensure that all students are learning.

Dispositions: Teachers must have appropriate dispositions, i.e., values, commitments, and professional ethics, that influence their behaviors to promote learning for all students. Dispositions are guided by beliefs and attitudes related to values such as caring, fairness, honesty, responsibility, and social justice. While an affective concept, and in the minds of teachers, dispositions may be seen in teacher behaviors.

ANALYZING CLASSROOMS FOR BEST PRACTICE IN TEACHING

While it is critical that teachers have a solid knowledge base of information related to student motivation, classroom management, and best practice in teaching, as discussed, having this knowledge base alone is not sufficient for teachers to consistently establish and maintain well-managed classrooms where motivated students achieve at high levels. Given the availability of so much information related to effective teaching, if this were the case, many teachers would be experiencing far fewer student motivation and classroom management problems than they presently do. And, students would be learning at higher levels than they are. Having information on best practice in teaching does not guarantee the appropriate application of this information to the teacher's behavior in the classroom.

Teachers must take charge of their own individual classrooms and act in informed and deliberate ways for those classrooms to reflect the best practice that they desire (Cangelosi, 2000). The role of the teacher in instruction is integrally involved in the teacher's role in student motivation and classroom management. The Teaching Process Model is recommended as a system for approaching classroom instruction in such a way that the instruction will be systematically responsive to issues of motivation and management. The model is comprised of six steps:

1. Determine needs of students,
2. Determine learning goal,
3. Design learning activities,
4. Prepare for the learning activities,
5. Conduct the learning activities, and
6. Determine how well students have achieved the learning goal.

The Teaching Process Model is offered here as it provides an advance organizer for systematically and effectively teaching organized, well thought out lessons and to, if needed, teach students to replace uncooperative behaviors or misbehaviors with cooperative, positive ones. Through the teacher's instruction, in particular through the first step in determining and understanding student needs, followed by clearly identifying learning goals and activities, the teacher will be able to proactively approach the teaching process in a way that will lessen the occurrence of unwanted student behaviors.

It is the ability of the teacher to reflect on and use this information that makes the greatest difference between a teacher who is a poor manager and motivator and one who is skilled in these areas. Recall Tameka's case study (*Tameka's Planning and Analysis*) presented in Chapter 1. Tameka reflected on her problems and made plans to deal with them. The Model for Reflection and Inquiry introduced earlier is recommended as being useful in guiding this reflection.

Reflection in and of itself, though, may produce little positive change. The key to the most effective reflection also includes the appropriate use of relevant information. The third step of the Model for Reflection and Inquiry is Collection of Relevant Data. It is in this step, where relevant information is deliberately sought, including through observations made, that teachers are performing a key step in the inquiry process. What teachers know about student motivation, classroom management, and best teaching practice greatly influences the benefits that will come from this step. The depth of information collected and the appropriate use made of it will, ultimately, determine the level of the quality of the teacher's problem solving.

The *System for the Analysis of Teaching Practices* that follows has been developed to assist teachers as they review their teaching behaviors. The *System* is built on the knowledge base of best practice in teaching and can serve as a helpful tool for teachers for self-review and in making decisions to strengthen the instructional process. Return to the *Seth's Confidence, Susan's Problem Ownership* or *Tameka's Planning and Analysis* case study from Chapter 1 and use the instrument as though you were one of the three teachers in the case studies.

System for the Analysis of Teaching Practices

Circle the appropriate number on the scale provided as you reflect on your teaching in each teacher characteristic area. Before making your selection, consider the accompanying statement(s) associated with each item as to how well the statement consistently describes your professional behavior.

	Seldom			Always	
1. **Clarity**	1	2	3	4	5

My students understand the words that I use in my teaching; I get my ideas across clearly without needing to repeat myself.

2. **Variability**	1	2	3	4	5

My teaching reflects the regular use of many different teaching strategies and resources rather than only a few.

	Seldom			Always	

3. Enthusiasm

| | 1 | 2 | 3 | 4 | 5 |

I am energetic, and my teaching reflects this energy; my enthusiasm shows in my teaching, my preparation, and the classroom environment that I establish.

4. Task-oriented

| | 1 | 2 | 3 | 4 | 5 |

I conduct my classroom in a positive yet business-like manner. Students know where they are headed in their learning activities; my teaching is focused on the desired learning outcomes at all times.

5. Students Learning Criterion Material

| | 1 | 2 | 3 | 4 | 5 |

My students know, in advance of the learning activities, what is important to be learned and how they will be evaluated. My assessments do not include "extras" that my students were not aware of.

6. Use of Student Ideas

| | 1 | 2 | 3 | 4 | 5 |

My teaching is characterized by a heavy involvement of student ideas. Students know from the way I teach that their ideas are important.

7 .Structuring Comments

| | 1 | 2 | 3 | 4 | 5 |

I use structuring comments at the beginning of my lessons and as I move through my lessons to help my students stay focused on my objectives and know what is expected of them.

8. Level of Difficulty

| | 1 | 2 | 3 | 4 | 5 |

My expectations are challenging but not beyond the reach of my students. Students are not "left behind" in my teaching; they know that they can be successful.

9. Success Rates

| | 1 | 2 | 3 | 4 | 5 |

My students are consistently successful; no student considers himself or herself a failure as my approach to teaching ensures success for all.

	Seldom				Always

10. Attitude   1   2   3   4   5

I know that if I plan my lessons thoroughly and select learning activities appropriately that all of my students can succeed. It may take extra effort, but I can make a positive difference with all of my students.

11. Use of Time   1   2   3   4   5

Students do not have idle time in my classroom, but stay actively and successfully engaged in meaningful experiences.

12. Organization   1   2   3   4   5

My classroom and teaching are organized, and my students recognize this. I am well prepared and my teaching transitions are smooth and controlled.

13. Communication   1   2   3   4   5

I communicate clearly to my students. This includes both verbal as well as nonverbal messages. I seldom need to repeat myself.

14. Focus   1   2   3   4   5

Students understand the purpose of my lessons, and my lessons stay focused. Spontaneous events do take place, but my students know where my lessons are headed and the outcomes that are desired.

15. Feedback   1   2   3   4   5

Students receive ample feedback related to their progress during my lessons and through my assessments. They regularly receive oral and written feedback that explains their progress to them.

16. Questioning   1   2   3   4   5

I routinely use both higher and lower order questioning. Students are asked many questions to develop their thinking and so I can know what they understand.

	Seldom			Always	

17. Probing Behaviors   1   2   3   4   5

My teaching includes probing students so that they may
go deeper into and expand on their ideas, especially
as their ideas relate to what I am teaching.

18. Pacing   1   2   3   4   5

My lesson pace is normally quicker as opposed to slower.

19. Review and Closure   1   2   3   4   5

I review at the beginning of my lessons what has just
been previously taught. I review again through closure
at the end of each lesson.

20. Criticism   1   2   3   4   5

My classroom environment is positive, open, and
inviting. I seldom use criticism with my students.

Scoring Your Analysis

Twenty items make up the *System for the Analysis of Teaching Practices* with a maximum possible rating of 5 on each item. The instrument is not intended for evaluation purposes, but as a guide for reflection and determining instructional directions for the future. It offers a way to analyze individual teacher behaviors as well as a teacher's performance in its entirety by combining individual ratings together. Each behavior is treated as having the same level of importance.

The following rating scheme may be used when seeking a combined rating of all items.

Points	Self-Rating
93–100	Excellent
86–92	Above Average
79–85	Average
70–78	Below Average
Below 70	Unsatisfactory

CONCLUSION

Chapter 4 has included a detailed overview of educational research related to what is popularly referred to as best practice in teaching. In so doing, information provided reinforces two important points. First, for teachers to be effective, they need to have a strong knowledge base of information regarding what is known about best practice in teaching, student motivation, and classroom management. The body of knowledge in these areas has continued to grow steadily since early studies were conducted and will continue to expand in the future. Second, teachers need to be able to use what they know to deliver more dynamic and effective instruction and to make sound decisions in the classroom. Knowing important information and not being able to use it leaves the teacher at a level of being less than optimally effective and students at a level where they are not learning at their greatest potentials.

The *System for the Analysis of Teaching Practices* was introduced as a way to help systematically analyze teaching performance in twenty teacher behavior areas. The *System* is built on the best teaching practices introduced throughout the chapter and is research-based in its make up. Teachers, and those who desire to be teachers, are encouraged to study and then use the instrument in real or hypothetical situations as it represents the most current thinking on characteristics and behaviors of effective teachers as related to student achievement.

It is also important to recognize that the knowledge base related to best practice in teaching, student motivation, and classroom management will never be complete as educators who are formal researchers, as well as those who are practicing teachers, continue to search for those instructional strategies and teacher behaviors that will enhance student learning. This is a critically important characteristic of the teaching profession. Just as students have expectations placed upon them for what they need to know, so too do their teachers. Teachers can not afford to be complacent with respect to their own need to remain active learners themselves. This learning must include the knowledge of teaching, motivation, and management, as well as the skills in how to best use this knowledge.

QUESTIONS/ACTIVITIES FOR REFLECTION

1. Evaluate Susan's teaching in the case study *Susan's Problem Ownership* as completely as you can using the *System for the Analysis of Teaching Practices*. Rate each item of the *System* and then total the scores. Discuss your ratings with another student in the class.

2. What are some strategies that a teacher might use to improve his or her questioning technique? Explain what it means to match questioning practices to the purpose of a lesson.

3. What can a teacher do to maintain high efficacy when working with students who are working below grade level?

4. All of the items on the instrument *System for the Analysis of Teaching Practices* have been given equal value. If it is the case that they all are not equal, which do you consider to be the five most important of the twenty included in the instrument? Why have you selected these five?

5. Many teachers strive for higher levels of Engaged Time in their teaching, but this is actually different from Academic Learning Time. What are the main differences between Engaged Time and Academic Learning Time and what can a teacher do to increase the amount of Academic Learning Time in the classroom?

REFERENCES

Alderman, M. (2004). *Motivation for achievement: Possibilities for teaching and learning* (2nd ed.). Mahwah, NJ: Lawrence Erlbaum.

Armstrong, D., Henson, K., & Savage, T. (1997). *Teaching today: An introduction to education* (5th ed.). New York: Macmillan.

Ashton, P., & Webb, R. (1986). *Making a difference: Teachers' sense of efficacy and student achievement.* White Plains, NY: Longman.

Ausubel, D. (1978). In defense of advance organizers: A reply to the critics. *Review of Educational Research, 48,* 251–159.

Bloom, B., Englehart, M., Furst, E., Hill, W., & Krathwohl, D. (1956). *Taxonomy of educational objectives. Handbook I: Cognitive domain.* New York: David McKay.

Borich, G. (1992). *Effective teaching methods.* New York: Merrill.

Brophy, J. (1981). Teacher praise. A functional analysis. *Review of Educational Research, 51*(1), 5–32.

Bruning, R., Schraw, G., & Ronning, R. (1995). *Cognitive psychology and instruction* (2nd ed.). Upper Saddle River, NJ: Prentice-Hall.

Burden, P., & Byrd, D. (2007). *Methods for effective teaching: Promoting K–12 student understanding* (4th ed.). New York: Pearson Education.

Cangelosi, J. (2000). *Classroom management strategies: Gaining and maintaining students' cooperation.* New York: John Wiley.

Cruickshank, D. (1985). Applying research on teacher clarity. *Journal of Teacher Education, 35*(2), 44–48.

Curwin, R., & Mendler, A. (1999). *Discipline with dignity.* Alexandria, VA: Association for Supervision and Curriculum Development.

Dempster, F. (1991). Synthesis of research on reviews and tests. *Educational Leadership, 48*(7), 71–76.

Eggen, P., & Kauchak, D. (2007). *Educational psychology: Windows on classrooms* (7th ed.). Upper Saddle River, NJ: Pearson Education.

Elawar, M., & Corno, L. (1985). A factorial experiment in teachers' written feedback on student homework. *Journal of Educational Psychology, 77*(2), 162–173.

Gallagher, J., & Aschner, M. (1963). A preliminary report of the analysis of classroom interaction. *Merrill-Palmer Quarterly, 9,* 183–194.

Glasser, W. (1990). *The quality school: Managing students without coercion.* New York: Harper & Row.

Good, T., & Brophy, J. (2000). *Looking in classrooms* (8th ed.). New York: Addison Wesley Longman.

Henson, K., & Eller, B. (1999). *Educational psychology for effective teaching.* Belmont, CA: Wadsworth.

Hunt, G., Touzel, T., & Wiseman, D. (1999). *Effective teaching: Preparation and Implementation* (3rd ed.). Springfield, IL: Charles C Thomas.

Hunter, M. (1984). Knowing, teaching and supervising. In P. Hosford (Ed.), *Using what we know about teaching.* Alexandria, VA: Association for Supervision and Curriculum Development.

Kagan, D. (1992). Implications of research on teacher belief. *Educational Psychologist, 27,* 65–90.

Karweit, N. (1989). Time and learning: A review. In R.E. Slavin (Ed.), *School and classroom organization.* Hillsdale, NJ: Erlbaum.

Lieberman, B. (2007). Educator to apply lessons learned to improve low-performing schools. Retrieved June 29, 2007, from www.signonsandiego.com/news/education.

Marzano, R. (2007). *The art and science of teaching: A comprehensive framework for effective instruction.* Alexandria, VA: Association for Supervision and Curriculum Development.

Marzano, R. (2003). *What works in schools: Translating research into action.* Alexandria, VA: Association for Supervision and Curriculum Development.

O'Flahavan, J., Hartman, D., & Pearson, D. (1988). Teacher questioning and feedback practices: A twenty-year retrospective. In J. Readence, R. Baldwin, J. Konopak, & P. O'Keefe (Eds.), *Dialogues in literacy research* (pp. 183–208). Chicago: National Reading Conference.

Poole, M., Okeafor, K., & Sloan, E. (1989, April). *Teachers' interactions, personal efficacy, and change implementation.* Paper presented at the annual meeting of the American Educational Research Association, San Francisco.

Rosenshine, B. (1988). Explicit teaching. In D. Berliner & B. Rosenshine (Eds.), *Talks to teachers* (pp. 75–92). New York: Random House.

Rosenshine, B., & Furst, N. (1971). Research in teacher performance criteria. In B.O. Smith (Ed.), *Research in teacher education.* Englewood Cliffs, NJ: Prentice-Hall.

Rosenshine, B., & Stevens, R. (1986). Teaching functions. In M. Wittrock (Ed.), *Handbook of research on teaching* (3rd ed., pp. 376–391). New York: Macmillan.

Rowe, M. (1986). Wait-time: Slowing down may be a way of speeding up. *Journal of Teacher Education, 37*(1), 43–50.

Snyder, S., Bushur, L., Hoeksema, P., Olson, M., Clark, S., & Snyder, J. (1991, April). *The effect of instructional clarity and concept structure on students' achievement and perception.* Paper presented at the annual meeting of the American Educational Research Association, Chicago.

Tauber, R. (1999). *Classroom management: Sound theory and effective practice* (3rd ed.). Westport, Bergin & Garvey.

Tiletson, D. (2005). *10 best teaching practices: How brain research, learning styles, and standards define teaching competencies* (2nd ed.). Thousand Oaks, CA: Corwin Press.

Tobin, K. (1987). Role of wait-time in higher cognitive level learning. *Review of Educational Research, 57*(1), 69–95.

Weinstein, C., & Mignano, A., Jr. (1993). *Elementary classroom management.* New York: McGraw-Hill.

Woolfolk, A. (2007). *Educational psychology* (10th ed.). New York: Pearson Education.

Chapter 5

SPECIAL PROBLEMS AND CONCERNS
IN STUDENT MOTIVATION
AND CLASSROOM MANAGEMENT

Many concepts related to student motivation and classroom management have been discussed in previous chapters in this text that are applicable to a wide variety of classroom settings across the entire PreK-12 continuum. While there is a wealth of important information available that addresses issues of student motivation and classroom management in a broad and general way, parents and teachers many times have their own specific questions concerning behavior management and student motivation. These questions frequently arise as a result of concerns that must be addressed in their local schools and communities. Some questions represent issues that are so unique to the situation that it is difficult to address them out of the context of the schools and communities where they arise. Others are broad and widespread enough that they can and should be discussed in a forum such as this that allows for greater applicability to their study and to possible answers. The problems and concerns chosen for discussion here were selected because of their relevance to many teachers and parents in individual schools, classrooms, and school districts across the country.

BULLYING: A SPECIAL TYPE OF AGGRESSION

Bullying among schoolchildren is a very old and well-known phenomenon (Olweus, 2003). Although many educators are acquainted with the problem, researchers only began to study bullying systematically in the 1970s. **Bullying** is *a negative behavior which is intentionally designed to cause real, or threatening injury or discomfort to another individual that may reflect physical harm, psychological harm, or both* (Olweus, 1993). In the wake of school shootings and lawsuits brought against individuals, schools, and school districts, numerous state governments have mandated that schools take active steps to reduce bullying (Cooper & Snell, 2003). South Carolina, for example, passed the Safe Schools Climate Act in 2006 (Safe Schools Climate Act, 2006). The Act calls for school districts to establish policies that include a statement prohibiting harassment, intimidation, or bullying of a student. Harassment, intimidation, or bullying is defined as a gesture, an electronic communication, or a written communication:

1. harming a student physically or emotionally or damaging a student's property, or placing a student in reasonable fear of personal harm or property damage; or
2. insulting or demeaning a student or group of students causing substantial disruption in, or substantial interference with, the orderly operation of the school.

"School" refers to in a classroom, on school premises, on a school bus or other school-related vehicle, at an official school bus stop, at a school-sponsored activity or event whether or not it is held on school premises, or at another program or function where the school is responsible for the child.

Although specific mandated actions vary by state, many schools recognize that the most effective approach to bullying prevention is one that is inclusive of school staff, parents, students, and community. There has been a considerable increase in recent years in the amount of literature addressing the topic of bullying in schools (Rigby, 2007). Many experts emphasize that bullying behavior occurs during repeated or successive encounters. Such acts can be carried out through physical blows, but bullying can also take the form of verbal attacks through insults, name calling, and other psychologically damaging words. Boys bully other students more often than girls do, and a relatively large percentage of girls, about 50 percent, report that they are bullied mainly by boys (Olweus, 2003).

Bullies are people who take advantage of weaker people. While weakness is often thought to be typically related to physical strength, this is not always the case. The imbalance between the bully and the victim might be related to more subtle differences such as social skills or language facility. Bullying, specifically, is a type of aggression aimed at a weaker (physically, socially, emotionally, or cognitively) individual that is designed to give the victim feelings of oppression. This oppression frequently builds up because bullying, by its very nature, happens repeatedly over time. Bullying begins with a desire to hurt which is followed by a hurtful action that is the result of a power imbalance (Rigby, 2007). This unjust use of power is typically used over and over for the enjoyment of the aggressor and the oppression of the victim.

Bullying is a very complex behavior. It is not apt to be controlled by telling the aggressor that his or her behavior is not nice or is unacceptable. Moreover, the imbalances in power may be very difficult to detect and hard to analyze; that is, bullying may be taking place when the observer cannot believe the victim could possibly be bullied by the perpetrator.

The National Council of Urban Boards of Education reported that many students commonly witness other children being bullied, physically or psychologically intimidated, or belittled (Croft, 2006). From a nationwide survey of 32,000 students, two particularly worrisome findings were that more than half of the students surveyed said that they had seen children being bullied at least once a month, and that almost 40 percent said teachers and schools could not stop the bullying. Manning and Bucher (2007) report that an act of bullying occurs every seven minutes.

In any given day, over 50,000 young people will be absent from school because they are being bullied; this is one-third of all truancies (Bindel, 2006). Research has identified an irrefutable link between bullying and truancy and persistent truancy and a young person's opportunities in later life. Reasons given by students for bullying-related truancy include the desire to be somewhere safe, where no one could bring harm and to remove oneself from environments where there are feelings of being worthless and hated. This link between poor behavior, truancy, and bullying is also linked to both affective and cognitive development.

A unique and growing type of bullying is cyberbullying or web bullying. While school officials have begun to attend to the student rumor mill and notes left in bathrooms, the Internet has now emerged as a major forum for bullying as well (Schreirer, 2006). Online threats are real and powerful. A recent poll identified that one in three teenagers and one in six preteens received threats or verbal abuse online. For the teens, this means the receiving of mean, threatening, or embarrassing messages online, mostly through instant messaging, email, or a Website posting. About 60 percent of the messages focus on a student's crush or friendship with a classmate; 38 percent said the messages were about physical appearance, such as weight or clothes. Other incidents involved race, religion, or sexuality. Joyce (2007), reporting from the Pew Internet and America Life Project, indicated that about one-third of all teenagers who use the Internet say they have been targets of menacing behavior online. The behaviors include receiving threatening messages; having their private emails or text messages forwarded without consent; seeing an embarrassing picture posted without permission; or having rumors about them spread online. The most common form of cyberbullying is reported as taking information once thought to be private and placing it across the Internet. The study also indicated that girls are more likely than boys to be targets and teens who share their identities and thoughts online are more likely to be targets than are those who lead less active online lives.

The typical bully used to torment victims out in the open, in school hallways or playgrounds, spitting out insults and disparaging remarks for anyone to hear and see. Bullying now has gone high-tech and anonymous (Tseng, 2006). The Internet and cell phone text messages are the new mediums for cyberbullies. They post nasty pictures or messages about others in blogs and on Websites, or exploit another person's online user name to spread rumors about others. Some school districts have introduced cyberbullying policies that prohibit this behavior on school computers. Parents must sign a form confirming they have read the policy and discussed it with their children. Punishment could range from a phone call home to an out-of-school suspension, depending on the offense. While not directed specifically and only to cyberbullying, the State of New Jersey, through the direction of the governor (Corzine: Train Teachers to Help Children Avoid Web Predators, 2007), has initiated a program in all New Jersey schools to train teachers and administrators in Internet safety. Through the program, teachers and administrators will be expected to use their training to instruct students, parents, and community groups on the potential dangers that can be found on the Internet.

Bullying today is actually an international problem. Ross (2007) reported that more than 150,000 students in the United Kingdom have been targeted by school bullies because they are gay. Two-thirds of lesbian and gay students surveyed indicated that they have experienced homophobic bullying, ranging from verbal abuse to violence and even death threats. About half of the teachers did not intervene when students used homophobic language like "dyke," "queer," or "rug muncher." The study indicated that 41 percent of gay and lesbian students had experienced physical abuse, 17 percent had received death threats, and 12 percent had been sexually assaulted. Some students reported that their teachers joined in with the abuse.

A relationship has also been drawn between bullying and suicide (Bullying Is Behind Teen Suicide, 2006). In Japan, at least six students being bullied were so desperate to stop the torment that the only way they could find to end their suffering was to kill themselves. Numerous victims have overloaded a hotline service wanting to tell someone how they were bullied at school because they could not tell their families. In one week, Childline Japan received over 27,500 calls, but could only answer 2,890 of them due to a shortage of lines. The Japanese government recently acted on schoolyard bullying with the Education Rebuilding Council calling for clearer standards for punishing student bullies. The panel recommended that teachers who turn a blind eye to bullying be disciplined and that pupils who want to change schools because of bullying be allowed to do so (Doi, 2006). Japanese law presently bars primary and middle schools from expelling students who bully or tease schoolmates. Even suspensions are rare. Of the 464 suspensions at middle schools in the past decade, only 24 cases involved bullying. Experts say concealment of bullying is part of a crisis in the educational system, leaving school administrators trying to save face.

Although bullying has been an issue in schools for a number of years, many educators are becoming more and more aware of how harmful the practice can be to the development and learning of the victims and the overall environment of the school. The cost to society of ignoring bullying is higher than it would be to develop antibullying strategies. Teicher (2006) notes that it is not normal to act like a bully and that, in anonymous surveys of several large middle schools, the vast majority of students reported that they had not hit, teased, threatened, excluded, or gossiped maliciously about classmates in the past thirty days from when the survey was conducted. But, a majority was also convinced that their own nonbully status was an exception to the norm. One observation of these data is that much of the bullying, violence, or substance abuse continues because the people engaged in it think that everyone else is doing it. The use of *social norms intervention* is felt to be applicable to dealing with this phenomenon. In this intervention approach, students are presented with credible bullying data from their own school, not just state or national average information. Through this approach, students come to realize that the behavior is not a behavior in which everyone is engaged. Basically, through the social norm intervention students come to understand that bullying is not the norm.

Amelia middle and high schools in Ohio are beginning a bullying prevention program that encourages bystanders to help put an end to intimidation and threats (Kranz, 2007). The program, Olweus Bullying Prevention Program, developed in Norway, was begun with help from Child Focus, a nonprofit mental health agency based in the community. The emphasis of the program is on the bystander and trying to empower that individual to help the victim. Components include developing policies and school rules against bullying, developing methods for reporting and recording bullying, identifying hot spots where bullying occurs, on-the-spot interventions by teachers and weekly classroom meetings on bullying issues. Most research shows that bullying begins in the elementary school, slows in the middle school, and re-emerges in the ninth grade. The model of the Olweus Bullying Prevention Program is as follows (Olweus, 2003).

General Prerequisite

• Awareness and involvement of adults

Measures at the School Level

• Administration of the Olweus Bully/Victim Questionnaire (filled out anonymously by students)
• Formation of a Bullying Prevention Coordinating Committee
• Training of staff and time for discussion groups
• Effective supervision during recess and lunch periods

Measures at the Classroom Level

• Classroom and school rules about bullying

- Regular classroom meetings
- Meetings with students' parents

Measures at the Individual Level

- Individual meetings with students who bully
- Individual meetings with victims of bullying
- Meetings with parents of students involved
- Development of individual intervention plans

Rigby (2007) has identified several steps that schools are taking to address bullying behavior; some are preventive in nature and others are strategies for intervention.

- Schools should have a clear definition of bullying so that all teachers, staff, and students recognize it.
- Schools should determine how frequent and severe the bullying problem is on campus.
- A school-wide antibullying policy needs to be developed that is supported by all school personnel.
- The prevention of bullying should be a significant part of the school's curriculum.
- Students need to be taught to become positive bystanders. Too often, students see others bullied and never report the information to teachers.
- Bullying needs to be responded to in a proactive way. This may be a procedure to help students problem solve or, in extreme cases, the use of sanctions may be necessary.

Central to any school-wide plan to address bullying behavior is the development of a defined, obvious, and easy-to-understand school policy statement. Rigby identifies the following features that should be found in such a policy.

- A clear statement of the school's position that bullying is inappropriate and will not be tolerated.
- A short, clear definition of bullying behavior that addresses both direct and indirect forms of harassment that includes cyber bullying.
- A statement that all people in the school community have the right to expect that the environment will be safe from bullying.

- A statement that defines the responsibilities of individuals who see other members of the community being bullied.
- General statements concerning what will take place to prevent bullying (e.g., instructional units and conflict management training) and how the faculty and administration will deal with those who bully others.
- A general statement outlining how the school proposes to interact with parents to address problems related to bullying.
- The description of a standard process to be used to assess the effectiveness of the process.

Resources recommended as helpful for better understanding bullying include:

- Center for the Study and Prevention of Violence–http://www.colorado.edu/cspv/blueprints,
- U.S. Department of Health and Human Services, Stop Bullying Now! Intervention, Prevention, Tips, and Games–http://stopbullyingnow.hrsa.gov
- National Youth Violence Prevention Center, Safe Youth–http://www.safeyouth.org
- National Society for the Prevention of Cruelty to Children–http://www.childline.org.uk/bullying.asp, and
- Channing Bete Company–http://www.channing-bete.com/education/bullying-violence-prevent.html

ZERO TOLERANCE

During the decade of the 1990s, many school districts adopted what have come to be referred to as zero tolerance policies related to student behavioral management. **Zero tolerance** is *a policy for managing student behavior, usually adopted on a school district-wide basis, represented by the use of certain predetermined consequences when particular rules are broken; the consequences are applied automatically regardless of the circumstances surrounding the rule being broken.* Zero tolerance policies actually grew out of national drug enforcement efforts and later were used by public schools to address an array of unwanted student behavior problems that were frequently dangerous in nature (Skiba & Peterson, 1999).

School systems began adopting tough codes regarding student behavior after Congress passed the 1994 Gun-Free Schools Act, which required a one-year expulsion for any child bringing a firearm or bomb to school. Zero tolerance policies in many states, however, also are written to address such areas as fighting, drug or alcohol use, and gang activity, as well as more frequently observed offenses like possessing over-the-counter medications, disrespect of authority, sexual harassment, threats, and vandalism. In 1997, more than 90 percent of the public schools across the country had zero tolerance policies for firearms or other weapons and more than 85 percent had the policies for drugs and alcohol (Koch, 2000). Manning and Bucher (2007) note that supporters of zero tolerance maintain that violence in schools has become lethal and must be addressed in a firm manner while critics of zero tolerance maintain that the approach affects a disproportionate number of students at risk, as well as students who are poor and minority.

Zero tolerance policies have become controversial in many areas. By 2004, the large number of reported cases where students were suspended for seemingly trivial offenses such as carrying legal, nonprescription pain killers (Advil, etc.), having small pocketknives in their cars, or having plastic knives in lunch boxes sparked broad public controversy (Zero Tolerance (schools), 2007). Yet, there are those who believe zero tolerance policies help educators create the best environments for learning. Some have argued that zero tolerance ensures that all students are treated equally, while others such as Skiba and his associates at Indiana University (2001) have reported that such policies are typically overly harsh toward minority students. Some educators believe that creating an environment where students know that minor offenses may be seen as reasons for suspension will make students more careful and, thus, better behaved. However, others fear that this type of environment is neither best for learning, nor best for student development (Ghezzi, 2006). Few adults have any tolerance at all when considering such behaviors as young people using drugs or drinking alcohol. All instances of student misbehavior, however, are not assessed this easily. For example, a zero tolerance policy becomes much less clear if the word "using" is replaced with "possessing." Consider the following all-to-common scenario: *a student in the elementary school was suspended from school because her mother put a butter knife in her lunchbox so that she could spread jelly on her sandwich.* The suspension took place because the school district had a zero tolerance policy against the possession of weapons (in this case knives) on any school campus. The student brought a knife to school in her lunchbox, and, therefore, the policy was applicable to her. While many people argue that the little girl should not be suspended, they still are in agreement that knives should not be allowed on school property. Just this one simple illustration points to the complexity of the issue.

One of the major complaints voiced about zero tolerance policies is that minor, sometimes seemingly innocent infractions receive the same punishments as more serious violations as was seen here in the example with the butter knife. Curwin and Mendler (1999), two well-known educators who have written a great deal about behavior management and student motivation, strongly support the validity of this complaint. They argue that the major problem with zero tolerance policies is that they treat all behaviors the same without allowing for a close examination of the motivation behind each individual behavior. Essentially, they are broadly used as opposed to applied to the situation. This, in turn, creates an unfair system, they aver, which treats a student whose behavior may reflect only a minor problem with the same consequences of a student whose behavior is clearly antisocial.

Many educators also find fault with the type of atmosphere felt to be created in a school where a zero tolerance policy is practiced (Black, 2004). Hyman and Snook (2000) posit that schools characterized by behavior controls such as zero tolerance policies are not as likely to develop attitudes and behaviors in students which are supportive of a productive democratic society. The philosophy of zero tolerance, with its strong foundation on external rules and harsh punishments, tends to exacerbate youth violence, not abate it. Dwyer, Osher, and Hoffman (2000) explain that their research indicates that educators should avoid using techniques which label students or try to oversimplify complex management and motivational issues. They caution that harsh penalties and zero tolerance policies are not the answer to problems of school violence. Instead of focusing on student behaviors in isolation, the critics of zero tolerance policies recommend that schools should promote management policies that focus on the individual differences among students and the motivation behind given student behaviors. Management models that do this tend to include input from a variety of individuals, including students, steps to correct unwanted behaviors through reflection, and interaction in a democratic, student-centered atmosphere (Curwin & Mendler, 2004; Dwyer et al., 2000; Skiba & Peterson, 1999; Wagner, Knudsen, & Harper, 1999/2000). Opponents of zero tolerance systems also find the approach to student behavior management offensive to the philosophy of student-centered schooling as well as basic democratic ideals.

Even though they enjoy a certain level of popularity, there presently is a lack of empirical evidence supporting the use of zero tolerance programs and their use may, in fact, be counterproductive (Skiba & Petersen, 2000). While supporters of zero tolerance policies credit recent declines in crime and school weapons cases to the implementation of the policies, there is little data to support this claim. In spite of the lack of compelling statistics, however, 85 percent of principals, 79 percent of teachers, and 82 percent of students credit zero tolerance policies with keeping drugs out of schools (Koch, 2000). Grant (2006) notes that people who support zero tolerance policies believe that they promote safety in schools and give everyone involved more peace of mind. But, those who oppose the policies believe that they lack rationale and logic and are far too extreme for schools. Largely brought about by the Columbine High School shootings in April, 1999, local zero tolerance policies have grown out of state and federal laws that give school administrators little leeway to individualize the consequences in punishing students for behaviors that are covered in the policies, such as bringing weapons to school, using drugs or alcohol, or making threats.

There is no question that certain types of student behaviors cannot be tolerated in school settings. Likewise, there are important issues that must be addressed concerning the severity of the consequences associated with certain student misbehaviors, the motivation behind the behaviors, and the developmental characteristics of students exhibiting the behaviors. Essex (2000), for example, makes a strong statement for the development of zero tolerance policies in cases of sexual harassment. And yet, there must be differences between how such policies are applied across the PreK-12 grade span such as in kindergarten versus high school settings. Taylor (2000) notes that zero tolerance policies should exist to protect middle level gay and lesbian students from being subjected to name calling and similar harassment. In selecting any system of behavior management or consequences for these types of unwanted student behaviors, at what point do students benefit most from sensitivity training and education to heighten social awareness as opposed to experiencing punishment for their behaviors? Is it possible that punishment will make the harassing students even more aggressive toward gays and lesbians? Many believe that it will.

Research suggests that zero tolerance policies have been only moderately effective at best. Blair (1999) identifies that four conditions must be present if the policies have any chance of making a positive difference in controlling student behavior:

1. clear consequences for misbehavior must be developed and applied consistently,
2. all stake-holders (e.g., educators, parents, students, etc.) must collaborate in developing the policies,
3. those developing the policies must have a knowledge base of what has worked and failed in other school districts, and
4. there must be an integration of a comprehensive health and education program to help individual students with their problems.

Today's world is one where some students bring guns to school and threaten or actually do harm to other students and teachers. Drugs are often found and sold within the walls of elementary, middle, and high schools. There are schools where young female students are frightened to walk down hallways because they are often touched and talked to in ways that are grossly unacceptable and where both young female and young male students alike are scared when they go into school restrooms. Parents and educators worry about the safety of young people on as well as off of school grounds because they cannot tolerate bad things happening to the children and adolescents they hold dear.

The challenge is how best to establish an atmosphere within all schools that is safe, healthy, and educationally productive. A major question that must be dealt with when considering zero tolerance policies is, "how far should school policies go to protect students at the expense of certain democratic principles and rights that should permeate society?"

EXPULSION

Tied closely to the concept of zero tolerance is the practice of expulsion (Wagstaff, 2004). **Expulsion** is *a process exercised by a school district's* *governing authority, generally the school board, of banning a student from attending school for the remainder of the school year or the remainder of the school year plus an additional period of time carried into the next school year.* An example of this might be when a student is expelled in May for the remainder of the school year plus all or a portion of the next school year. The enforcement of an expulsion and the determination of the length of the expulsion are made by the school board in a session where the student is allowed to have legal representation. Zero tolerance rules often result in either suspension, where the student is not allowed to return to school for a short period of time (e.g., three or four days), or expulsion (Richards, 2004). Schools with higher numbers of African American and Latino students are more likely to have zero tolerance policies and, when students are suspended or expelled, they are more likely to enter the juvenile justice system (Jones & Jones, 2007).

A serious concern also has been raised regarding the results of expulsion policies in observing that African Americans, as a group, are the recipients of a disproportionate amount of suspensions and expulsions (Townsend, 2000). A survey of twelve large school districts showed that in some districts black students are three to five times more likely to be expelled or receive suspensions than white students. In Phoenix, Arizona, for example, blacks made up only 4 percent of the high school population, but received 21 percent of the expulsions and suspensions. White students made up only 18 percent of the expulsions or suspensions, but made up 74 percent of the population. Figures from the U.S. Department of Education identified that in 1997, black students represented 17 percent of the public school enrollment nationwide while also making up 32 percent of those suspended (Koch, 2000). An Allegheny County, Pennsylvania, report in 2006 of students under court supervision identified that, of the 555 students under supervision between September and June, 463 were black and 90 were white (Grant, 2006). Expulsions add to the problems already experienced by many African American youths resulting in poorer educational opportunities and, ultimately, a greater rate of dropping out of school. The high rate of expulsions among African Americans is sometimes felt to be due to or at least influenced by the cultural differences between these students and the predominantly white, middle class teaching work force. These cultural differences often lead to misunderstandings and misinterpretations of attitudes, behavior, tone, and working styles (Townsend, 2000).

This problem is, for many, at the heart of the expulsion issue. Students who are most likely to be expelled and alienated from the system are the same students who often are already having problems in school and who perhaps could benefit most from a quality public school education before entering the job market. Students who have difficulty learning and fitting into the middle class school society become unhappy, alienated, and less likely to comply with their teachers' expectations. Middle class children come to school to be educated and are reinforced for the values and mores of their society. Low socioeconomic status (SES) minority students come to school to be educated and to get changed. This change is frequently painful and hard to accept. In response to what is often interpreted as "forced change," many of these students rebel and threaten the safety and learning of others. They often fail, drop out, or are expelled and enter the world lacking the skills needed to support themselves, become nurturing parents and productive members of the community. Such children ultimately have their own children (too often before they become adults they become parents) and these children then come to school without the necessary parental and home support to be successful. The cycle continues and repeats itself seemingly *ad infinitum.*

Expulsion is the most serious strategy used in student behavior management. When expulsion is used, the student's right to a public education is forfeited. In expelling a student from school, the position has been taken that the negative impact of having the student in the school setting outweighs or is greater than the negative impact on the student's life when the student is removed from school. While some students have the financial means to attend a private school or pay tuition to attend school in another school district, many if not most expelled students do not have such options and spend their time out of school in unsupervised activities. This type of situation often leads to even greater problems. The decision to manage behavior through expulsion can have a profound negative impact on the lives of students and their families and should never be approached lightly.

Expulsion and Exceptional Students

The management and motivation of exceptional students raises unique questions in the minds of many educators and parents regarding expulsion. The expulsion of exceptional or special students is an issue that creates its own set of complex concerns. If special education students are held to different disciplinary standards, they are not fully a part of the mainstream curriculum. An effective disciplinary code that applies to all students can help create a more productive learning environment. The misperception that educators are supposed to tolerate different behaviors for special education students, in fact, is largely the result of unclear administrative procedures (Taylor & Baker, 2002). Still, it has been suggested that there is a double standard with respect to the management of exceptional students *vis-a-vis* other students and a number of court cases can be identified that support the point that current laws place an inordinate burden on educators when questions of the management of exceptional students arise (King, 1996). Some feel that current laws may actually encourage exceptional students to demonstrate a lack of responsibility for their behavior and a lack of respect for the system. Before they are suspended or expelled, educators must offer proof that the unacceptable behavior of exceptional students is not a manifestation of the student's condition of exceptionality. Morrison and D'Incau (2000) studied special education students in California who had been referred for expulsion and identified that the causes of the unwanted behaviors were often triggered by events outside of the school. Even though they were performing poorly in school, it was often determined that the school system was not providing the needed services to help them deal with their deep-seated, lingering problems. King (1996) identifies that some educators actually believe that it should be easier to remove students with exceptionalities from the school setting when their behavior seriously interferes with the learning or safety of others. Others (Morrison & D'Incau, 2000) argue that schools need to do more to help exceptional students and support them within the regular school environment. Decisions regarding expulsion, in particular when they involve students with exceptionalities, are extremely difficult to make and typically require legal guidance.

There are obvious concerns about the rights of all students with special attention being given to the rights of students with exceptionalities under Public Law 94-142, the Individuals with Disabilities Education Act (IDEA) of 1975 (Eggen and Kauchak, 2007). The law requires that educators working with students having exceptionalities do the following:

1. Provide a free and appropriate public education (FAPE).
2. Educate children in the least restrictive environment (LRE).
3. Protect against discrimination in testing.
4. Involve parents in developing each child's educational program.
5. Develop an individualized education program (IEP) of study for each student.

The courts have, for the most part, supported school districts when their rights to expel individual students have been challenged. Even in cases where due process questions have arisen, the courts have consistently backed school district decisions (Zirkel, 1997; Zirkel & Gluckman, 1997). One reason given for the courts having supported school districts is that expulsion frequently takes place as a result of extreme circumstances such as violence, drug-related behavior, and general antisocial behavior which often impacts on the learning and safety of other students and which society strongly condemns. Little tolerance is shown for such behaviors when they are school-related.

This is not an argument to abolish expulsion as an approach to behavior management. Schools cannot be allowed to become sites for drug deals or arenas for violence. It is an argument, however, for being especially careful and reflective before using expulsion as a management strategy. If used at all, expulsion should be the last resort to solve student management problems. Educational research shows that expelled students who do not attend alternative classes are less likely to re-enter school at a later point in their lives and more likely to get involved in gang activity, drug usage, and otherwise run afoul of the law (Koch, 2000). Expulsion should be used only when educators are certain that the impact of a student's negative behavior on the learning environment and safety of the school and other students outweighs the fact that the behavior of the student being expelled may deteriorate beyond help in the future after the expulsion.

TEACHING EXCEPTIONAL STUDENTS

When managing students who have exceptionalities there is more to be concerned with than just the legal, social, and educational ramifications of expulsion. Public Law 94–142 directs educators to ensure that students addressed in this legislation receive the most appropriate education possible in the least restrictive environment (LRE). Special students are diagnosed, an individualized educational plan (IEP) is developed for each student by a team of educators, usually with parent participation, and the students are included as appropriate in a regular classroom setting for either the entire or part of each school day. Management and motivational problems associated with many exceptional students are related to the difficulty that they have in competing academically with other students, in receiving positive attention from their teachers and other students, and in feeling equal to and accepted by other students (Curwin & Mendler, 2004).

If a teacher has a student with an exceptionality who is characterized by exhibiting unacceptable behaviors in a regular classroom setting, it is important that a plan or specific strategy be developed to help the student adjust to the setting in which he or she has been placed. If the teacher chooses to ignore the student's special needs and continues to teach as if the student were like all other students in the class, problems most definitely will occur and the student's rights will have been violated. If ignored, the student's unacceptable behavior will likely continue and probably worsen. The teacher's behavior in not addressing the problem will be running contrary to federal law and, in fact, ethical practice. Teachers cannot let problems go unresolved, but must make adaptations in their instructional programs to accommodate the unique characteristics of exceptional students (Curwin & Mendler, 2004).

Gottlieb and Weinberg (1999) report on four reasons that some students have difficulty fitting in the mainstream of American public education. These reasons were identified following a study to determine if differences exist between students who are referred and those who are not referred for special education services. Gottlieb and Weinberg note that:

1. referred students come from families that are more transient than those of non-referred students,
2. most of the students who were referred received a referral because they were behavior problems, weak academically, or highly unmotivated,
3. referred students were late to school substantially more often than non-referred students, and
4. most referrals were made by a very small number of teachers who lacked training in the use of behavior management and instruc-

tional techniques that could be used as interventions that might reduce the need for the referrals.

Many students are referred for special education placements for reasons of being difficult to teach, presenting management problems for their teachers, and being different from the other students. When these students are included in regular classrooms, they many times are being sent back into environments where, too frequently, they already have shown a history of unacceptable behavior and poor performance. This can lead to increased management and motivation difficulties for their teachers as well as enhanced learning problems for the students themselves.

When principals and teachers work with special students, it is important that they have an understanding of the laws that protect their legal rights when behavior management techniques are being considered. Teachers and administrators need to be familiar with the basic features of IDEA, Section 504 of the Vocational Rehabilitation Act of 1973, the Americans with Disabilities Act of 1990, and the IDEA Amendments of 1997 (Smith & Colon, 1998). Since 1975, Congress has amended IDEA three times, 1986, 1997, and 2004. The Amendment in 1986 extended the rights and protections of IDEA to children aged three through five, and held states accountable for locating young children who need special education. The 1997 Amendment, IDEA 97, brought about the features identified earlier in this chapter, i.e., FAPE, LRE, protection against discrimination in testing, the right to due process, and IEP. Osborne (1998) explains how the 1997 Amendments to the IDEA have clarified much of the gray area that previously existed concerning the discipline of students with exceptionalities noting that the Amendments expand the authority of school officials when such students are found to have drugs or weapons in their possession. The Amendments aid in the determination of whether or not a student's unacceptable conduct is related to the student's exceptionality and clarify that educational services must be continued for the student, even when the student has been suspended or expelled for misconduct unrelated to the disability.

The provisions of the IDEA Amendments of 1997 also impact the behavior management responsibilities of IEP teams (Smith, 2000). The Amendments identify that a special education student can be placed in a 45-day interim placement in an alternative setting as a result of behaviors involving weapons, drugs, or dangerous activity (Dayton, 2000). When this 45-day interim placement is used, however, the IEP team must conduct an assessment of the behavior to determine if a link exists between the misconduct and the student's exceptionality. The team must also develop an intervention program, an IEP that addresses the unwanted behavior, and designate an interim alternative educational setting for the student.

When regular classroom teachers, special educators, and school administrators manage the behavior of exceptional students, many factors must be considered related to their actions. Weatherly (2000), an attorney who specializes in case work for students with exceptionalities, recommends that school officials follow specific guidelines in such cases. These guidelines include:

- suggesting appropriate individualized education services for each student,
- getting all appropriate educators together with parents for IEP meetings,
- setting all final decisions for education and placement in IEP meetings,
- not letting cost or availability of services interfere with decisions,
- avoiding the inclusion of unnecessary details in the IEP,
- giving due consideration to outside private evaluations of students,
- sending parents written notice of any proposed changes in the educational program,
- developing a behavioral-management plan for disruptive students,
- showing care when suspending or expelling disabled students, and
- remembering that the right to a free and appropriate public education belongs to the student, not the parents.

Regular classroom teachers who have included students have much to consider regarding their approaches to classroom management and student motivation (Curwin & Mendler, 2004). In preparation for working successfully with such students, it is advised that teachers first address their own feelings toward the realities of working with exceptional learners. Teachers of students with exceptionalities must learn to deal with the frustrations and defeats that may come after long hours of planning and dedicated instruction. Teachers also need to be prepared to give an appropriate level of responsibility for behavior and learning to the special student himself. Many teachers actually take too much responsibility for the behaviors of their students. They must recognize that they cannot accept excuses for behavior from students that are not legitimate and that they cannot solve all of their students' problems for them. Teachers can and should, however, set clear and appropriate limits and expect students to follow them. Exceptional students, as with regular students, must learn to take responsibility for their own behaviors and take an active part in their own problem solving and decision making. It is essential for teachers to be able to communicate with the special students in their classrooms, even if the students themselves have communication difficulties. In so doing, teachers need to be prepared to give special students honest feedback. This feedback might often include praise, but may well need to also include constructive criticism. Teachers actually can, when carefully done, help an exceptional student by publicly acknowledging their own mistakes. This strategy of communication and openness tells the student that it is acceptable to try and sometimes fail. The classroom should be an inviting as well as structured environment. Many, if not most, students with exceptionalities perform best in environments that are highly structured and, therefore, predictable.

Most recently, Congress enacted IDEA 2004 (Eggen & Kauchak, 2007). This Amendment included the following features:

- reduced paperwork by deleting short-term objectives and benchmarks from IEPs (except for students who take alternative assessments),
- began a fifteen-state paperwork demonstration project to pilot three-year IEPs,
- created discipline provisions that allow districts to remove students who "inflict serious bodily injury" from the classroom to an alternative setting during the appeals process,
- established methods to reduce the number of students from culturally and linguistically diverse backgrounds who are inappropriately placed in special education,
- provided districts with more flexibility in meeting the highly qualified teacher requirements of No Child Left Behind legislation of 2002,
- provided professional development for special educators, and
- included students with disabilities in accountability systems.

Levin and Nolan (2007, pp. 260-262) note that, instead of considering specific behaviors or interventions for separate categories of special needs, it may be better to focus on general guidelines that will be helpful in thinking about working with special need students, but also all other students who struggle with behavior. These guidelines assume that the teacher is regularly modifying instruction to meet the student's needs and to enable the student to experience success. The following guidelines are offered with this consideration:

1. Help the student to develop a sense of belonging in the classroom. Model a positive attitude of welcome and acceptance and also create opportunities for the students in the class to get to know each other and to work cooperatively.
2. Parents of special needs students typically have a better understanding of their child's behavior than their teachers do. This is especially true in the early part of the academic year. Parents understand what situations and contexts are likely to help the student maintain self-control and those that make self-control more difficult. Involving students and parents in the problem-solving process is critical and helping special needs students to understand and be able to label their own strengths and weaknesses is a powerful tool for helping them make better choices about behavior. Self-control is the ultimate goal.
3. Use the expertise of other specialists as part of the problem-solving process. Read the student's IEP carefully and consult regularly with special education teachers, school psychologists and counselors, physical, speech, and occupational therapists, and therapeutic support staff and paraprofessionals who work with the student.
4. Your ability as a problem solver will be the most important tool that you possess to help students be successful and in controlling their own behavior. Be a student of the student's behavior. Observe the student carefully and record as much information as possible about the student's behavior. Try your best to document those events and contexts that trigger inappropriate student behavior and those events that lead to increased self-regulation. Investigate by collecting data through answering such questions as: "What times of day seem better for self-control?" and "What types of learning activities and materials seem to lead to better self-control?"

5. Recognize and encourage positive behavior and effort whenever possible. Help the student to keep track of progress in his or her behavior over time.

6. Teach to the student's strengths whenever possible and gradually move from strengths to areas of weakness. The teacher's goal in maximizing student success should be to use the teaching modalities (visual, aural, kinesthetic, tactical, and so on) as much as possible that match the student's preferred ways of learning.

7. Make both instruction and your daily schedule predictable. Many special needs students function better when they are able to predict events that will occur and prepare themselves emotionally.

8. Keep instruction brief, clear, and to the point. If there is a long series of steps that students must follow in order to complete a given task, sequence the steps and introduce one or two at a time instead of giving all of the directions at once.

9. Hold appropriate but high expectations by focusing on the quality of work that the student does rather than the quantity. Help the student to clearly understand what high-quality work looks like by providing exemplars and rubrics, and by ensuring that students understand the criteria that you use to judge their work.

10. Work to make sure that students have the opportunity to learn the social skills that they lack. When students are lacking the social skills that they need to interact positively with classmates, it is important that they be given the opportunity to develop those skills.

11. Teach students self-management skills that they can use to gain or regain control when they experience problems. Breathing and relaxation techniques; anger management strategies, such as slowly counting to ten; or stop-relax and think, as well as non-punitive time out are tools that students can use to keep it together when things start falling apart.

ADDRESSING DIVERSITY

Across the country, many schools and classrooms are characterized by students of diverse socioeconomic backgrounds, skin colors, religious practices, and national origins. While this kind of diversity can form the foundation for rich and varied educational experiences for all students, it can also contribute to problems in communication and understanding between teachers and students, teachers and parents, and even students and students. These problems can be manifested through instructional challenges in making the curriculum relevant, interesting, and appropriately rigorous, and through classroom management and student motivation difficulties.

The majority of educators in schools today are from white, middle-class backgrounds. However, of the almost 50 million students in schools during academic year 2001-2002, 35 percent were from minority ethnic groups; this is a percentage that is expected to increase to 44 percent by 2020 and to over 50 percent by 2040. In the nation's 5th largest school district, Broward County, Florida, students come from 52 different countries and speak 52 different languages while the percentage of teachers from minority groups is about 13 percent. Nearly half of the schools have no minority teachers. This situation, predictably, can lead to misunderstanding, conflict, distrust, hostility, and negative teacher expectations (Levin & Nolan, 2007). Students who come from a different segment of society, having different cultural backgrounds and life experiences, can quickly find it difficult to communicate and feel comfortable with many of their teachers and administrators. Some teachers have problems helping students of color for many reasons, including the fact that many teachers and administrators may even hold negative perceptions of and expectations for their students (Banks, 1994). These negative perceptions and expectations generally emerge from a lack of understanding of the students' backgrounds and a difficulty in communicating openly and honestly with them. Nevertheless, behavioral expectations must be high for all students (McEwan, 2003). If a student comes from a difficult family situation with an impoverished background and holds values different from those held by his teacher, he still must be required to exhibit acceptable conduct as is expected of others. To expect less is to violate the student's right to an equal educational opportunity. If negative student behaviors are ignored by a teacher based solely on a student's background, in time the teacher will most assuredly be faced with a troublesome student discipline problem. This was discussed earlier as related to teacher expectations and teacher efficacy. One of a teacher's greatest challenges is to hold appropriately high expectations for all students while meeting the sometimes unique needs that students from diverse backgrounds bring to the school and classroom.

The term *diversity* is a term used frequently in educational literature today. It perhaps is used so often by so many people in so many different ways that, even though it is commonly used, its meaning is taken for granted or even misunderstood. **Diversity,** *in the school or classroom, pertains to the variety of backgrounds or circumstances from which students come as they enter the schooling environment.* The key issue is a simple one to understand. Most teachers and administrators come from white, middle-class backgrounds while working with many students who do not. Even teachers themselves who do not come from a white, middle-class background, but, who come from a background of a different culture, may not be prepared to deal with the challenges that they find in the classroom when called upon to serve students from a different socioeconomic status or culture from their own. Many have predispositions toward their students and are quick to form stereotypes that unfairly label and characterize them. This lack of understanding of ethnic and cultural sensitivity on the part of some teachers and administrators can quickly lead to a total misunderstanding of student behaviors. For example, students coming from some cultural backgrounds may have adopted a set of behaviors that are accepted and considered appropriate in the home, but which are not considered this way at school. A situation such as this may lead these students to react in unanticipated ways to many of the traditional approaches to behavior management used by their teachers. Teacher expectations and procedures used at school in conducting classroom instruction may also be very foreign to them (Zabel & Zabel, 1996). Teachers are advised to be cautious not to assume that, just because children or families are from a specific ethnic or racial group, they necessarily share a common cultural experience. There are differences within cultures and within families. Students who are able to maintain comfort with behaviors that are valued in their home as well as those valued in the wider society, including the school, may be more likely to have positive views of themselves in both cultural contexts (Marshall, 2001).

Inappropriate behaviors, however, should not be ignored. Helping students from diverse backgrounds includes having an understanding and appreciation of the customs of their backgrounds and an understanding of why they have different values and behaviors than those traditionally found in and rewarded in schools. Change can be both difficult and slow. But, it can only take place positively if educators are informed, patient, and nonjudgmental. Indeed, students in underrepresented minority groups have culturally relevant knowledge and diverse cognitive abilities that schools can use to promote learning. When teachers teach and assess in ways that respect different student strengths, students learn and perform better (Sternberg, 2006). Wiest (2003) suggests that a part of the challenge includes getting students to know, accept, and respect each other. Having students think critically about culture can help them toward achieving this end. To do this, students themselves must better understand the meaning of culture. Wiest recommends that in their schooling experiences students have opportunity to (1) define culture, (2) take another's perspective, (3) analyze social behavior, (4) speculate on the meaning of observed actions and interactions, (5) interpret language, (6) analyze and compare cultural customs, (7) explore change in and alternatives to habitual behavior, (8) examine sociotypes and stereotypes, (9) identify sources of intercultural conflict, (10) propose solutions to intercultural problems, and (11) devise social action measures. By exploring these different aspects of culture, students will better understand each other, and through the instructional experiences that bring this understanding about, teachers also will better understand their students, in particular those of different cultural backgrounds.

There is no doubt that socioeconomic factors have a major impact upon the quality of education any student receives, regardless of the school. A 1994 report from the Children's Defense Fund identified that almost one-fifth of all school children live in poverty and over 40 percent of that group come from families whose income is less than one-half the poverty level (Children's Defense Fund, 1994). Children from such backgrounds are at risk of failure, especially in the present day world of high-stakes accountability and standardized testing. They also are at risk of being misunderstood, not having their personal and learning needs met, and subject to higher levels of disciplinary actions, suspensions and expulsions from school (Townsend, 2000). Cummings and Haggerty (1997) report on the program *Raising Healthy Children* that is designed to reduce the problems associated with adolescence for at-risk students. Emphasis in the program is placed on developing a bond between students, their family members, and the school. *Raising Healthy Children* offers teachers training in proactive classroom management strategies, motivation skills needed for at-risk students, and techniques for teaching social skills and reading. Through the program, parents participate in workshops designed to help their children (students) socially and academically while collaborating with their teachers. Such programs as this, that offer specific skills to teachers while developing a strong parenting component, represent positive approaches to dealing with problems that may result from social and cultural diversity.

Matus (1999) observes that many disadvantaged students attend high schools in urban communities and describes many of the unique challenges that they face. Many of the adolescents from such communities hold full-time jobs, making it virtually impossible for them to consistently complete the homework that their teachers assign. Because of their work schedules, they also are often tired and easily distracted at school. Teachers and administrators need to use a "humanistic approach" to management with such students, including peer mediation programs and flexible scheduling of classes and assignments to help them adjust simultaneously to school and work expectations. Conflict Resolution, an example of a peer mediation program, was introduced in Chapter 3. The importance of treating students with respect, not yelling or speaking harshly to them, and rewarding them when they do well cannot be overemphasized. For teachers to be effective, they must be sensitive to the needs of their students. They must make a direct attempt to understand the reasons for their students' behaviors, when such behaviors may seem to be unacceptable, and be informed by these reasons when seeking solutions to their problems.

As previously noted, public schools are institutions built upon middle-class values and mores and run by a teaching work force that comes from a predominantly white, middle-class background. Many students in the public schools, however, are neither middle class nor white, resulting in a greater chance for miscommunication and misunderstanding between teachers and students. Efforts at behavior management, which can create tension in any situation, can bring about especially unique classroom problems where miscommunications and misunderstandings in this context can prove to be particularly damaging. While all students need to be held to high standards of conduct in the school setting, regardless of their personal backgrounds and circumstances, teachers and administrators also need to be knowledgeable of and appreciative of the unique needs of a diverse student body and of each student in the student body. This type of sensitivity in teachers and administrators can come only from an understanding of the reasons for certain behaviors that students exhibit. Having this understanding will enable educators to be more effective in helping all students conduct themselves in acceptable ways. Lack of sensitivity can quickly create a "me against them" attitude or feelings of pity on the part of teachers and administrators. Either of these attitudes will lead to feelings of alienation on the part of at-risk students. All students can learn, and the student's culture is a significantly important part of the learning package and potential the student brings to the school. To engage students from diverse cultural and linguistic backgrounds, teachers must see them as capable learners (Villegas & Lucas, 2007). Teachers must hold the view that all students can learn and, in the case of culturally different students, be prepared to have a specific framework for addressing their learning needs. For example, teachers must be prepared to: (1) understand how their students construct knowledge, (2) learn about their students' lives, (3) be socioculturally conscious, (4) hold affirming views about diversity, (5) use appropriate instructional strategies, and (6) be advocates for all students.

VIOLENCE

No topic has drawn greater controversy and attention to public schools in recent years than school violence and the resulting demands for safer learning environments in schools. The public is horrified every time a story of injury, attack, or violent death in a school setting is in the news. The tragedy of Columbine High School in Littleton, Colorado, in April, 1999, where two teenagers killed twelve fellow students and a teacher before committing suicide, was brought into living rooms across the country by virtually twenty-four hour news coverage. The shooting deaths of two students and the wounding of thirteen more by a fifteen-year-old boy at Santana High School in Santee, California (2001), along with more recent shootings in Red Lake, Minnesota (2005), Las Vegas, Nevada, and Tacoma, Washington (2007), have served as stark reminders that school violence can still occur and the cause for concern still remains. The number of weapons confiscated in and around Boston's public schools has risen 42 percent in the last five years, mirroring a citywide rise in youth violence (Tracy, 2007). School police found 577 weapons, mostly knives, in the 2005–2006 school year, compared with 407 during the 2001–2002 school year. Violent crimes, mostly assaults and robberies, increased

14 percent during the same period with 902 occurrences in the 2005-2006 school year. The crimes include assaults against teachers, other school staff, and students. The United States has been reported as having the highest rates of childhood homicides, suicides, and firearm-related deaths of any of the world's 26 wealthiest nations (Aspy, Oman, Vesely, McLeroy, Rodine, & Marshall, 2004). Events and statistics such as these frighten parents as well as students and have elicited questions about school safety across the nation. Concern for discipline in schools and school safety were well documented in Chapter 1.

While recent and tragic school shootings such as the one at Virginia Tech University in Blacksburg, Virginia (April 16, 2007), where 32 people were killed and 25 were wounded before the student doing the shooting committed suicide, have reminded the nation that violent death at school is intolerable no matter how rare an event; however, it should also be noted that students actually are safer in schools today than in the community or the home. Overall school violence continues to drop, according to an annual report card on school crime published by the U.S. Department of Education. Since 1992, crime against students–including theft, rape, sexual assault, robbery, aggravated assault, and simple assault–has decreased by nearly a third. Research released by the U.S. Department of Education confirms that schools remain among the safest places for children and youth. In 2001, 90 percent of the nation's schools reported no serious violent crime, and 43 percent said that they experienced no crime at all (*Community Update*, 2001). Less than 1 percent of the 2,500 child homicides and suicides during the last six months of 1997 took place at school or on the way to and from school. There were also significant decreases between 1993 and 1997 in the percentages of high school students who carried a weapon on school property or were involved in a physical fight at school (Good News About American Education, 2000, p. 22). Even with this information, however, school violence has led many administrators and school boards to develop stronger behavior management policies in their schools, and zero tolerance policies for violent acts and weapons of any sort have become the standard in many communities. As was discussed earlier, however, these policies do not always solve the problems they are intended to address.

Lasting solutions to problems of school violence really lie in effective measures of problem prevention, in being proactive, not in dealing with problems once they have occurred. Students who are at the point where they are ready to commit violent acts against their class-mates or teachers are not likely to be thwarted by discipline threats or zero tolerance policies. More systemic solutions (i.e., well-planned preventive solutions) must be developed and implemented which involve the school, the family, and other support agencies found in the community.

Wallace (2000), a teacher in Jefferson County, Colorado, reacted to the reasons why two students shot and killed a number of their class-mates at Columbine High School. Wallace asserts that a problem exists in society in general when high status and recognition is granted to some students, e.g., athletes, members of certain clubs, and those who excel in less glamorous activities such as band or drama are ignored by comparison. Students who do not excel in high-profile activities often feel alienated, especially if they lack popularity with those who do excel. Schools must make every effort possible to address the needs of the gifted, the introverted, and those interested in nonmainstream activities. It is important that those students who enjoy high status in the school do not malign those who do not and are seen as nonconformist.

Early identification of students who are at risk of committing violent acts in the future is critical (Sprague & Walker, 2000). Several models exist that can be used to predict future violent behavior that focus on pathology within the student, ecological factors, and past behaviors. For example, youth who have shown a number of antisocial behaviors in multiple settings are more prone to be violent in the future than students who do not display these behaviors. Such factors as living in poverty, living with adults who abuse drugs and alcohol, and being a victim of child abuse are among the factors that can interact with other characteristics to predict the probability of future dysfunctional behaviors. One recommended model for the prevention of violent behavior has three distinct tiers (Sprague & Walker, 2000).

1. All students in the school are given instruction in such funda-mental skills as conflict resolution and violence prevention in an effort to create a positive learning environment throughout the school,
2. Identify those students who exhibit a pattern of factors that indi-cate that they are apt to be involved in future violent behavior and provide them with a specialized intervention program de-signed to lessen the impact of their risk factors, and

3. Identify students who are already engaged in dysfunctional, anti-social behavior. These students must receive specialized, professional help designed to change their attitudes and behavior patterns.

Although most classroom problems are minor and are easily resolved, during behavior escalation, where both the teacher and student become engaged in a confrontation, classroom instruction comes to a standstill and other students become anxious or curious spectators (Shukla-Mehta & Albin, 2003). The following twelve practical strategies have been identified as empirically effective in preventing behavioral escalation.

1. **Reinforce calm and on-task behaviors**–because most behavior is maintained by virtue of some kind of reinforcement, e.g., teacher attention, peer approval, teachers should immediately reinforce students when they display target behaviors like working calmly and being on task.

2. **Know the triggers**–most student behavior is set off by something; anything that prompts an action from others is a trigger; teachers need to learn these triggers.

3. **Pay attention to anything unusual about the student's behavior**–when the student arrives at school each day, note if the student appears distraught, anxious, or preoccupied.

4. **Do not escalate along with the student**–teachers are models for socially appropriate behavior and should maintain that stature; if teachers lose self-control, then both student and teacher will escalate together and act inappropriately.

5. **Offer students opportunities to display responsible behavior**–most behavior is a matter of choice; students choose to display a given behavior on the basis of their past experience with using the behavior to obtain specific outcomes.

6. **Intervene early in the sequence**–by intervening when less severe problem behaviors occur, teachers can avoid potentially more serious incidents.

7. **Understand how such behavioral incidents ended in the past**–whether an incident is minor or major, how it ends will determine the likelihood of future occurrences; teachers should evaluate the effectiveness of their strategies on the basis of the effect they have had on a student's prior behavior.

8. **Know the function of problem behaviors**–most students use problem behavior to either get access to something they find pleasant or to avoid or escape something they find unpleasant.

9. **Use good judgment about which behaviors to punish**–it is important to make sure that the consequence matches the severity of the problem behavior; do not use severe punishment for mildly disruptive behavior problems or the same consequence for all types of problem behavior.

10. **Use extinction procedures wisely**–extinction is the withdrawal of the consequent stimulus that previously maintained the problem behavior; it is better to use extinction in combination with differential reinforcement of alternative responses that are more socially acceptable.

11. **Teach students socially appropriate behavior to replace problem behavior**–teachers should use their knowledge of the main reasons for the occurrence of behavioral problems and teach alternative social and communication skills that will succeed in producing the same effect as the problem behavior does for the student.

12. **Teach academic survival skills and set students up for success**–there is little question that academic failure is positively correlated to behavioral problems; teachers should teach academic survival skills to students and promote their active engagement so that they are less likely to be challenged with disruptive behavior.

The following listing of behaviors represents early warning signs of potential violent behavior in students. Teachers and students are advised to be observant for these behaviors and respond proactively and accordingly. Ignoring known warning signs is definitely not the appropriate course to take.

1. Social withdrawal
2. Excessive feelings of isolation and being alone
3. Excessive feelings of rejection
4. Feelings of being picked on and persecuted
5. Low school interest and poor academic performance
6. Uncontrolled anger
7. Patterns of impulsive and chronic hitting, intimidating, and bullying behaviors

8. History of discipline problems
9. Intolerance for differences and prejudicial attitudes
10. Drug use and alcohol use
11. Affiliation with gangs
12. Inappropriate access to, possession of, and use of firearms
13. Serious threats of violence
14. Being a victim of violence
15. Expression of violence in writings and drawings
16. Past history of violent and aggressive behavior

One major concern related to violence in schools is the existence of organized gangs. Dowling-Sendor (1998a), an appellate defender from North Carolina, provides important information for school administrators when reacting to the existence of gangs within their schools. First, all school policies must be comprehensive and should serve to prohibit gang activity while also working to motivate students not to engage in such activity. Second, when dealing with the prohibition of certain types of dress or symbols, a student's First and Fourteenth Amendment rights cannot be violated. Third, a student should be allowed the opportunity to deny any accusation that an item of clothing or symbol has any gang significance. Educators should seek help from students, parents, law enforcement, and community agencies to provide students with alternatives to gang activities (Dowling-Sendor, 1998b). Parent involvement at the time gang behavior is suspected is especially important (Curwin & Mendler, 2004). Levin and Nolan (2007) note that, if the school and its teachers have started to build a positive relationship with parents before a problem really begins, parental contacts concerning problems are more likely to result in greater parental cooperation. Three factors are identified as influencing parent involvement: (1) the belief about and acceptance of the role of parents as it relates to providing home support for the school, (2) parents' sense of efficacy concerning their ability to help, and (3) the perception of the invitation for parental involvement in the school. School principals should appeal to parents for their assistance in finding immediate resolutions if problems are identified. Parents should be told that the school will not tolerate gang activities and that the principal is prepared to take action, to include contacting any authorities and agencies as necessary, in order to maintain a safe school environment. After parents have had an opportunity to react and propose solutions to the identified problems, students should join the dialogue in order to hear their parents say that the problems will come to an end. Violent behavior is not acceptable and will not be tolerated.

Obviously, personality factors and peer relations impact school violence; however, the overall impact of the school's culture also has a significant influence on violent behavior. Bryner (2007) and Reis, Trockel, and Mulhall (2007) have pointed out that certain characteristics of middle schools can be predictors of aggressive behavior in students. Reis and her associates found three cultural features that lead to a reduction in school violence; they are:

- teaching that emphasizes understanding, not memorization,
- student participation in making school rules, and
- education about cultural diversity.

Violence in schools is a problem that parents, educators, and students alike agree cannot be allowed to occur. Though school violence is not a new phenomenon, the tragic events of recent years have aroused parents, educators, and school boards to take what are sometimes felt to be dramatic actions to prevent further violence from taking place in their communities. While popular with some, stringent school rules for behavior and zero tolerance policies do not always prevent radical, dysfunctional behavior. Educators have come to recognize that dealing with crime and violence requires a total community effort (Rossman & Morley, 1996). Many schools have formed effective alliances with other agencies in their communities, e.g., law enforcement and mental health, to combat crime and violence in a more comprehensive way. Because school violence is something that must be prevented, and not just dealt with after the fact, it is in a school district's best interest, and the best interest of all involved, to have a sound prevention plan in place. Any comprehensive strategy to curb school violence will need to deal with both school safety programs and access to guns (Dealing With School Violence, 2006). These two issues go hand in hand, in addition to the financial resources that must be invested in problem solutions from the federal, state, as well as local levels.

SCHOOL UNIFORMS

One possible, and in some places popular solution to school violence, gang activity, and difficult student behavior problems that received high interest beginning in the 1990s is having students wear school uniforms. The view in support of this strategy has been that, if all students are dressed alike, unique gang clothing and symbols would be easier to detect. School uniforms make it more difficult for drug pushers and other undesirable persons to come on school campuses during school hours without being spotted by authorities. It also has been argued that the wearing of school uniforms is an effective strategy to lessen the differences of socioeconomic status that are often apparent in diverse schooling situations.

Many educators as well as noneducators favor requiring school uniforms. The third Phi Delta Kappa Poll of Teachers' Attitudes Toward the Public Schools (Langdon, 1996) indicated that 53 percent of the general public favored school uniforms while approximately two-thirds of the teachers favored them. Though a strategy viewed favorably by many teachers, and to a lesser degree by the general public, having students wear school uniforms to significantly improve the learning environment of a school still needs further research.

There have been, however, reported successes. A mandatory uniform program was adopted in the elementary and middle schools of Long Beach, California (Stanley, 1996). After one year of the program being in operation, there were significant decreases in suspensions, assault/battery, assault with a deadly weapon, fighting, sex offenses, robbery, extortion, possession of both drugs and weapons, and vandalism. There also were fewer disruptions in class, overall unacceptable student behavior, uncooperativeness, bad attitudes, and poor work ethics. Parents felt that the uniform policy had led to positive results and were in greater support of the school. The students, however, were less than enthusiastic about wearing the uniforms and denied that the uniforms had led to positive results, though observed by others. In Anne Arundel County, Maryland (Butler, 2006), advocates say that dressing uniformly eliminates the social pressures and the expense of buying fashionably and encourages children to behave better and get serious about learning. There is some research that indicates a correlation exists between appropriate dress and academic performance and a greater sense of community. Currently, about 25 percent of public elementary schools in the country have some form of mandatory uniform policy, up from a handful in the mid-1990s.

Kommer (1999), using his experiences as a former middle school principal in Los Angeles, California, adds support to the development of school uniform policies in identifying the following positive results of school uniform programs. School uniforms:

1. help to reduce gang influence,
2. create a more positive and businesslike atmosphere,
3. increase pride in the school,
4. reduce problems for students related to choosing what to wear to school,
5. reduce strife between students and parents concerning what to wear, and
6. lower the stress and expense for parents related to buying school clothes.

Kommer advises those who wish to institute a uniform policy to make uniforms mandatory, not voluntary. Mandatory programs are seen as working better than those that are voluntary. It is wise, however, to provide an optout option for parents who are adamantly opposed to uniforms or whose child transfers into the school after the beginning of the school year. A uniform policy will work if parents and students are involved throughout the decision-making process. If it is decided that a school uniform program is to be implemented, it is recommended that students be given the ultimate decision as to what the uniform will look like.

Hamilton (1999), a principal of an elementary school in Plainfield, New Jersey, has had experiences similar to those previously described and also stresses the importance of getting parents and students involved early in the decision-making process. Parents who are in favor of the uniform policy can be encouraged to talk with those parents who are opposed to the idea. This positive support from parent peers, along with as much data as possible from the school, usually convinces those in opposition to at least try the new program. Parents who find buying uniforms a financial burden can receive assistance to ease this problem through local businesses or charitable organizations (Hamilton, 1999; Stanley, 1996).

There are, however, those who are as opposed to school uniform policies as there are those in support of them (Caruso, 1996; Evans, 1996). Arguments against uniform policies include the view that:

1. such policies are an infringement on First Amendment rights,
2. having such a policy is a tool of power for school administrators,
3. uniforms represent an unnecessary cost burden given to parents,
4. gangs and violence still exist even with uniforms being worn, and
5. uniforms do not do away with class distinctions between the "haves" and the "have not's."

All of these issues are important and must be addressed when the possibility of initiating a school uniform policy is being considered.

It has been suggested that the real push behind school uniform policies has been more political than research-based (Black, 1998). A study conducted by Educational Testing Service (1998) shows no apparent relationship between the use of school uniforms and student achievement or behavior. It may be concluded that there is little meaningful research evidence to support that having students wear school uniforms will improve discipline, increase student respect for teachers, promote school spirit, raise academic performance, equalize social status, or any other claims made by those promoting uniform policies. While some evidence does exist for elementary and middle schools, little evidence exists to support school uniforms for high school students. In spite of differing views, and in an attempt to solve student management problems in schools, some educational leaders and school boards still have instituted school uniform policies, and a number of the communities that have such policies report positive results. Those who oppose such policies, nevertheless, continue to note that, at this time, there is little empirical data, certainly no compelling data, supporting a link between the utilization of school uniform policies and desired student behavior outcomes. The approach clearly deserves further study.

DRUG ABUSE

Drug abuse has been seen as a major problem in and out of schools across the country for many years. Each year approximately 150,000

young people under the age of 18 are admitted to drug abuse programs in the United States (Morral, McCaffrey, Ridgeway, Mukherji,
Beighley, 2006). Like many other societal problems, substance abuse
has a powerful negative impact on young people. Drug use among
young people remains at levels near or even above the peak years of
1979–1980 (Curwin & Mendler, 2004).

In a major survey of over 10,000 high school students, researchers
investigated the relationship between school violence (i.e., carrying a
weapon, being in a physical fight, damaging and stealing property,
threatening with a weapon, and missing school due to safety concerns)
and substance abuse (Lowry, Cohen, Modzeleski, Kann, Collins, &
Kolbe, 1999). A little more than half of the respondents reported
drinking alcohol and approximately one-fourth reported using marijuana. Approximately one-third reported that they had been offered,
sold, or given illegal drugs on school property in the last year. Nearly
60 percent noted that they had used one or more of the substances in
the previous month. The study also reported that the prevalence of
school violence factors was greater for those students who had used at
least one of the substances than for those who had not. Researchers
with the U.S. Department of Education and the Centers for Disease
Control and Prevention in Atlanta, Georgia, suggest that drug abuse
and school violence are so closely related that the problems associated with each one should be approached in a coordinated fashion.
Addressing these serious problems in an isolated manner, or in a fashion that separates one from the other, risks less than optimum attention being given to either one.

Another related study was conducted to determine knowledge levels, feelings, and attitudes of kindergarten students regarding alcohol,
tobacco, and other drugs. The sample for the study was drawn from
high-risk elementary schools in Lexington, Kentucky (Hahn, Hall,
Rayens, Burt, Corley, & Sheffel, 2000). Results indicated that approximately one in six kindergartners were able to identify marijuana,
crack cocaine, LSD, injectable drugs, or other illegal substances. Although most of the children in the study voiced negative attitudes
toward drug use, some of the kindergarten students viewed drug use
positively. The recognition of cigarettes and alcohol was not related to
demographic factors. Minority children, however, were much more
likely to be knowledgeable about illicit drugs than nonminority children. How do such young children know so much about illegal sub-

stances? It has been reported that young people are highly influenced by their close friends and their parents as this relates to their knowledge and their likelihood of becoming involved in drug use (Curwin & Mendler, 2004).

Many substance abuse programs have been developed in recent years in an effort to help control the drug use problem among young people. Jones (1997) describes an evaluation of forty-seven such programs with only six earning high marks. The six rated most favorably were Alcohol Misuse Prevention Study (AMPS), Life Skills Training, the Michigan Model, Project ALERT, Project Northland, and Drug Abuse Resistance Education (DARE). However, virtually all drug prevention programs get mixed reviews. Adair (2000) evaluated fifty drug prevention programs and suggested that Jones (1997) was correct only in the high rating of Project ALERT, believing that Project ALERT is especially good for middle school students. In their assessment of drug prevention programs, Elias, Gager, and Leon (1997), have drawn a different position on DARE, finding the program to have only two of what they report as being the necessary characteristics of a good program. They identified that QUEST was the best program with Here's Looking at You, 2000, Growing Healthy, and Social Decision Making-Social Problem Solving (SDM-SPS) also being good programs. Some suggest that all drug abuse prevention programs fall short of meeting students' needs and that even the ones considered best lack complete utility because they do not focus on student capabilities and do not provide honest information to students (Brown, 1997). Many federal and state mandates stand in the way of best-practice alternatives. While it is difficult to get agreement among the experts as to which prevention programs work best, it is clear that there is obvious room for improvement in most programs. Factors have been identified that are important to acknowledge concerning the quality and completeness of any program (Jones, 1997). Successful programs help students with problem solving, social skills, and goal setting while providing training and support for teachers as well as family and community involvement. Good programs also provide students with accurate information about drug use. In an effort to take a proactive stance, random drug testing of student athletes has become as routine as study hall and lunch at many high schools across the country (Kansas Schools Take Drug Testing to Extreme, 2006). Acknowledging no quick fixes, efforts such as these to recognize the importance of engaging the problem, as well as its causes, are in an effort to address what is regrettably a growing problem among school-age youth in the United States.

An important perspective on working with students who may be involved with illegal substances is that teachers and parents should guard against accepting excuses and empty promises (Curwin & Mendler, 2004). Students who use drugs typically do not complete their schoolwork at the level of those who do not abuse drugs, and teachers must adhere to strict consequences for such behavior. When teachers notice changes in the behavior of a student that may indicate drug use, the student needs to be told about this observation. This should be done without accusation of drug use, but, as a caring teacher sharing an observation regarding a change in student behavior with a student. If the teacher has tried to communicate this information to the student, and the behavior goes unchanged, the teacher should then approach the student with the suspicion of drug use. It is important for the teacher, when taking this action, to listen to the student and interact in a caring, nonaccusatory and nonthreatening manner.

There is evidence that solitary substance use can be related to poor academic achievement and educational attainment (Tucker, Ellickson, Collins, & Klein, 2006). Schools today are under tremendous pressure to improve the scholastic performance of students, and much time and money is being dedicated to the academic preparation of students, teachers, and administrators. All feel accountable, and pressure, for reaching higher and higher levels of student achievement. Teachers must not forget, however, that many students have needs that go far beyond the academic concerns of the school, community and even the state. It is important to recognize that a coordinated program should be offered which will help to reduce the prevalence of problems such as drug usage and underage drinking (Wooley, Eberst, & Bradley, 2000). The strongest coordinated program will include the school, family, and appropriate community agencies.

THE FIRST YEAR OF TEACHING

The first year of teaching is a time of great challenge, complexity and adjustment, as beginning teachers must be able to face many new and different demands and respond to them effectively. In a review of a large number of studies focusing on important problems faced by beginning teachers, classroom discipline heads the list and motivating students is second (Tauber, 1999; Veenman, 1986).

Martin and Baldwin (1996) studied how beginning teachers are different from experienced teachers in the way they perceive classroom management and how school counselors can help them develop better learning environments in their classrooms. They found that teachers who had taught three years or less had more controlling attitudes toward students than did those who had taught more than three years. It is suggested that this controlling attitude toward students can result in less favorable learning conditions and damage to student self-esteem and that school counselors should be used to coordinate mentor programs between experienced and novice teachers. School counselors could also lead support groups where new teachers can brainstorm solutions to shared problems and provide consultation to new teachers concerning best practice techniques for managing and motivating students.

Beginning teachers need a well-planned, extensive, and continuous induction program with a strong mentoring component with master teachers that lasts for at least the entire first year of teaching if not longer. Experienced teachers need be encouraged to assist first-year teachers by providing them with practical information, political *savoir-faire*, and professional support (Morgan, 1997). Practical information involves important, everyday matters such as how to fill out purchase orders, the location of preferred parking places, and even which copy machine to use. Political *savoir-faire* deals with how certain things are perceived and what may or may not be acceptable behavior in certain situations such as dealing with parents and colleagues. Professional support involves sharing lesson plans, guidance on ways to motivate certain students, and methods of classroom management. When inexperienced teachers receive this type of advice from supportive, experienced teachers, they typically become less frustrated and more likely to remain in teaching longer. Strong (2006) reports that, the more comprehensive induction support that a new teacher receives, the more likely the teacher is to remain in the profession. In a study where seventy-two teachers were examined six years after they were enrolled in a induction support program that provided them with veteran teachers released full-time as mentors, 84 percent of the teachers were still teaching after four years. This compares to a nationwide figure of 67 percent after the same period of time. These numbers suggest that comprehensive induction support is effective in increasing teacher retention.

Principals also must be key figures in the mentoring of new teachers. Brock and Grady (1998) report findings from a study done to gather information from principals and first-year teachers that explored the needs of beginning teachers and how principals can best assist them. The study showed that most principals offer new teachers some type of orientation program, assign mentors to new teachers, and spend time working with new teachers on an individual basis. Although the new teachers in the study felt that the orientation and mentoring programs were helpful, most indicated that they would have preferred to have had more time with the principal, in order to get clearer perspectives on the principal's expectations for them, and more immediate feedback on their performance.

While there are many teacher education programs throughout the country that prepare candidates for initial certification, there is often a wide variance across these programs in the abilities of their graduates, even among graduates of the same program. In spite of its agreed upon importance, few teacher education programs make available and even fewer programs require students to take specific courses in the area of classroom management (Tauber, 1999). This is surprising, and questionable, in particular given the repeatedly high rating of concern that teachers give to working with student behavior problems. Much of what teachers learn with respect to classroom management techniques comes through school district efforts in in-service training or what some more offhandedly refer to as "on-the-job training." Because district programs vary in their approaches to preparing teachers, and because individuals are naturally different in many ways, all first-year teachers are not equally prepared to teach, manage, and motivate students. This is especially true since the level and ultimate effectiveness of their preparation may be relative to the type of school in which they are teaching. For example, a first-year teacher who might be well prepared to teach in a rural school setting may find it difficult to be successful in an inner-city setting. Likewise, teaching in a suburban school site near a large metropolitan area like Chicago or Miami would present a different set of challenges from those found on an Indian reservation in Oklahoma or in an Appalachian area in North Carolina.

Teacher training institutions must continue to improve in preparing their graduates to teach in present-day, standards-driven, diverse school settings. Principals also must understand the significant role that they play in the development and success of first-year teachers and, at times, teachers-in-training. Many of the frustrations that drive young teachers out of the profession could be significantly reduced by more real-world-based initial preparation; effective instructional leadership; strong induction programs; and supportive, experienced colleagues willing to share with and support first-year teachers. Professionals already in the field should see it as their responsibility to do everything in their power to ensure the success of beginning teachers.

The following checklist represents advice given by first-year and veteran teachers to assist those entering their first year of teaching (What to Expect Your First Year of Teaching, 1998).

- Plan relentlessly: Create back-up plans for teaching students of varying abilities.
- Set high, consistently reinforced expectations for behavior and academic performance.
- Show and require respect in the classroom at all times.
- Reach out to parents and your administration, preferably early on and before a problem arises.
- Consider participating in an extracurricular activity, which strengthens relationships with students and can be enjoyable as well.
- Seek mentors, team teaching assignments, and regular exchanges with fellow first-year teachers.
- Be flexible and ready for surprises: For example, one teacher was assigned a classroom of students from kindergarten through fourth grade.
- Work closely with counselors or other school personnel authorized to respond to children's social problems.
- Take care of yourself physically and spiritually.
- Love learning, love kids, and love teaching.

TEACHER STRESS

It seems as though each academic year the demands on teachers increase and reports of teacher stress increase proportionately. Educators are continually subject to higher levels of consistent stress than are professionals in most other fields (Crute, 2004). Overcrowded classrooms, pressure to produce high student test scores, increasing amounts of paperwork, and anxious parents and students are some of the factors that contribute to stress-related burnout in the teaching workforce. This level of stress has resulted in many young teachers leaving the classroom in only their first years of teaching. National Education Association data indicate that one-third of new teachers leave the profession, often because of stress-related issues, in the first five years of teaching.

Dealing with disruptions and students who are unmotivated are consistently identified as two of the primary sources of stress for classroom teachers. If this stress is sustained over long periods of time, the result can be teacher burnout. A teacher who suffers from **teacher burnout** is characterized by having reached a *point of extreme stress where the teacher has lost his or her enthusiasm for teaching and has little energy to focus on helping students learn.* Coming to work is difficult for such teachers who often complain of headaches, exhaustion, frustration, irritability, outbursts of anger, and many other similar symptoms, including depression (Curwin & Mendler, 2004; Hendrickson, 1979). Teacher preparation programs rarely include skill development, at least indepth skill development, to help teachers deal with overwrought individuals. But, understanding conflict and stress is the first step toward managing it. Reducing stress for all parties will allow teachers to focus on the more important aspects of their jobs. Stress undermines physical, emotional, and intellectual energies precisely when strength in these areas is needed most (Morris, 1998).

Although related, teacher burnout and attrition (i.e., leaving the profession) are not the same thing. Some teachers leave the profession because they are experiencing symptoms of burnout but many others leave for other reasons. And, all teachers who burn out do not quit. Some remain in the classroom though they have lost virtually all zest for their work (Zabel & Zabel, 1996). If the negative effects of being burned out cannot be reversed, it is in the best interest of the students, and the schools and communities they are there to serve, when these teachers leave the profession.

There are certain identifiable factors that exist in a teacher's world which augment the possibility of burnout (Zabel & Zabel, 1996). The number of students assigned to a teacher can be seen by the teacher as creating an unfair burden, though in some cases this feeling may be more a result of perception than reality. Such a feeling is important, however, if it is real to the teacher. Stronger feelings of support from parents, other teachers, and especially administrators can ease the perception of being overburdened. The type of student assigned to teachers also can be a determiner of teacher stress (Curwin & Mendler, 2004). Students with exceptionalities, for example, especially those with emotional or behavioral problems, can behave in ways that are stressful to their teachers as well as classmates. Additionally, teachers can become burned out if the expectations that they have for their jobs are greatly different than the realities of their jobs. Most teachers enter the profession for the intrinsic rewards that come with teaching, not extrinsic rewards such as salary. If a teacher does not receive intrinsic rewards from students, parents, or colleagues and teaching in general; if sufficient external rewards are not present; or if teaching in some way disappoints a perhaps overly idealistic view of the profession; job-related stress may be the end result. Disparity between expectations for teaching and the reality of teaching can be a real cause of stress. Many teachers become frustrated and develop feelings of inadequacy as a result of poor student performance. In the current era of high-stakes testing and accountability, increased expectations for student achievement have placed great stress on teachers and students alike. Because of these and other complex factors, many teachers are caught in a cycle of unfulfilled expectations and negative feelings, behaviors, and reactions from students, parents, colleagues, and administrators. In the end, they become frustrated because circumstances are not as they had expected which, ultimately, can lead to negative behaviors in the classroom. Negative teacher behaviors in the classroom often result in increasingly negative behaviors on the part of students (i.e., disruptive behaviors). Increased levels of discipline problems, in turn, bring about increased levels of stress and frustration for teachers and the cycle continues.

In discussing the areas of teacher stress and teacher burnout, Larrivee (2005) notes that teachers can enter into either a burnout cycle or renewal cycle as a result of the approach they take in responding to stressful problems with students. In the Burnout Cycle, the teacher responds to student misbehavior in one of two ineffective ways. The teacher either avoids the misbehavior (overlooks, ignores, denies, rationalizes, surrenders, or pleads) or attacks the misbehavior (orders, interrogates, blames, puts down, threatens, argues, provokes, punishes, or seeks revenge). As a result of this approach, there typically is no improvement in the student or the student's behavior worsens, and the teacher is often hurt or humiliated. The teacher's anxiety increases and the teacher either withdraws or blows up. Consequently, student misbehavior increases. When the cycle becomes repetitive, burnout is the end result. Teachers may suffer both physical and mental side effects; be preoccupied with negative thoughts; lack motivation to go to work; be fatigued and irritable and even experience muscular tension, high blood pressure, or ulcers. In the Renewal Cycle, the teacher responds to student misbehavior in one of two effective ways. In the first way, the teacher is proactive and initiates action (expresses feeling, clarifies teacher expectations, accepts ownership, provides rationales, invites participation, solicits information, enlists cooperation, or requests help). In the second way, the teacher is reactive in responding to something the student has initiated (validates student feelings, acknowledges student needs, respects student perspective, asserts teacher needs, provides options, offers assistance, mutually explores resolutions, or negotiates a plan). Through either of these approaches, the student behavior typically improves and there is less confrontation. And, the teacher feels valued and respected. Through effective use of the Renewal Cycle, teacher self-efficacy improves, the teacher remains engaged and enthusiastic, and there is increased appropriate student behavior. The Renewal Cycle clearly is the desirable and appropriate approach for the teacher to take in that it produces positive results, not only for the teacher and his or her own health and effectiveness as a teacher, but also positive results for the student in terms of student behavior and learning.

If the stress cycle is to be broken, teachers need to be able to examine their own feelings and emotions as an important first step toward stress reduction. In so doing, teachers must be prepared and capable of assessing how their feelings and behaviors affect their relationships with their students and colleagues (Rizzo & Zabel, 1988). Nissman (2006) offers the following suggestions to teachers as approaches to dealing with teacher stress.

- Recognize that stress is not a problem, but a symptom. Focus on what is causing the stress, e.g., classroom management, administrative pressure, lack of community support, home responsibilities, or lack of sleep, and take action.
- If stress is extreme, seek professional assistance.
- When experiencing a stressful situation, write down in a log the situation and how you are dealing with it. After a period of time, evaluate the log and see if a pattern develops. This information will assist you in making appropriate changes in your teaching.
- When experiencing anxiety, share your feeling with the people with whom you are dealing. This may lower your level of stress after an incident.
- Make a concerted effort to separate your stress-producing problems and handle them one at a time. Once you have coped with one situation, that success often alleviates other situations that have led to a stressful reaction.
- Evaluate your reactions and be sure you are not overreacting to the responsibilities placed upon you. You cannot solve everyone's problems.
- Be open to investigate other professional areas in and out of education. Such an investigation or change can bring back the enthusiasm you once felt as a classroom teacher.

Since behavior management problems are a primary cause of teacher stress and burnout, teachers must give special attention to the way their own behaviors affect their students if stress is to be reduced and brought under control. A teacher who dislikes or is feeling dissatisfied with his or her teaching quickly conveys these feelings to students who, recognizing this, often exhibit unwanted behaviors that then create more stress for the teacher. For this situation to improve, teachers must confront their feelings of stress and do something proactive in order to be able to appropriately cope with them. Teachers who avoid holding back their emotions by finding safe ways to vent their feelings are much less likely to become overly stressed. Withheld emotions often lead to negative and depressing thoughts. Teachers who are able to think and act more positively are more likely to project an acceptable image to their students, which then improves life in the classroom for everyone concerned (Curwin & Mendler, 2004).

Among other characteristics and strategies, a good sense of humor is a wonderful aid when combating burnout. Though easy to say yet hard to do, if a person can simply learn to laugh at himself or herself and not take too many things on a personal level, stress can be reduced. At times, however, too much stress can lead to dangerous depression or seriously aggressive acts. When serious problems of this nature are identified, it is advisable for the teacher to seek professional assistance from someone who specializes in issues dealing with job-related stress.

Administrators can and need to help teachers who are having stress-related problems (Pawlas, 1997). Principals should always take time to listen to a teacher's frustrations. A problem that may sound trivial to the principal is likely to be truly stressful to the teacher who took the first step to visit the principal to talk about the problem. Principals should be supportive and, whenever possible, make a point of looking for something good to share with a frustrated teacher. Giving reassuring advice or help to a teacher who seems to have encountered a particularly frustrating situation can be especially beneficial. The principal, for example, might speak to a disruptive student or request a meeting with the student's parents as a strategy to be of special assistance. Supportive, reassuring behavior by the principal can do a great deal to lift a teacher's morale. Some principals have actually created special support groups within their schools as a strategy to help teachers get help in stress reduction. Activities such as yoga, meditation, breathing exercises, and dance, to name a few, have been used as strategies to make the work place more enjoyable and reduce the stress related to the responsibilities of teaching.

CONCLUSION

A discussion of zero tolerance policies, expulsion, teaching special students, addressing diversity, violence, school uniforms, and drug abuse began this review of special problems and concerns related to student management and motivation. These topics are identified as recurring issues for discussion when teachers share their concerns about managing and motivating students in contemporary school settings. The discussion has sought to provide current information that will help teachers advance their skills and knowledge to meet the demands of a dynamic and challenging profession while encouraging further investigation and study.

The last two topics discussed in this chapter are of a slightly different nature. Special concerns of beginning teachers and the impact of stress and teacher burnout are seen as having special importance in any investigation of issues of best practice in classroom management and student motivation. Management and motivation concerns are uniquely related to both of these topics as issues of management and motivation are tightly intertwined with many of the problems related to the first year of teaching and the ongoing pressures of working in the profession. Consequently, they, in turn, are potential causes of teacher stress and burnout. This chapter has sought to extend the understanding of management and motivation in the classroom with respect to identified special problems, while reinforcing the important need for educators at all levels to continue their study in these critical areas.

QUESTIONS/ACTIVITIES FOR REFLECTION

1. What is your personal assessment of zero tolerance policies related to student behavior management? Do you see zero tolerance as positive or not positive? If you were a building administrator interested in adopting such a policy, how would you begin the process? What would be important questions that need to be addressed?

2. Many teachers hold the view that expelling certain chronic misbehaving students from school is needed for the greater good of helping other students who exhibit positive behaviors. Others see expulsion as an act of discarding a human being into a world of little hope or positive future. Evaluate the strategy of expulsion as a means of dealing with student misbehavior. Explain why you have made the evaluation that you have made.

3. The practice of including exceptional students in regular classrooms has resulted in greater diversity in classrooms than ever before. Many regular classroom teachers are strongly in support of this practice while some believe that the presence of exceptional learners in regular classrooms helps neither the regular students nor those that are exceptional. If you were a teacher in a regular classroom with exceptional learners, what are the important questions that you would need to ask and have answers to in

order to maintain a well-managed classroom with highly motivated students?

4. If you were a teacher new to the profession, what personal plan might you put in place in order to address the potential problems of teacher stress and burnout? What would be the key elements of the plan and how would you go about ensuring that the plan was successful?

5. A number of early warning signs related to potential student violence were introduced in the chapter. Interview three teachers working in classrooms today and review the signs on the list with them. What is their assessment of the problem of violence in schools and classrooms today and the accuracy of the warning signs on the list?

REFERENCES

Adair, J. (2000). Tackling teens' no. 1 problem. *Educational Leadership, 57*, 44–47.

Aspy, C., Oman, R., Vesely, S., McLeroy, K., Rodine, S., & Marshall, L. (2004). Adolescent violence: The protective effects of youth assets. *Journal of Counseling and Development, 82*, 268–276.

Banks, J. (1994). *An introduction to multicultural education.* Needham Heights, MA: Allyn & Bacon.

Bindel, J. (2006). Absent enemies. Retrieved November 21, 2006, from http://education.guardian.co.uk/schools/story.

Black, S. (1998). Forever plaid? *American School Board Journal, 185*, 42–45.

Black, S. (2004). Beyond zero tolerance. *American School Board Journal* (9)191. Retrieved May 21, 2007, from asbj.com journal.

Blair, F. (1999). Does zero tolerance work? *Principal, 79*, 36–37.

Brock, B., & Grady, M. (1998). Beginning teacher induction programs: The role of the principal. *Clearing House, 71*, 179–183.

Brown, J. (1997). Curriculum: Listen to the kids. *American School Board Journal, 184*, 38, 40, 47.

Bryner, J. (2007). Study: School culture affects student violence. *LiveScience*, 1–4. Retrieved May 21, 2007, from LiveScience database.

Bullying is behind teen suicide wave in Japan. (2006). Retrieved November 20, 2006, from http://news.monstersandcritics.com/asiapacific/article.

Butler, A. (2006). Uniforms take pressure off. Retrieved August 31, 2006, from www.baltimoresun.com/news/education.

Caruso, P. (1996). Individuality vs. conformity: The issue behind school uniforms. *NASSP Bulletin, 80*, 83–88.

Children's Defense Fund. (1994). The state of America's children 1994. Washington, DC: Children's Defense Fund.

Community Update. (2001, February/March). U.S. Department of Education, Issue No. 85.

Cooper, D., & Snell, J. (2003). Bullying–Not just a kid thing. *Educational Leadership, 60*(6) 22–25.

Corzine: Train teachers to help children avoid web predators. *South Jersey News Online.* Retrieved August 4, 2007, from http://blog.nj.com/gloucester/2007/08/corzine_train_teachers_to_help.html.

Croft, G. (2006). Back-to-school: Books and bullies. Retrieved September 19, 2006, from http://abcnews.go.com/Primetime/story.

Crute, S. (2004). Teacher stress: Stressed out. *NEA Today.* Retrieved May 10, 2007, from www.nea.org/neatoday.

Cummings, C., & Haggerty, K. (1997). Raising healthy children. *Educational Leadership, 54,* 28–30.

Curwin, R., & Mendler, A. (2004). *Discipline with dignity.* Alexandria, VA: American Association of Supervision and Curriculum Development.

Curwin, R., & Mendler, A. (1999). Zero tolerance for zero tolerance. *Phi Delta Kappan, 81,* 119–120.

Dayton, J. (2000). Discipline procedures for students with disabilities. *Clearing House, 73,* 151–156.

Dealing with school violence. (2006, October). Retrieved October 17, 2006, from www.startribune.com.

Doi, E. (2006). Schoolyard bullying in Japan leads to rash of student suicides. Retrieved December 7, 2006, from www.mercurynews.com/mld/mercurynews/news/world.

Dowling-Sendor. B. (1998a). Watching what students wear. *American School Board Journal, 185,* 12–13.

Dowling-Sendor, B. (1998b). Gangs and rosaries. *American School Board Journal, 185,* 22, 24.

Dwyer, K., Osher, D., & Hoffman, C. (2000). Creating responsive schools: Contextualizing, early warning, timely response. *Exceptional Children, 66,* 347–365.

Educational Testing Service. (1998). Beyond assumptions. *American Educator, 22,* 32–35.

Eggen, P., & Kauchak, D. (2007). *Educational psychology: Windows on classrooms* (7th ed.). Upper Saddle River, NJ: Pearson Education.

Elias, M., Gager, P., & Leon, S. (1997). Selecting a substance abuse prevention program. *Principal, 76,* 23–24, 27.

Essex, N. (2000). Classroom harassment: The principal's liability. *Principal, 79,* 52–55.

Evans, D. (1996). School uniforms: An `unfashionable' dissent. *Phi Delta Kappan, 78,* 139.

Ghezzi, P. (2006, March 20). Zero tolerance for zero tolerance. *Atlanta Constitution.*

Good News About American Education. (2000). Washington, DC: Center on Education Policy and the American Youth Policy Forum.

Gottlieb, J., & Weinberg, S. (1999). Comparison of students referred and not referred for special education. *Elementary School Journal,* 187–199.

Grant, T. (2006, August). Back to school: Zero tolerance makes discipline more severe, involves the courts. Retrieved September 6, 2006, from www.post-gazette.com/pg/06243/717806-298.stem.

Hahn, E., Hall, L., Rayens, M., Burt, A., Corley, D., & Sheffel, K. (2000). Kindergarten children's knowledge and perceptions of alcohol, tobacco, and other drugs. *Journal of School Health, 70*, 51–55.

Hamilton, K. (1999). Implementing a school uniform policy. *Principal, 79*, 46–47.

Hendrickson, B. (1979). Teacher burnout: How to recognize it, what to do about it. *Learning, 7*, 36–38.

Hyman, I., & Snook, P. (2000). Dangerous schools and what you can do about them. *Phi Delta Kappan, 81*, 488-498; 500–501.

Jones, R. (1997). More than just no. *American School Board Journal, 184*, 30–32.

Jones, V., & Jones, L. (2007). *Comprehensive classroom management: Creating communities of support and solving problems.* Boston: Pearson Education.

Joyce, E. (2007). I'm, like, so being harassed online. Retrieved June 29, 2007, from www.internetnews.com/stats/article.php/3685726.

Kansas schools take drug testing to extreme. (2006). Retrieved September 14, 2006, from www.msnbc.msn.com.

Kranz, C. (2007). Program urges students to put a stop to bullying. Retrieved January 16, 2007, from http://news.enquirer.com.

King, A. (1996). Exclusionary discipline and the forfeiture of special education rights: A survey. *NASSP Bulletin, 80*, 49–64.

Koch, K. (2000, March 10). Zero tolerance. *Congressional Quarterly Researcher.* Washington, DC: Congressional Quarterly, Inc., 187–204.

Kommer, D. (1999). Beyond fashion patrol: School uniforms for middle grades. *Middle School Journal, 30*, 23–26.

Langdon, C. (1996). The 3rd Phi Delta Kappa poll of teachers' attitudes toward the public schools. *Phi Delta Kappan, 78*, 244–250.

Larrivee, B. (2005). *Authentic classroom management: Creating a learning community and building reflective practice* (2nd ed.). Boston: Pearson Education.

Levin, J., & Nolan, J. (2007). *Principles of classroom management.* Boston: Allyn & Bacon.

Lowry, R., Cohen, L., Modzeleski, W., Kann, L., Collins, J., & Kolbe, L. (1999). School violence, substance use, and availability of illegal drugs on school property among U.S. high school students. *Journal of School Health, 69*, 347–355.

McEwan, B. (2003). *The art of classroom management: Effective practices for building equitable learning communities* (2nd ed.). Upper Saddle River, NJ: Merrill.

Manning M., & Bucher, K. (2007). *Classroom management.* Upper Saddle River, NJ: Pearson Education.

Marshall, H. (2001). Cultural influences on the self-concept: Updating our thinking. *Young Children*, November, 12–22.

Martin, N., & Baldwin, B. (1996). Helping beginning teachers foster healthy classroom management: Implications for elementary school counselors. *Elementary School Guidance & Counseling, 31*, 106-113.

Matus, D. (1999). Humanism and effective urban secondary classroom management. *Clearing House, 72*, 305–307.

Morgon, M. (1997). Dear colleague: A letter from a new teacher to experienced teachers. *Clearing House, 70,* 250–252.

Morral, D., McCaffrey, D., Ridgeway, G., Mukherji, A., & Beighley, C. (2006). The relative effectiveness of 10 adolescent substance abuse treatment programs in the United States. *Rand Technical Reports TR-346.* Retrieved May 14, 2007, from www.rand.org/pubs/technical_reports.

Morris, R. (1998). Conflict: Theory must inform reality. *The Kappa Delta Pi Record,* Fall, 14–17.

Morrison, G., & D'Incau, B. (2000). Developmental and services trajectories of students with disabilities recommended for expulsion from school. *Exceptional Children, 66,* 257–272.

Nissman, B. (2006). *Teacher-tested classroom management strategies.* Upper Saddle River, NJ: Pearson Prentice-Hall.

Olweus, D. (2003). A profile of bullying at school. *Educational Leadership, 60*(6), 12–17.

Olweus, D. (1993). *Bullying at school: What we know and what we can do.* Cambridge, MA: Blackwell.

Osborne, A. (1998). The principal and discipline with special education students. *NASSP Bulletin, 82,* 1–8.

Pawlas, G. (1997). Seven tips to reduce teacher stress. *High School Magazine, 4,* 42–43.

Reis, J., Trockel, M., & Mulhall, P. (2007). Individual and school predictors of middle school aggression. *Youth and Society, 38*(3), 322–347.

Richards, J. (2004). Zero room for zero tolerance policies: Rethinking federal funding for zero tolerance policies. *University of Dayton Law Review, 30,* 91–117.

Rigby, K. (2007). What is bullying? Bullying in schools. Retrieved April 19, 2007, www.education.unisa.edu.au/bullying.

Rizzo, J., & Zabel, R. (1988). *Educating children and adolescents with behavioral disorders: An integrative approach.* Boston: Allyn & Bacon.

Ross, T. (2007). 150,000 pupils targeted by homophobic bullies. Retrieved June 28, 2007, from http://education.independnet.co.uk/news/article2710599.ece.

Rossman, S., & Morley, E. (1996). Introduction. *Education and Urban Society, 28,* 395–411.

Safe Schools Climate Act. (2006). Retrieved June 7, 2007, from http://ed.sc.gov.

Schreier, L. (2006). Crime prevention group tracks cyberbullying. Retrieved August 18, 2006, from www.contracostatimes.com/mld/cctimes/news/nation.

Shukla-Metha, S., & Albin, R. (2003). Twelve practical strategies to prevent behavioral escalation in classroom settings. *The Clearing House.* November/December,

Skiba, R. (2001). *Zero tolerance, zero evidence: An analysis of school disciplinary practice.* Bloomington, IN: Indiana Educational Policy Center, Indiana University.

Skiba, R., & Peterson, R. (2000). School discipline at a crossroads: From zero tolerance to early response. *Exceptional Children, 66,* 335–346.

Skiba, R., & Peterson, R. (1999). The dark side of zero tolerance: Can punishment lead to safe schools? *Phi Delta Kappan, 80,* 372376; 381–382.

Smith, C. (2000). Behavioral and discipline provisions of IDEA '97: Implicit competencies yet to be confirmed. *Exceptional Children, 66,* 403–412.

Smith, J., & Colon. R. (1998). Legal responsibilities toward students with disabilities: What every administrator should know. *NASSP Bulletin, 82*, 40–53.

Sprague, J., & Walker. H. (2000). Early identification and intervention for youth with antisocial and violent behavior. *Exceptional Children, 66.* 367–379.

Stanley, M. (1996). School uniforms and safety. *Education and Urban Society, 28*, 424–435.

Sternberg, R. (2006). Recognizing neglected strengths. *Educational Leadership, 64*, 30–35.

Strong, M. (2006, January). Mentoring new teachers to increase retention: A look at the research. *Research Abstracts.* Santa Cruz: CA: New Teacher Center.

Tauber, R. (1999). *Classroom management: Sound theory and effective practice* (3rd ed.). Westport, CT: Bergin & Garvey.

Taylor, H. (2000). Meeting the needs of lesbian and gay young adolescents. *Clearing House, 73*, 221–224.

Taylor, J., & Baker, R. (2002). Discipline and the special education student. *Educational Leadership, 59*(4), 28–30.

Teicher, S. (2006). Social norms strategy aims to tame bullying. Retrieved August 17, 2006, from www.csmonitor.com.

Townsend, B. (2000). The disproportionate discipline of African American learners: Reducing suspensions and expulsions. *Exceptional Children, 66*, 381–391.

Tracy, J. (2007). School crime rises, reflects Hub violence. Retrieved January 2, 2007, from www.boston.com/news/local/massachusetts.

Tseng, N. (2006). Districts grapple with web bullying. Retrieved August 9, 2006, from www.orlandosentinel.com/orl-cyberbullies.

Tucker, J., Ellickson, P., Collins, R., & Klein, D. (2006). Does solitary substance use increase adolescents' risk for poor psychosocial and behavioral outcomes? A 9-year longitudinal study comparing solitary and social users. *Psychology of Addictive Behaviors.* Retrieved May 18, 2007, from www.rand.org/health.

Veenman, S. (1986). Perceived problems of beginning teachers. *Review of Educational Research, 54*, 143–178.

Villegas, A., & Lucas, T. (2007). The culturally responsive teacher. *Educational Leadership, 64*, 28–33.

Wallace, M. (2000). Nurturing nonconformists. *Educational Leadership, 57*, 44–46.

Wagner, M., Knudsen, C., & Harper, V. (1999/2000). The evil joker. *Educational Leadership, 57*, 47–50.

Wagstaff, L. (2004). Zero-tolerance discipline: The effect of teacher discretionary removal on urban minority students. Unpublished dissertation, University of Texas, Austin.

Weatherly, J. (2000). Special rules for special ed. *American School Board Journal, 187*, 26–27

What to Expect Your First Year of Teaching, A Checklist of Tips. (1998). Retrieved July 9, 2007, from www.ed.gov/pubs/FirstYear/checklist.

Wiest, L. (2003). Twelve ways to have students analyze culture. *The Clearing House,* January/February, 136–138.

Wooley, S., Eberst, R., & Bradley, B. (1999/2000). Creative collaborations with health providers. *Educational Leadership, 57*, 25–28.

Zabel, R., & Zabel, M. (1996). *Classroom management in context: Orchestrating positive learning environments.* Boston: Houghton Mifflin.

Zero tolerance (school). (2007). Retrieved July 10, 2007, from http://en.wikipedia.org/wiki/zero/tolerance_(schools).

Zirkel, P. (1997). The Midol case. *Phi Delta Kappan, 78,* 803–804.

Zirkel, P., & Gluckman, I. (1997). Due process in student suspensions and expulsions. *Principal, 76,* 62–63.

Chapter 6

RESPONDING TO STUDENT MOTIVATION AND BEHAVIOR PROBLEMS

The ability to respond to specific classroom behavior problems so that the problems are effectively addressed represents a special skill, or perhaps more accurately a set of skills, that requires development and refinement over time. Effective teachers as reflective practitioners must individually analyze unacceptable behaviors exhibited by students in order to develop appropriate ways to address each behavior and manage and motivate those students who are not conducting themselves in ways appropriate to the classroom.

This chapter will examine several instances of student conduct that are seen by most teachers as representing motivation and behavior problems (Charles, 1976; Hunt et al., 1999). The use of the Model for Reflection and Inquiry, introduced in Chapter 1 to help effectively address problems of classroom management and student motivation, will be illustrated through the use of behavior management scenarios as practical examples of typical classroom problem situations.

TEACHER REACTIONS TO STUDENT MISCONDUCT

Teachers can and do prevent many problems from occurring through the effective use of managerial and motivational techniques that they regularly incorporate into their teaching. It has already been noted that effective teachers have to address fewer student behavior problems than teachers who are considered to be not effective. Kounin (1983), in his initial research, compared the behavior of effective and ineffective teachers as classroom managers and concluded that the primary difference between the two groups of teachers was not in how they handled disruptive behavior, but in the dispositions of the teacher to quickly and accurately identify a problem behavior and act on it. As previously discussed in Chapter 3, a key teacher disposition here is the quality of *withitness*. Even with well thought out preventive measures and preparations in place, however, the occasion will occur in virtually any classroom when a student acts in an undesirable fashion. This may be represented by a minor infraction of rules such as talking too loudly or not waiting for others to finish talking before speaking. Or, the problem could be of a more serious nature such as a student endangering the safety of other students or doing something that directly interferes with the learning of classmates. Teachers need to be prepared on a daily basis to alter (some might say correct) the behavior of some students. As introduced in Chapter 1, teachers need to be prepared to discipline those students who do not respond to the teacher's instructional, motivation, and management plans.

It has been suggested that any one of three different approaches to classroom leadership (i.e., management) can be used by teachers to modify student behavior (Schlechty, 1976). This position, influenced by the earlier work of social psychologists such as French and Raven (1959), is that, to be effective, teachers must earn or otherwise gain a type of social power or leadership over the students in the classroom. If the teacher does not maintain leadership of the group, leadership will be gained by someone else, in this case one or more students. Teachers are felt to manage their classrooms through the use of one of the following three strategies: *normative, remunerative,* or *coercive.* **Normative strategies** are *behavior strategies used by the teacher in maintaining a well-managed classroom based on all involved doing what is traditionally expected of them because each person knows his or her expected role;* teachers are expected to direct or ask students to do certain things, and students are expected to do what their teachers direct or ask them to do. **Remunerative strategies** are *behavior strategies used by the teacher that are based on the power of rewards.* Rewards can take the form of special privileges, extra time to participate in enjoyable activities, or more tangible rewards such as candy or tokens (Borich, 2006; Borich & Tombari, 1997). **Coercive strategies** are *behavior strategies used by the teacher that are based on the power of punishment.* If students do not behave properly, they will be punished. Some educators believe that an over reliance on coercive strategies may alienate students to the point that they withdraw from the learning process (Borich, 2006). Many teachers, however, even with this potential concern, try to manage the learning environment through the use of coercive power. Coercive strategies, however, often can produce short-term gain coupled with long-term loss.

Normative power is dependent on the teacher's ability to gain respect from students. When teachers are seen as knowledgeable, trustworthy, fair, and concerned, students more readily respond to their requests (Goodlad, 1984). When teachers treat students with respect, students develop a greater sense of belonging in the classroom. Students respond more consistently to a system of management based on normative strategies when a respectful and trusting environment has been established. Glasser (1986) stresses the importance of such a relationship between students and their teachers if effective management is to be realized. Normative power is positional in that the role of *teacher* carries with it, by its very nature, a high degree of influence and authority. If teachers conduct themselves the way students feel teachers should conduct themselves, students will more readily respond positively to their teacher's use of normative strategies and do what their teachers ask, simply because it is their teachers who are making the requests.

Operant conditioning forms the foundation of remunerative management. Chapter 4 included a discussion of the Applied Behavior Analysis management theory that is based on B.F. Skinner's theory of operant conditioning. The basic purpose that drives remunerative management is the motivation by reward of students so that they will continue to exhibit, and even intensify, acceptable conduct. The parent who gives money to a child for every "A" on the report card, the teacher who shows a special film because the students all made good grades on a mathematics test, or the principal who hosts a pizza party for all students who make the Honor Roll all represent the use of remuneration to motivate and manage students. One of the most important aspects of remunerative management is that it focuses on the positive, not the negative aspects of students' behaviors. In spite of this, many educators criticize management and motivation by the use of remuneration approaches suggesting that students should not be expected to exhibit appropriate behavior only for the purpose of receiving rewards (Kohn, 1993).

Coercive management relies on the use of physical or psychological pain or discomfort, taking away belongings or privileges, or threatening either of these measures in order to persuade (i.e., motivate) students to discontinue unwanted behaviors. An important concern regarding the use of coercive strategies is the fear that their use may increase student antagonism and lead to students becoming alienated from their teachers and the learning process (Borich, 2006). Since coercive strategies focus on the negative aspects of student behavior, it is important that teachers avoid the use of consequences that belittle, embarrass, or attack the character of a student. When consequences are given for undesirable behavior, teachers should focus on just that, the undesirable behavior, not the student. What should be emphasized in efforts to extinguish a student's unwanted behavior is that it is the behavior that is unwanted, not the student. Comments such as, "I don't know what you get away with at home, but you cannot do that in my room," or "Stop acting so immaturely," are attacks on the student's character or that of the student's parents. Attacks such as these result in hurt and embarrassment with the typical end result being alienated, angry, or otherwise disenfranchised students. In some cases, such attacks may also produce alienated and angry parents.

If a student does something that is considered inappropriate, the teacher should deal with the misbehavior and the consequence swiftly. Identifying the consequences for undesirable behavior early in the school year emphasizes to students that they have an important responsibility for their own self-control (i.e., self-regulation) and forewarns them of the end result if they do not take this responsibility seriously (Emmer et al., 2006; Evertson, Emmer, & Worsham, 2005; McCormick & Pressley, 1997). Early identification also helps to make clear in the communication process between the teacher and his or her students just what is considered as being unacceptable and what is not. In establishing these ground rules, the teacher will have taken an important preventive step in dealing with potential management problems in the classroom.

THE PROACTIVE TEACHER

Being characterized as proactive as opposed to reactive in teaching says a great deal about how the teacher approaches his or her responsibilities in the profession. The **proactive teacher** is *a teacher who has the ability to "head off" most management problems before they occur and* *respond to management problems when they do occur in such a way that sets the stage for learning to continue in the future.* Given that there will be cases of student misconduct from time to time in all classrooms to which teachers will need to respond, it is important that teachers remain appropriately focused on the purpose behind any use of their power. The teacher's primary purpose in reacting to student misconduct is to change the behavior of the student so that the school environment will be safe and conducive to learning for all students, including the student(s) exhibiting the misbehavior. The purpose is not simply to react to a disturbance or unacceptable behavior so that the disturbance or behavior is eliminated. In reacting to student misbehaviors, the teacher's emphasis should be on eliminating the unacceptable behaviors so that students displaying these behaviors, and their classmates, will gain the greatest benefit from their schooling experiences. Effective teachers also see their responses to student behavior problems as additional opportunities to teach their students so that the learning environment will be improved. They, in effect, teach their students what proper behavior, in some ways proper social behavior, i.e., prosocial behavior, is all about and how they can exhibit this proper behavior. In doing this they also teach, and reinforce, which behaviors are considered to be not proper, i.e., antisocial. Their responses to student behavior problems focus specifically on the undesired student behaviors while avoiding personal attacks on students; this is a crucial aspect of effective management. Teacher responses seen as personal attacks on the students themselves will only increase the probability of future disruptive behavior. More importantly, such responses by the teacher can result in a decrease in learning. Teachers who concentrate their efforts on motivating students to do better, as opposed to focusing their attention upon policing them to not misbehave, establish more productive learning environments and fruitful relationships with their students.

A number of teacher behaviors can be identified that research indicates are associated with a behavior management system that will help teachers create a learning environment that encourages students to conduct themselves appropriately (Cotton, 1999). When used, the behaviors and system also decrease the likelihood that students will misbehave in the future. The following behaviors are recommended:

1. set behavior standards that are similar to the standards set in the building conduct code,

2. tell students that there are high standards for conduct in the classroom and clearly explain rules and consequences for their behavior,
3. have standards that are conscious of cultural influences on conduct,
4. provide a written set of behavior standards to students and review the standards periodically,
5. establish clear and specific rules at the beginning of each year or semester,
6. allow students to help in the establishment of rules and procedures in grades 4–12,
7. provide appropriate amounts of review and reteaching of rules in PreK–3 settings,
8. link discipline sanctions to the students' inappropriate behaviors and avoid using or threatening to use corporal punishment,
9. focus on teaching positive, prosocial behaviors, especially when students consistently repeat inappropriate behaviors,
10. quickly stop students who are disruptive in order to avoid loss of learning time,
11. focus on inappropriate behaviors, not the students' past offenses or personalities,
12. handle disciplinary problems themselves with referrals to administrators only in rare situations, and
13. actively seek new methods and strategies to improve students' behavior management skills.

Teachers who exhibit these behaviors are considered proactive in their approaches to student motivation and classroom management. Instead of waiting for a disruption to occur before acting, or being reactive, they use behaviors and strategies designed specifically to create an environment that decreases the potential for inappropriate conduct occurring in the first place. Hunt et al. (1999) discuss eight behaviors that characterize teachers who create environments designed to promote positive student behavior and diminish student misbehavior. The teacher should:

1. thoroughly prepare in order that all students stay on task with activities suitable for their individual rates, styles, and abilities of learning,

2. develop classroom routines that help students get through non-instructional times when behavior problems are most frequent,
3. communicate with parents to develop a strong support system in order to better work with specific management problems,
4. maintain a professional demeanor when carrying out their duties and responsibilities,
5. recognize inappropriate student behaviors and deal with them rapidly while ignoring insignificant conduct,
6. exhibit calm, confident behavior when correcting inappropriate student conduct,
7. immediately follow up on directives when students do not respond positively, and
8. focus on preventing problems instead of reacting to problems.

These behaviors focus on the development of classroom learning environments where teachers can rely mainly on a normative management system with the teacher and students together forming a positive learning relationship founded on trust and respect. They also reinforce the need for the teacher to utilize effective teaching practices that will keep students focused and involved in constructive learning activities and reduce "down times" when most misbehavior occurs.

Maintaining a professional demeanor, exhibiting calm and confident composure, and reacting only to truly inappropriate as opposed to minor student misbehaviors are all ways for teachers to earn the trust and respect of students. Following through with appropriate consequences when students fail to respond to directives is an essential behavior used by effective teachers to develop consistency in their management. Schlechty (1976) and Hunt and Bedwell (1982) note that teachers who retreat (i.e., ignore students who do not respond positively to a teacher request) greatly increase the probability of having more management problems in the future. The need to know how to prevent problems has similarity to the need for the teaching profession to become more science than art, and for teachers to recognize their need to know what works specifically and in what situations (Marzano, Pickering, & Pollock, 2001). For this to happen, educators must have a desire and commitment to change. Knowing how to prevent problems, for example, requires being willing and able to learn from past mistakes as well as accomplishments along with seeking and utilizing the assistance of other professionals. Freiberg and Driscoll (2004) use the term **advancework** in referring to *the process of preventing problems before they begin rather than reacting to problems after they have already occurred.* Advancework requires teachers to gather data to develop a better understanding of their students, the community and school, and the impact the content being taught has on the behavior of their students.

Good and Brophy (2007) include one further aspect of effective management not yet discussed to this point. Teachers who desire to minimize their management problems set as a goal the development of inner self-control in students. It is not sufficient for teachers to be satisfied merely in being able to manage their classrooms and students. A major part of the enculturation that should take place in any school is for students to learn to manage themselves in order to live in a supportive environment with others. Without self-control it is difficult, if not impossible, for students to resolve the various conflicts that may develop in their lives on any given day. The development of self-control was previously discussed in reference to students becoming self-regulated learners.

The first days of the school year or the beginning of a semester are critical for the teacher to develop a system (i.e., rules and procedures) for effective classroom management. Various research studies have identified that one important quality that characterizes effective teachers as managers is that they establish their expectations for student behavior during the first few weeks of the school year or semester and consistently reinforce them thereafter (Emmer et al., 2006; Freiberg & Driscoll, 2004). Evertson et al. (2005) suggest that teachers should use the first weeks of the school year to clearly communicate their rules and procedures to their students, observe student attitudes and work habits, and begin instruction with a high level of energy and enthusiasm. This will help greatly to establish a solid foundation upon which the teacher's academic program can be built.

Effective teachers project themselves as leaders in the classroom while creating a learning environment based on concern, trust, and respect. Students maintain a high level of productivity because they are regularly engaged in learning activities appropriate for their learning styles, interests, and abilities. Students have a clear understanding of the rules and procedures for classroom behavior and the consequences that accompany the breaking of rules or not following procedures. They observe that the teacher quickly and consistently takes action to ensure that all students follow established rules and procedures. Students understand that there exists a high standard for conduct and that they must assume responsibility for their own behavior.

Teachers who aspire to meet these expectations and who follow these guidelines will have students who more regularly conduct themselves in an appropriate fashion. As any experienced teacher can attest, however, it is unrealistic to believe all student misbehavior can be prohibited. Behavior management problems can still occur even in what may appear to be the best of classroom situations. As a result of their study and prior planning, however, effective teachers are prepared to handle these problems swiftly with minimum interruption to the learning process. Hunt et al. (1999) organize effective teaching concerns related to motivation and management into three categories: *personal considerations, instructional considerations, and environmental considerations* (Figure 6–1).

Personal Considerations	Instructional Considerations	Environmental Considerations
Conduct one's self in a calm, confident fashion.	Able students must be challenged.	The classroom should be a clean, comfortable setting.
Be prepared for unexpected events.	Low ability students should not be placed in unduly frustrating situations.	The classroom should be void of major distractions to learning.
Praise positive behavior.		
Show respect and affection for learners.	Instruction should be both exciting and enjoyable.	A few rules for acceptable conduct should be clearly stated.
Treat students in a consistent fashion.	A variety of questioning patterns should be utilized.	Parents and administrators must offer support.
Ensure that student ideas are valued.		The atmosphere should be one of acceptance.
	All students should experience success.	

Figure 6.1. Considerations for the prevention of management problems.

ADDRESSING SPECIFIC MANAGEMENT PROBLEMS

The teacher's role in student motivation and classroom management should be examined in the context of the ideas and recommendations presented throughout the entire body of this text and not in any one chapter. As emphasized, the most productive learning environments are those where high levels of motivation and the absence of student misbehaviors are found. Nevertheless, in spite of the teacher's best efforts to be well planned and motivating, and even with a sound management plan, the time will inevitably come when some students will behave in ways that are felt to not be acceptable and where the teacher will need to take action to correct these behaviors.

What is unacceptable behavior? It is important for teachers to have the answer to this question clearly in mind, and have it understood by students as well, as effective teachers do not react to just any student behavior that appears undesirable. Consider the following four definitions of unacceptable behavior:

1. any behavior that disrupts the learning of one or more students,
2. any behavior that threatens the safety of one or more students,
3. any behavior that is in direct violation of written school-wide or classroom rules, and
4. any behavior that is a violation of accepted social mores (e.g., the use of profanity, inappropriate touching, etc.)

In addition to these four definitions, teachers will likely wish to identify rules for student behavior specific to their individual classrooms as a part of their own individual management and discipline plans. That which is unacceptable in one teacher's classroom may be acceptable in another teacher's, while some behaviors are always unacceptable in every classroom. For example, some teachers may have the expectation that students should speak only after first raising their hand and being recognized. Other teachers may encourage more open discussion and actually expect and desire spontaneous participation from their students. However, if there are school-wide rules for certain behaviors (e.g., that no candy is to be eaten in classrooms or no hats are to be worn inside the school building) all teachers are expected to enforce these rules.

The number of rules a teacher has influences how much time the teacher will spend monitoring and managing student behavior. The more rules there are the more time will be spent in seeing that they are followed. As presented previously, teachers should only have those rules considered to be most important and which relate specifically to promoting the instructional program of the classroom. The fewer rules the better with no more than five or six being considered maximum by many teachers. Not only do greater numbers of rules create added monitoring problems for teachers, large numbers of rules create problems for students in trying to remember them and the consequences that will occur when they are not followed.

Many authors have identified and categorized various kinds of student misbehaviors found in classrooms and made suggestions concerning strategies teachers can use when confronted with them. Student misbehavior needs to be analyzed and then addressed in a situational manner as such behaviors are contextual. What may prompt a behavior in one student may not in another. Likewise, what may prove to be an effective remedy to one problem in one situation may or may not be as effective in another (Gootman, 2001). The following section of the chapter examines eight frequently observed student misconduct behaviors and provides suggestions for teacher intervention. The suggestions are recommended as important ones to be considered when a teacher is faced with specific student misbehaviors. Even with this information, however, teachers need to analyze and evaluate each situation independently, and then apply the most suitable solution called for. The behaviors included here are: *inattention, disruptive talking, attention-seeking, chronic avoidance of work, dishonesty, unruliness, defiance, and aggression.* Some of the behaviors are considered as being more serious than others; they are examined here from least to most serious in nature.

Inattention

Inattention behaviors are defined simply as *students not paying attention when the teacher is conducting instruction or when participation in an instructional activity is expected.* Common inattention behaviors exhibited by students are daydreaming, staring into space, doing unrelated work, doodling, or even playing with some object, e.g., calculator, toy, ruler, during instructional time. Inattention is seen as the least severe management problem, in part, because the inattentive student tends not to disturb other students in the classroom. Inattention is still considered to be unacceptable behavior; however, inasmuch as, when students are inattentive to the teacher or the teacher's planned activities, they are not engaged in the learning process. And, if not addressed, their inattention can be adopted by other students in the classroom if the inattention is seen by them as being acceptable.

Working with Students with Inattention Problems

If a teacher's lesson is progressing well, the teacher who has twenty-five students in a classroom is advised to not interrupt the instructional process that is being effective with twenty-four students for one student who may be inattentive. While it is important that all students attend to the teacher's lesson, there are more subtle ways of effectively handling the problem of a student being inattentive than to disrupt the learning of the rest of the students in the class to eliminate the inattentive behavior of one or even a few students. Moving physically closer to an inattentive student, for example, will usually help bring the student's attention back to the learning task or to what the teacher is saying. This use of what is sometimes referred to as proximity control will allow the teacher to modify the student's behavior without ever having to say a word. When teachers are physically close to students, the likelihood of student misbehavior diminishes.

Teachers can do a number of things to be proactive in preventing student inattention with the first step being to evaluate the physical arrangement of the classroom. Researchers established years ago that students sitting in certain parts of the classroom get less teacher attention than other students and are, therefore, more likely to be inattentive if they are so inclined (Adams & Biddle, 1970). It is recommended that seating arrangements be developed so that those students most inclined to be inattentive sit as near the teacher as possible. The corners of the classroom farthest from the teacher are areas to avoid for students prone to inattentiveness. The distance between the student and the teacher is an important variable when determining the likelihood of a student being inattentive.

Another important physical factor affecting inattention is spacing. Students who are seated too closely to one another automatically have greater opportunities for distractions. When students are seated at tables, adequate space must be provided so that each student has a comfortable work area that does not encroach on the area of other students. It is best when a space is provided away from the student's immediate study or work area for the storage of excess books and supplies that can become distractions. Lack of adequate space and comfort increases the probability that distractions and, eventually, inattentiveness will take place.

Room temperature is another physical factor that affects attention. While comfort level as far as temperature is concerned varies from individual to individual, it is generally better to have the room temperature slightly cool rather than warm. If the room temperature gets too warm, activity may slow down and some students are likely to become sleepy.

A final physical factor affecting inattention is the presence of distractions in the classroom. Most elementary school students sitting beside a window overlooking a playground are almost certain to be distracted. Similarly, many students at the secondary level sitting beside an open door leading to a busy hallway may also lose their focus on the teacher's lesson. Although there are some distractions over which teachers have little control (e.g., construction workers, the first snow of the year, the onset of important events, etc.), to the degree possible, distractions should be eliminated or at least minimized in order to help students stay on task.

The teacher's own instruction can be another factor that can impact student attentiveness. Student inattention will increase when the teacher's instruction lacks excitement and enthusiasm, i.e., energy. Though some may say that teachers cannot be exciting every minute of the day, this is little consolation when students are inattentive or exhibiting some other form of unwanted behavior. Instruction that is not stimulating may reflect insufficient preparation on the part of the teacher in terms of preparing for instruction, motivation and management at the same time. Effective teachers are enthusiastic and often animated. They think about their students individually when they plan their lessons in terms of how a particular activity will draw students into the center of the instructional process or leave them on the edge. Teachers who have students who are inattentive are often characterized by (1) doing the same thing over and over, (2) lacking in spontaneity and excitement, (3) teaching subject matter that students see as having little importance or meaning to them or as being too difficult for them to master, and (4) not engaging students actively in the learning process. Teachers are encouraged to use a variety of different instructional strategies, vary stimuli in order to encourage student interest, and use multi-media presentations and hands-on activities to add excitement to their instruction. Even though quiet, sedentary activities have a place in the classroom, many students, especially younger students, have difficulty maintaining attention when involved in activities that do not require their involvement for extended periods of time. Classrooms where students are given the opportunity, and are even expected to actively participate in the learning activities, as well as the actual planning of the activities, as appropriate depending on their age, constitute environments that foster student attentiveness. Students who are involved in learning activities that are meaningful to them are seldom inattentive.

Beyond questions of classroom environment and instruction, certain personal characteristics of the teacher may augment student inattention. The monotonic voice that drones on has become a symbol of the uninteresting, stereotypical bore. Teachers who talk in this manner should not be surprised if their students become inattentive or even disruptive. Voice inflections are recommended along with complementary gestures to enliven the teacher's instructional delivery. The use of humor at the moment students are starting to let their minds wander also is an effective strategy. Teachers should never underestimate the effectiveness of an appropriate joke or humorous anecdote with students of all ages.

The source of some attention problems also can be found in the students themselves as opposed to the teacher or the physical environment. Some students may be inattentive, even though the teacher is doing an excellent job teaching a dynamic curriculum, due to personal problems either at school or outside of school that are so severe that it is difficult, if not impossible, for them to attend to their class work. Too, students who have been allowed to be inattentive at other times in other classes or during other lessons may have developed a pattern of behavior or habit of not attending to the lessons that their teachers present. They may have developed shorter attention spans simply because they have never been encouraged or required to be attentive. In order to help a student become attentive, the teacher first must understand the reason why the student is not attentive. Gaining this understanding will require problem solving and analysis on the part of the teacher. If the cause of the student's inattention is a personal problem, counseling may be needed. If the student simply has poor learning habits, it is the teacher's responsibility to reinforce the student when good attention is shown and not give reinforcement when it is not.

Developing an effective questioning technique can be a very effective strategy to help students be more attentive (Good & Brophy, 2007). Teachers are encouraged to ask a variety of questions and direct these questions to a variety of students. When a teacher asks a question first and then calls on a student for an answer, this questioning approach encourages all students to listen to the question, in case they may be called on. It also helps the students focus on the answer that is eventually given to the question. Teachers should remain aware of to whom they have directed their questions to make sure that their questions are uniformly delivered throughout the classroom. This strategy was discussed in Chapter 4 in reference to the equitable distribution of the teacher's questions. It is easy to fall into a pattern of directing questions to only a few students, typically to those who are more normally responsive and attentive. This pattern of question asking allows, or even encourages, students who are not involved in the questioning process to become inattentive as they become more and more distant and disconnected from the lesson. Asking questions can draw students actively into the instructional process or embarrass them publicly in the classroom. A teacher who calls on a student knowing that the student is being inattentive, thinking that putting the student "on the spot" in front of his or her classmates will cause the student to be more attentive in the future, can be making a major mistake in judgment. Not only may the student not be attentive in the future, the student may also resent the teacher for the public embarrassment and be motivated to be involved in more serious forms of misbehavior than inattention.

Teachers are encouraged never to reinforce or reward student inattention; unfortunately, this is an error that is easy to commit. When a teacher gives directions and students do not pay attention, the teacher is actually reinforcing undesirable behavior when the directions are regularly repeated or when students are allowed to ignore the directions that have been given. This teacher behavior also sends the message to the other students in the class that being attentive is not necessary. Good listening habits represent learned behaviors, and students who habitually fail to be attentive will only improve their abilities to pay attention if their behaviors are shaped by the teacher to do so. This will take time. Teachers must be patient yet firm.

Disruptive Talking

Disruptive talking is *talking that interferes with the learning process by interrupting the teacher while teaching or students as they are listening to the teacher or as they are involved in completing activities that the teacher has assigned.* Different teachers set different standards for acceptable student talk in the classroom, and this fact itself can cause confusion for students who move from teacher to teacher during the school day. There may be no other standard for unacceptable student behavior that varies as much from teacher to teacher as the one that serves to define acceptable talking in the classroom.

Working with Students with Disruptive Talking Problems

Different teachers invariably have different views of what is and is not an appropriate level of student talk in the classroom. Individual teachers may even vary during the school day or from day to day as to what they consider to be a permissible level of student talk. This variance could even be determined by the type of lesson that is being conducted. For example, a teacher normally will accept more student talk when a cooperative group activity is taking place than when students are involved in a more traditional teacher-led discussion. All students can understand and adjust to these differences when they clearly know what the teacher expects, i.e., when the ground rules are clear. Problems are created for students, however, when they do not know just what teachers expect or when teachers change what they consider to be the acceptable level of talk based on reasons unknown to the students. It is confusing to students when teachers fluctuate from situation to situation for no apparent reason in the amount and level of talk that is seen as being acceptable. Teachers need to be consistent with their standards in this area and avoid punishing a student one day for a behavior that was looked upon as acceptable on another.

Students become involved in disruptive talk for many reasons. Although the need to talk with peers is a strong drive for many students, teachers can and should take steps to prevent or eliminate such unwanted interaction when it is disruptive to the instructional process. One strategy to address this type of problem is for the teacher to be certain that directions and instructions are stated clearly. Students often talk to classmates as they try to figure out what the teacher wants them to do. Teachers should observe students for nonverbal indications of confusion and ask questions to be certain that their directions are clear to everyone before having students start an activity or moving on to the next segment of a lesson. Idle talk also can be a result of unmotivating lessons. As is true with inattention, much unwanted talk will disappear if students are involved in motivating lessons that require their participation and that hold their interests.

The prevention of disruptive talk begins with the teacher. Students who are given an assignment which is stimulating and meaningful enough to hold their interest, and adequate to keep them occupied for the entire instructional period, are much less likely to become involved in unwanted talk. This is an important point to remember as disruptive student talk can also occur when students have been given work that is too simple and which results in an abundance of idle time. It can also develop when they have been given work that is too difficult which leads to frustration as students do not perceive themselves as being able to be successful on what the teacher wants them to do. It is critical that teachers understand the abilities and interests of their students in planning and delivering their instruction, in particular as this relates to student talk and attention.

It is not uncommon for certain special events in the school or classroom to lead to unwanted talking and teachers must be prepared for this. For example, teachers should explain to students what they consider to be appropriate behavior when guests come to the classroom, when the class goes to an assembly, or when students go on field trips. Teachers should talk to students about these and other similar events before they occur and review with them what they may expect. These are all considered as preventive measures on the teacher's part. Students will have a natural curiosity and will want to ask questions and talk when special events such as these occur. If the teacher prepares for this beforehand, instead of waiting until the level of student excitement is at its highest, there will be less unwanted talking, confusion, and frustration on the part of the student as well as the teacher.

Certain instructional activities also will naturally stimulate what may initially seem to be unwanted talking, especially with younger students. If issues of excessive student talk develop, teachers are encouraged to discuss the problem and its causes with the entire class. While it is difficult for students to objectively examine their behavior when they are excited, it is possible for them to look back at a later time and reflect on what they did that may have been considered as inappropriate and discuss ways to avoid what may have been unacceptable behavior. Glasser (1998) believes that teachers who lead by example, instead of bossing students, and who develop positive relationships with their students (i.e., they are liked and respected), will have positive results from the class meetings that he recommends be used to address an issue such as this.

Although some undesired talking can be explained by unexpected events or the use of certain instructional activities, some students have problems with excessive talking regardless of what is taking place in the classroom. In many cases, these students can be better controlled through the classroom seating arrangement and teacher movement during instruction. There are some students who will talk excessively if they are allowed to set together, and simply separating their seats will usually reduce if not eliminate this behavior. As with inattentiveness and the use of proximity control, nearness to the teacher in many cases can act as a preventive measure for unwanted talking. Teacher movement will also add an additional dynamic to the lesson that will increase the likelihood of students attending to the teacher rather than to each other.

Nissman (2006) suggests that the following strategies be considered when working with students with disruptive talking problems:

- Use proximity to get right in the middle of the classroom, possibly touching a noisy student's shoulder to keep class discussion flowing without bringing peer attention to the student.
- Allow students free time to chat. This may cut down on the talking out of turn.
- Confer with parents and possibly help them establish a reward system for good days.
- During seatwork time, allow students to communicate through writing notes or whispering. Abuse of his privilege will result in some predetermined consequence.
- Give a warning or warning signal (e.g., flicking the lights on and off); if talking persists, use a predetermined consequence.

- If students' calling out is a problem, have a class meeting and have the students make recommendations to solve the problem, including the type of discipline to be used for students who continue to disturb the class.
- Students calling out may be motivated by enthusiasm or the fear that something will be forgotten. Have students keep a pad and pencil on their desks to write down their thoughts so that they can refer to them later when they are called upon.

A word of caution, however, is important with respect to student talk. Teachers are encouraged to rethink their goals in teaching if they desire to teach in classrooms where student-to-student talk is generally discouraged or considered inappropriate. Instructional settings are also social settings and student interaction with peers as well as teachers is essential if optimal levels of achievement are to be reached. While some teachers may have strong views concerning problems of excessive student talk, the ability to appropriately communicate ideas is one of the most important life skills an individual can develop. It would be regrettable to think that any teacher's classroom was structured in such a way as to discourage the development of open communication. Conversation can be contagious, and teachers cannot allow students to talk and chatter freely to the extent that they and their peers have problems learning and the teacher has problems teaching. At the same time, it is also important not to let the classroom be represented by unrealistic expectations for a level of silence which may be more appropriate for a library than for an environment where active student exploration is to be desired and encouraged.

Attention-Seeking

It is commonly understood by teachers at all grade levels that some students misbehave simply to get the attention of their classmates or the teacher. **Attention-Seeking** behavior is *a student misbehavior problem often manifested in tattling by younger students to get their teachers' attention or by older students acting as the class clown or the show off as a way to get attention from the teacher as well as other students.* Tattling, due to peer pressures and other social considerations, tends to become less frequent as students grow older.

Working with Students with Attention-Seeking Problems

Regardless of the method chosen by an attention-seeking student (i.e., tattling, clowning, etc.), attention-seeking behavior should not be reinforced by the teacher or other students in the class. As with students exhibiting any form of misconduct, attention-seeking students, for some reason important to them, need special attention in the social setting of the classroom. Teachers should not doubt or deny that it is the case that some students have a special need for attention. Teachers should provide such students an opportunity to receive the attention that they need in an appropriate manner. Instead of clowning to get attention, an attention-seeking student might be given the opportunity to receive attention by helping the teacher in some meaningful way, sharing ideas, stories, or reports to the class at an acceptable time.

Some attention seekers are characterized by insecurity because they do not receive the attention that they need at home, in the peer group, or from the teacher. A teacher must avoid demeaning or publicly chastising an attention-seeking student for his or her behavior as there is, at least for the student, an important motive behind it. Effective teachers seek to learn more about the cause of the undesired behavior and ways to satisfy the student's need appropriately. Such students, in fact, might benefit from receiving praise in front of the group when they conduct themselves properly.

It is best to redirect the inappropriate behavior of an attention-seeking student through private, not public, conversations. Although it may be a temptation for some teachers when dealing with chronic attention seekers to tell them to "act their age" or "stop acting silly," these responses harm more than help the situation. The best procedure to follow in working with an attention-seeking student is to ignore unwanted attention-seeking while channeling the student to a way of getting attention in an acceptable manner. Teachers should make every effort to give attention to students when possible, but only reinforce them when their behavior is appropriate (Good & Brophy, 2007).

It is important for the teacher to prepare the environment in order to prevent problems with attention seekers as it is with other forms of student misbehavior. This is best done by communicating the guidelines for appropriate behavior early in the school year and then consistently following those rules and procedures that have been established (Levin & Nolan, 2007). Some student tattling can be prevented simply by telling students early in the year what kinds of information they should and should not report to the teacher (Evertson et al., 2005). This is also true for other forms of student attention-seeking. When all students know what is considered as proper behavior in the classroom, the attention-seeking student can often be quickly cut off and directed back to an appropriate activity by being reminded of what has and what has not been identified as acceptable behavior.

A part of preparing the environment to eliminate or reduce attention seeking from certain students could involve a special consideration of the teacher's instructional program. If teachers closely monitor the unwanted behaviors of their students, they might well discover that some students are seeking attention when they have nothing else that seems meaningful or interesting to do. If this is the case, it provides an important message for the teacher regarding the importance of ensuring that all students are actively involved in high-interest and meaningful learning activities. When this is established, the frequency of student attention-seeking behaviors, and likely all student misbehaviors, will be reduced.

Possible teacher strategies or responses to consider when faced with attention-seeking behavior on the part of a student include the following (Nissman, 2006):

- Carefully examine the cause of the behavior. Is it due to poor self-concept or being ignored, or, is there a potential learning disability or some other problem? Examine the reaction to the behavior and then change the reaction if the reaction behavior triggers a negative response on the part of the student.
- Role-play. Give students a situation and have them play out acceptable and unacceptable behavior.
- Use various modalities when giving directions. Write as well as say the assignment so all understand. Give examples and check the students' progress by moving around the room.
- Attach consequences to the undesirable attention-seeking behavior. Keep an accurate record of when each behavior occurs for objective evaluation. Post a chart in the front of the room delineating the rules to be followed (e.g., raise your hand if you wish to talk; wait to be called on; listen while others talk, etc.).
- Give an abundance of praise. Most students will strive for positive reinforcement.

- Ignore the student's annoying comments, but provide praise when there are real achievements to be acknowledged.
- Assign the student to a small group to which he or she must primarily participate as a follower.
- Arrange a parent conference to discuss any factors that may be contributing to the student's problem in school, (e.g., sibling rivalry, problems with classmates, etc.).

Chronic Avoidance of Work

All teachers are aware that some students habitually do not complete the assignments that they have been given (Evertson et al., 2005). **Chronic Avoidance of Work** is *a misbehavior demonstrated by a student who consistently fails to complete his or her assigned work following repeated teacher effort to get the work completed.* This can represent a serious problem if students find that when they fail to do their assigned work that no negative consequence results. If not completing their work has no meaning, students will become less and less likely to complete their work as the school year progresses. Teachers need to have a management system in place to regularly follow up on the assignments they give to students to make sure that the assignments are being completed in the manner and time frame expected. Avoidance of work, while perhaps not openly disruptive to the class, is a serious matter since the student involved is not taking part in important learning activities. Too, if one student does not finish assignments as expected with no consequences, other students are apt to follow suit. This is an example of what Kounin (1970) referred to as the *ripple effect.*

Working with Students with Chronic Avoidance of Work Problems

In a situation where assignments are not completed in a timely manner, the teacher needs to determine if the student's ability to complete the assignment is the primary cause of the problem. The teacher should determine this before any interaction with the student takes place. This actually should be determined before the assignment is given. If a student has learning difficulties or otherwise lacks the necessary prerequisite skills or knowledge to complete the teacher's assignments, an adjustment in what is assigned needs to be made.

Students should not be held responsible for work that they are not able to complete if the problem of completing the work is based on a basic lack of ability on their part. Assignments that teachers give need to be made with an understanding of student ability in mind. In cases where a student is overwhelmed by the totality of an assignment given, but yet has the ability to complete the work, it may be beneficial for the teacher to break the assignment up into smaller units.

Where a student has the ability to do the assigned work, but is for some reason choosing not to do so, early intervention on the teacher's part is needed (Evertson et al., 2005). Before taking any action, however, the teacher frequently will need additional data or pertinent information about the student to be able to determine why the assignments are not being regularly completed, especially in a classroom where other students are successfully completing the same assignments. This normally requires collecting and checking student work frequently while carefully maintaining and recording the results. This activity represents an application of the third step in the Model for Reflection and Inquiry. Using these records, teachers can more easily and specifically determine to what degree a student is not completing homework and/or classroom assignments. Follow-up conversations with the student and possibly with other teachers who are familiar with the student and the student's work may then be used to determine why the work assigned is not being completed.

It has already been identified that some students do not finish their work because an assignment may be too challenging for them. Personal problems may also interfere with a student's ability to do what the teacher desires. Death or illness of a loved one, divorce or separation of parents, difficult home environment where a student has neither the time nor place to complete assignments, and abuse are a few examples of the many types of problems that can interfere with a student completing his or her schoolwork. A teacher who discovers that a student has such a problem should work closely with the student, giving help and support until the situation has improved or the student is more in control of the situation. The school counselor can often help such students deal with their personal problems and become better able to meet their responsibilities at school and in the classroom.

After inquiring into the situation, the teacher may discover that neither personal problems nor learning problems are the causes of the student's incomplete work. Some students simply choose not to complete their assignments because they are not appropriately motivated to do so. Evertson et al. (2005) suggest that a parent conference is one of the best techniques to use in intervening to change the behavior of students who elect not to finish homework and classroom assignments. When this strategy is used, it is important to be able to show parents the records that have been kept of the student's past performance. What students are telling parents at home may be different from what is actually taking place in school. A record of past homework or classroom assignments that were never completed is important evidence to show a parent who has been told by the student that no such assignments were made or that assignments were turned in. A monitoring or recording system should be developed where the teacher can send a list of homework assignments with needed materials home on a regular (e.g., daily or weekly) basis for the parents' review. Jones and Jones (2007) identify that a part of the teacher's role includes working with parents. Students' attitudes about school are influenced by their parents and, when they feel good about their teachers and school, the students are more likely to receive reinforcement for desirable behavior. Parents need to be informed about student academic performance and behavior so that they can be involved in their child's school experience. Parent involvement can have a positive impact on students' attitudes toward school, belief in the relationship between effort and school performance, and persistence at schoolwork.

Parents and teachers, together, might want to explore setting up a reward system to encourage a student to regularly complete assignments that are given. A behavior contract, discussed earlier in Chapter 3 as recommended by William Glasser, can be an effective tool to use in a situation such as this. Teachers need to be careful, however, not to decrease penalties or increase grades simply because the student may make a slight improvement over time. It is easy to send a message that doing half of the work is acceptable when this is not the case. In order to have the optimum effect, if a reward system is used it must encourage students to put forth the maximum effort.

The following strategies are also suggested as possible ways to approach problems of students not completing work assigned (Nissman, 2006).

- Assign homework on a regular basis so that students are aware and come to expect that homework is a regular part of the classroom routine.

- Make assignments brief and manageable: fifteen to twenty minutes.
- Assignments should involve review or reinforcement of skills covered in class that day.
- Discuss with the class the value of homework. Allow students to air their complaints if they have any. Do not assume that students understand the reasoning for homework.
- Use an assignment pad which requires your initials and parents' initials for students who do not return assignments. Make clear to the student that it will be his or her responsibility to write down the assignments. The teacher should initial the assignment as correct. Parents should initial the assignment as completed.
- Use progress charts as a way to encourage daily responsibility of homework. Have meaningful rewards available for high achievers.
- Whenever possible, plan assignments that revolve around high student interest.
- Establish goals with each student and reinforce them with frequent review and personal interaction. Evaluate/mark students' work as quickly as possible to eliminate frustration and prevent reinforcement of erroneous concepts.

Dishonesty

Dishonest behavior represents *one of the most serious forms of student misconduct often exhibited through cheating and/or stealing and telling untruths or lying.* Cheating and stealing generally have a more devastating impact on the entire classroom as they automatically effect others and are more difficult to deal with in a positive, proactive fashion. In a recent international study where students gave themselves high marks for ethical behavior, around 60 percent of American high school students reported having cheated on a test, 28 percent admitted stealing from a store, and 23 percent said they stole from a parent or other relative (Sixty Percent of U.S. High School Students, 2006). Ninety-two percent of the students indicated that they were satisfied with their personal ethics and character, and 74 percent agreed with the statement, "When it comes to doing what is right, I am better than most people I know." Following high-stakes school testing and accountability sweeping the nation about five years ago, some key lawmakers now say they want to make sure that testing results are credible. Much of this is a reaction to reports of cheating from around the country where some high test scores have been reported to be the result of "adult interference" (Kummer, 2006). Benton and Hacker (2007) report that tens of thousands of students have cheated on the Texas Assessment of Knowledge and Skills (TAKS) test every year; this includes thousands on the state's graduation test. The analysis conducted found cases where over 50 percent of students had suspicious answer patterns that researchers say indicate collusion, either between students or with school staff. Some teachers have rated dishonesty as one of the most serious problem they must deal with in the management of their students (Charles, 1976; Hunt et al., 1999).

Working with Students with Dishonesty Problems

One problem that teachers encounter when dealing with dishonesty in the classroom is that children and adolescents, at least young adolescents, are still in the formative stages of their moral development. What is right and wrong for many students is often very much determined by the situation. Certainly at young ages, students are still learning right from wrong, appropriate from inappropriate, etc. Because of this, teachers are advised to focus on the intent as well as the impact and results of such behavior. For example, children in the early elementary grades often do not have a clear understanding of *truth* and *ownership* as would be expected of them if they were older. Young adolescent students may decide to steal a test paper from their teacher's desk as much for the excitement of the adventure and the accomplishment as from a desire to cheat and improve their grades. The advent of modern technology has only served to acerbate the problem. As technology makes it easier than ever to cheat, educators are combating the intractable problem on at least three fronts: setting clear standards and consequences, using technology to fight back, and talking with students and parents about ethics and pressure (Noguchi, 2006). Also at issue is the actual definition of dishonest behavior. With more and more encouragement regarding the used of cooperative learning and students-working-together on instructional activities, teachers need to clearly define just what is honest or dishonest, cheating or noncheating, behavior when students are, in fact, encouraged to work together and to share their work products in route to completing assignments.

Regardless of the motivation, teachers have the responsibility to guide students in their learning of acceptable standards of conduct and cannot condone dishonesty. No matter the age of the student, dishonesty should always be cast in a very unfavorable light. Nonetheless, teachers again must remember that many students do not come from backgrounds that reflect and promote middle class standards of behavior that are typically common to teachers and school environments. Many students must learn acceptable behavior at school, in this case honesty, though the home and community should and will no doubt play an important role in this learning process as well. Such behavioral development typically can be long-term in nature.

When dealing with a student who has possibly been dishonest (e.g., cheating, stealing, or lying), the teacher must be cautious not to label the student when approaching the student being suspected of having committed the misbehavior. If a student is labeled as a *cheat, thief,* or *liar,* the possible ill effects on the student's future behavior and self-concept is a consequence that needs to be avoided. If a student is caught cheating, for example, the teacher is advised to talk to the student in private, present the reasons for suspecting cheating, express concern and try to find out why the student cheated, explain the consequences, and then discuss the consequences for subsequent cheating (Weinstein & Mignano, 2007). Be sure that the consequences fit the situation. Telling students they are bad or dishonest may cause them to genuinely think of themselves negatively and begin to consistently assume these roles. Students would then be following the teacher's prophecy or expectation for or about them as was discussed earlier in this text. As with confronting students with other forms of misbehavior, the teacher should never publicly accuse a student of having been dishonest with other students, or teachers, serving as an audience.

Since it is important to help students understand the importance of honest behavior, there needs to be consequences for dishonest behavior. For example, the student could lose valued privileges or the lowering of a grade if the dishonesty was of an academic nature. Teachers need to realize that what is dishonest for mature adults may not be for some students and their peers. It could be helpful to plan activities that improve the students' perception of honesty and how to implement it in everyday situations. It also could be helpful to use activities that will build feelings of mutual respect with peers and adults (e.g., group projects that involve working in the community). Finally, it is recommended that the teacher discuss with the class the consequences of stealing in the outside world, instruct students to keep valuables in a safe place, and to discourage bringing valuable items to school.

Beyond trying to determine appropriate consequences, however, it is also important to determine the cause of the misbehavior. If a student cheated on an assignment because the assigned work was at too difficult a level, a new assignment should be made in the future that will allow the student to achieve success without cheating. The need for the teacher to have an accurate understanding of a student's ability and make appropriate assignments based on this understanding has been previously emphasized under the heading Chronic Avoidance of Work. One characteristic of students who have a history of failure is a reliance on getting help from others (perhaps through cheating) as opposed to relying on their own ability to study and learn. Feelings of learned helplessness and low self-concept must be overcome before a meaningful and long-lasting change in behavior can be expected (Weiner, 1985).

Unruliness

Unruliness is *a state of general student misbehavior characterized by a lack of self-control which may be exhibited by such behaviors as talking loudly, running in hallways, using unacceptable language, getting out of seats without permission, and playing practical jokes.* Unruly students are not generally aggressive or defiant, but habitually break school and classroom rules. One reason why this behavior syndrome is considered less severe than other behaviors is because unruly students, as a rule, typically do not desire to hurt others or be disrespectful, but just lack personal self-control. They frequently seem out of control to teachers and other students alike.

Working with Students with Unruliness Problems

Some students are unruly simply because unruly behavior has been modeled around them on a regular basis. They have copied and adopted this behavior and may have even been rewarded for it. A child growing up in a family where the adults there disregard manners normally looked upon as acceptable, show constant criticism of mainstream values, curse, and question authority, will often go to school and display these same types of behaviors. This unruliness, over time, becomes ingrained in the student and represents an adopted personality trait. Unruly students, however, also come from family backgrounds that do not model such traits. This fact reinforces that a student's home environment cannot always be looked upon as the determiner of a student's behavior. Whatever the origin of a student's unruliness, if nothing is done to correct the behavior, it will augment over time. To accent the problem, unruly students can become negative role models that other students may choose to emulate if the teacher does not intervene and respond to the problem.

Many students find the social and academic adjustments in a school setting difficult and uncomfortable where they do not receive satisfaction from academic and social activities. This lack of satisfaction can trigger rebellious or unruly behaviors. When teachers react to unruliness, they may very well be dealing with the symptom, not the true cause of the misconduct if they have not investigated the situation thoroughly. Students who are unruly generally need closer supervision than other students, and an effective technique to use with them is close monitoring. Close monitoring is important but can be a challenge under certain conditions such as field trips, laboratory work, and other activities where consistent teacher supervision is more difficult.

Unruly students need to experience success in school as do all students. Repeated failure increases the likelihood of repeated misconduct. Although there must be consequences when students break established rules, teachers must be certain to separate their reaction to a negative behavior from a reaction to the student as a human being. Unruly students are often unpopular with many of their peers and, unfortunately, many of their teachers. It is important to build within them a sense of self-worth and belonging. Such students need to be in controlled situations where they have an opportunity for success, are reinforced when success is achieved, and not be overly stimulated to a point where they will lose self-control. When encountering an unruly student, teachers should have the frame of mind that they are dealing with someone who needs support and nurturing more than discipline and control.

It is recommended that student isolation be given serious consideration when it becomes necessary to discipline an unruly student. If isolation is used, it needs to take place in a non-stimulating area. Students should see the isolation as an opportunity for them to calm down and regain their self-control, rather than as punishment, and it should be clearly explained to them why they are there. Though it should not be seen as a punishment, neither should it be seen as a reward. A student who sees being isolated as a reward may be saying volumes about how he or she sees being in the teacher's regular classroom environment. After the prescribed period of isolation is over, and a student who has been isolated is back in the normal classroom setting, the teacher should guide the student to exhibit desired behaviors and reward these positive actions appropriately. The behaviors of unruly students will change in positive ways when they begin to experience more success, in particular on activities that are meaningful and of value to them. This change in behavior will also result in more social acceptance by their peer group.

It is recommended that the teacher let the student know, in private, how his or her behavior is impacting the classroom and what is expected in terms of desired behavior. Success will be built on establishing a trusting relationship. The teacher should listen carefully to what the student has to say and try to channel the student's talents into a more productive direction. For whatever the motivation, the teacher should make it clear that the student's solution to his problem is the responsibility of both student and his teacher. It may also be helpful to identify some aspect of the curriculum where the student is interested and capable and give him independent work in this area and observe carefully any change in behavior.

Defiance

Defiant behavior is *a serious form of student misbehavior where a student refuses to do what the teacher asks of him or her or boldly talks back to the teacher in a hostile or threatening way.* Defiance is a serious type of misbehavior because it threatens the leadership position of the teacher. If a student is allowed to be defiant to the teacher, with no meaningful consequence to follow, it is possible that other students will act similarly, resulting in a total loss of classroom control. This is one of the worst possible things that could happen to a teacher, and the teacher must think and act quickly when faced with student defiance.

Working with Students with Defiance Problems

Teachers are encouraged to use caution when dealing with any defiant or hostile student because such a student is not likely to comply to normal verbal commands. A student who challenges a teacher usually realizes that serious, deviant behavior has already taken place and may allow his or her emotions to intensify. Rather than take offense at what has been said or done, it is recommended that the teacher stay calm and, if possible, direct the student out of the classroom into an area where a teacher-to-student conversation can be held privately. Removing the student from the immediate classroom setting has three major advantages:

1. the student is given time to get his or her emotions under control,
2. the peer audience in the classroom will not be able to stir emotions and reinforce further defiance, and
3. the need of the student to keep face in front of the rest of the students in the class will be gone.

In rare situations, some students may become so emotionally hostile that they refuse to leave the classroom. With a younger or smaller student, the teacher can simply escort the student from the classroom. If the student is larger, however, and refuses to leave the classroom, it is advisable for the teacher to send another student for an administrator or another teacher for help. It is not advisable that the teacher risk having a physical confrontation with the student.

When talking with defiant students, the teacher is encouraged to exhibit as much openness as possible. Rude remarks from students should not be taken personally and should not be followed by similar remarks from the teacher. Sarcasm is never warranted, and its use can quickly cause the situation to worsen. The teacher is advised to not participate in an argument with a defiant student and should try to separate the student as a person from the student's undesirable conduct. Given these considerations, the teacher has a responsibility to explain to the defiant student that the behavior that has been shown will result in consequences and that these consequences will be carried out in a just and timely manner (Evertson et al., 2005).

Nissman (2006) identifies possible teacher strategies that can be helpful in working with students who challenge or defy authority.

- Talk to the student in private to ascertain the reason for the misbehavior.
- Give students reading and/or writing assignments that deal with antagonistic behavior and ask them to comment on different socially acceptable ways of handling conflict situations.
- Provide the students with models of appropriate communicative behavior through role-playing activities.
- Emphasize to the students the difference that exists between acceptable communication behaviors in school and those that are used at home and/or in the community.
- Do not use an accusatory tone or confront the student in a group situation; do not back the student, or yourself, into a corner; leave room for options. Do not make threats that cannot be carried out; allow your emotions to cool before approaching the student.
- Try to discover what led to the confrontation and avoid repeating those circumstances.
- If you made an error, admit it.
- Clarify exactly what defiant behavior the student has exhibited and what the consequences will be; be consistent with whatever is tried.

Causes of defiance are often deep-seated, and defiant behavior is frequently accompanied by a level of anger and frustration that may have reached a point that can no longer be contained. This hostility could be a result of problems at school, both academic and social, as well as problems found in the student's home life. In cases where students have chronic problems with these types of outbursts, professional help may be warranted. Regardless of whether the student displays frequent defiance or has simply had a momentary loss of control, an understanding teacher who is willing to listen and help can be an important support for the student. A private teacher-to-student conference may allow the student to see the teacher as being fair and concerned when this may not have been what was initially thought. Through this building of rapport and trust, the teacher may be able to understand why the student acted the way he or she did. Since the teacher is encouraged to interact with defiant students on a one-to-one basis, the teacher also may feel freer to admit mistakes, if they were made, and discuss ways to improve the classroom climate to lessen stress and frustration. While a teacher cannot afford to ignore a defiant act since it challenges the teacher's authority, it is important for the teacher not to react to defiant students in a confrontational way.

Aggression

Aggressive behavior is *a serious student misbehavior often represented by fighting although lesser forms of aggressive behavior are not uncommon such as name-calling or other verbal attacks, pushing and shoving, and overly physical play.* Aggressive behavior is a serious problem in schools and classrooms because, when aggressive behaviors are displayed, there exists the possibility that one or more students may be injured. Since even nonfighting aggression can result in physical combat if allowed to escalate, the teacher must deal with aggressive behavior in a quick and decisive manner.

Working with Students with Aggression Problems

A key strategy to use in working with students who have been fighting, name calling, or pushing and shoving is to allow them to "cool-down" before any interaction with them or teacher follow-up takes place. It is best to keep students who have been fighting away from one another and from their peers when possible immediately after the fight has taken place. Classmates have a tendency to fuel an already volatile situation when emotions are running high. Evertson et al. (2005) suggest that, when the students are mature enough, having each student write his or her version of why the fight or aggressive behavior began is a good "cooling-off," defusing activity. After the students have calmed down, the teacher then can meet with each of them individually to discuss whatever problem had precipitated the aggression. The teacher should stress the inappropriateness of the behavior, the need to solve problems in a more acceptable way, and discuss with the students how their problem could have been resolved differently. If the teacher finds it difficult to get an accurate explanation of why the problem started from the students involved, it is appropriate to ask uninvolved students for additional information. It is best not to do this in front of the combatants, however, as this will only increase the likelihood of further emotional outbursts.

Virtually all schools and school districts have established procedures to follow when handling student fights and aggressiveness.

Teachers must clearly understand the policies and procedures that are in place in their schools and districts and these procedures should always be followed. Typical procedures involve school administrators, parents, and guidance personnel and are designed to ensure the safety of all students on the school grounds. Conflict resolution and peer mediation programs, presented in Chapter 3, have been successful in dealing with this type of student behavior at the middle and high school levels.

Many teachers are concerned about whether or not they should actually try to step in and physically break up a fight that is underway. Only if the teacher feels that it is safe to do so, perhaps with younger students, is it recommended to separate students who are fighting. In a situation where a fight occurs, the first step should be to have all other students leave the immediate scene so that they will not be injured. Such an environment is not safe for spectators and may tend to spur on the combatants. If the teacher does not feel safe separating the fighting students, a loud command to stop fighting, i.e., desist, should be issued, and someone should be sent to quickly bring help (Evertson et al., 2005). One difficulty in dealing with aggressive behavior is the fact that aggressive behavior situations frequently escalate quickly, and the teacher often has little time to react. Nevertheless, through their own alertness and *withitness* in being aware of what is taking place throughout the classroom, the teacher can deter many problems and certainly diffuse many situations before they become violent or physical encounters. When violent outbreaks do occur, however, teachers need to remain calm in facing such situations and, through their prior planning, know just what they are going to do before such occasions take place.

Although most aggression in the school setting is manifested in momentary outbursts as a consequence of frustration, some students have problems that can only be effectively addressed by professional assistance such as would be provided by a counselor or psychologist. There are times when help beyond that which the teacher can provide may be required. Some students come from homes and communities where they see aggression modeled frequently and believe that the use of aggressive behavior is a normal and acceptable way to solve problems. Other aggressive students have histories of academic failure and frustration at school and have become alienated from the mainstream of the school environment. They often display aggressive behavior as a type of defense mechanism. Finally, situations where students have been physically or emotionally abused, or perhaps seen a parent and/or sibling abused, can represent the background of an aggressively behaving student. These students, all too frequently, become aggressive and abusive themselves as a reaction to what they have experienced at home. Regardless of the reason, teachers cannot allow aggressive behavior to exist in the classroom environment. A display of aggressive behavior that the teacher does not respond to represents a true threat to the teacher's ability to teach and to be the classroom leader.

Long-term solutions to aggressive behavior require that teachers make it clear to students that such behaviors are unacceptable. Teachers should listen patiently when discussing problems with aggressive students and refrain from verbal chastisements and emotional outbursts as this will only further arouse their aggressiveness (Brophy & McCaslin, 1992). As with all forms of student misbehavior, it is necessary to understand the sources of the frustrations of aggressive students in order to be able to help them regain and then maintain their self-control.

APPLYING THE MODEL FOR REFLECTION AND INQUIRY

As discussed in Chapter 1, the Model for Reflection and Inquiry, essentially the model of the scientific method, is a recommended process for the teacher to follow when dealing with student misbehaviors and/or motivation problems. Possible applications of this model will be examined in the following section of the chapter where teachers are confronted with some of the common problems that have been previously discussed.

Janice's Problem

Janice is a sixth grade student in a middle school organized through the use of integrated instructional teams. During the first six weeks of school, Janice's performance was very much like what would have been expected based on the grades she received in school prior to this year. On her first grade report, Janice received a "B+" in mathematics and an "A" in all other subjects. However, soon after the next grading period began, Janice's behavior began to change. Her teachers all noticed she no longer completed all assignments, and, too often, failed to even attempt much of her homework. These problems were discussed at a team planning meeting, and it was determined that Janice was likely to receive a "D" in language arts and no higher than a "C" in all other courses on her next report card.

At least one problem in this case is easy to define. Janice, who in the past has been an excellent student, no longer completes her class and homework assignments. This has had a major negative impact on her performance in all subjects. Since there seemed to be no obvious or apparent problems in her classes at school that the team members who served as Janice's teachers could identify, they hypothesized that perhaps the change in Janice's behavior was due to a new boyfriend (not an uncommon problem with sixth grade preteens) or to some problem at home. Ms. Greene, Janice's mathematics teacher, called Janice's mother to share insights. Janice's mother was certain Janice did not have a boyfriend, though interest in the opposite sex was certainly increasing, and assured Ms. Greene that Janice was getting along fine at home. She did share that Janice often said that school didn't seem very interesting to her anymore and that she saw little purpose in most of her school work. She preferred to spend her evenings on the phone or listening to music while reading magazines rather than studying or completing assignments for school.

Upon learning this, the teachers changed their hypothesis; Janice, it was now believed, had lost her motivation and interest in school. Perhaps school was no longer purposeful, challenging, or fun for her. Ms. Greene was now able to talk with Janice with a broader background of information gained from the parent conference, collective teacher observations, and discussions in class. Janice admitted that she had lost interest in school and actually disliked many of her assignments. In her opinion, they took her away from more interesting thoughts and activities. With this new information allowing for a better understanding of the problem, the teachers decided to challenge Janice with more sophisticated assignments that they hoped would pique her interest while helping her to better see the importance of learning to her future. By working with Janice's mother, they were able to develop a system to motivate Janice through rewards related to her interests when she successfully completed her schoolwork.

George's Problem

George is a first-grade student who had his kindergarten experience through home schooling. Early on, Ms. Williams, his teacher, observed that George had difficulty in his relationships with other students. Even during the first weeks of school, there had been complaints from other students about George hitting and even biting other students. Ms. Williams talked with George and used isolation in the "Timeout" area as a consequence. However, during the fourth week of school, George lost his temper on the playground and threw a rock that barely missed hitting another child. George was so upset he had to be physically restrained until he calmed down so that he would not hurt the other child or himself. Ms. Williams realized she had a more serious problem to deal with than she had at first thought.

Like Janice, George's problem can be identified. George has bouts of aggression that can disrupt the instructional environment and endanger the safety of others. Ms. Williams, George's teacher, has a serious problem that must be addressed immediately. Since George had been home schooled up until this time, there were few if any school records that could provide helpful insight into his previous schooling experiences and behaviors. Through her observations of George, her experience with other children, and her consultations with Ms. Langston, the principal, Ms. Williams hypothesized that George had a problem with aggression and that this was not just a simple problem of adjusting to school. Ms. Williams wondered if George's staying home the previous year was actually related to this problem. Additional information was gained through a conference with Mr. and Mrs. Cobb, George's parents. Ms. Williams learned that George had shown signs of aggression early in life and that there was a history of problems at church, in day care, and with other children in the community. George was kept home the previous year in hopes that he would "grow out" of the problem. Unfortunately, the problem did not lessen and the Cobbs admitted that they were anxious to get help. Ms. Williams' hypothesis had been correct. Through the resources of the school system, the Cobbs were able to get professional help for George so that he could function in the least restrictive environment in his schooling. In dealing with a problem of this nature, George's parents, teacher, administrators, counselor, and psychologist all recognized that they would need to patiently but deliberately work together as a team over time to achieve the results that they desired.

Monica's Problem

Monica is a senior in high school who has always made above average grades in her classes with the exception of French I which was a struggle for her to achieve a "C-", her final grade last year. Monica made a very respectable score on the SAT and has been accepted to the state university where both of her parents graduated. Monica's parents, Mr. and Mrs. Pepper, both teach at the high school she attends and are very proud of her. They have promised to buy Monica a new car for graduation in order that she can more easily visit home from the university next year. One day, the Peppers were called by Mr. Long, the principal, to come to the office at the end of school. When they arrived Mr. Long told them that Mr. Davis had caught Monica cheating on a French II examination.

The problem identified is that Monica has cheated on a test; this cannot be treated as a minor infraction. Neither Monica nor her classmates can be allowed to think that cheating goes without consequences. Mr. Davis, Mr. Long, and Monica's parents all hypothesized that Monica cheated because she needed the two units of French to graduate from high school and to complete her admission to the university. She did not want to disappoint her parents and ruin her plans for next year, but felt that she could not be successful without cheating. Mr. Davis was wise enough to also hypothesize that Monica had a low level of self-confidence and a self-efficacy problem that left her feeling helpless to pass French II through her own individual efforts. Mr. Davis realized that, as long as Monica held such an external locus of control, she would continue to have problems with motivation and confidence and that this could also cause serious problems for her after she eventually completed high school and began taking classes at the university. After talking with Monica's French I teacher from the previous year, Mr. Davis met with Monica and developed a program of study where, through her own efforts, Monica would be able to pass French II. Monica did face the consequences of her serious misconduct that meant that she would have to accept a lowered grade, retake the test that she had cheated on, and do additional work in the class. However, due to her teacher acting in a proactive manner and as a caring and reflective educator, she came out of a difficult situation a stronger, better person.

In each of these cases just presented, the teachers involved, with help from others, systematically identified the problems they were dealing with, planned workable solutions, and were able to help their students. The students were able to become more successful in school through the use of reflection, inquiry and genuine concern on the part of their teachers. Instead of simply reacting to misbehaviors in isolation, the teachers collected data from a variety of sources that helped them make more informed decisions in order to effectively address the problems with which they and their students were dealing. When faced with problems of classroom management and student motivation, reflective educators do not enter into "me against you" conflicts or arguments with their students. They seek to eliminate their students' misbehaviors with an eye on gaining needed skills and motivation in order that such mistakes will not hamper their learning or adjustment in the future.

CONCLUSION

This chapter has provided information and recommended appropriate strategies when responding to specific types of student misbehaviors. Recommendations related to the teacher's role in establishing a strong management system were also included. These recommendations pertain to the teacher giving attention to identified personal, instructional, and environmental considerations. As has been the case in other areas of the text, the need for the teacher to be proactive and well planned in dealing with issues of student motivation, classroom management, and instruction, as well as being able to address problems when they occur, has been emphasized.

The chapter also addressed types of student misbehaviors felt to be both common and serious to the teacher's ability to effectively teach students and manage the learning environment. These misbehaviors were: inattention, disruptive talking, attention-seeking, chronic avoidance of work, dishonesty, unruliness, defiance, and aggression. All of these misbehaviors represent threats to teachers in carrying out their instructional responsibilities. The information provided defined the misbehaviors and then gave guidance as to possible ways to respond to them.

Finally, the chapter concluded with three short situations for analysis and illustrated the use of the Model for Reflection and Inquiry as a tool to guide the teacher in logical problem solving with respect to responding to student misbehaviors. Two important aspects of dealing with problems of student motivation and management are evident. First, teachers must have a genuine understanding of each of their students and their issues in these areas, as well as a broad knowledge of motivation and management, to be able to effectively address the problems that they encounter in the classroom. Second, teachers have to have the ability to use their understanding about students and knowledge about motivation and management in a reasoned and logical way in order to put this information to its greatest use. Having knowledge about students, motivation, and management, and not knowing how to use it will cause the teacher to fall far short of what is needed in effective teaching. Likewise, having knowledge about reasoned decision making and logical problem solving, without a solid understanding of pertinent information on which to base problem solutions, also will cause the teacher to fall short of what is needed. It is felt that the knowledge base of information presented here on student motivation and classroom management, and effective teaching practices, along with a model to guide reflection and decision making, together, will allow the teacher to effectively resolve most problems that will be encountered in the classroom. With this achieved, the teacher will then be able to advance the instructional program for the greatest benefit of all involved.

QUESTIONS/ACTIVITIES FOR REFLECTION

1. Analyze the statement, "teachers can frequently prevent most problems before they ever occur." In your opinion, what does this statement mean? Do you agree with it? Explain.
2. Though criticized by some, coercive management strategies are used by many teachers every day. How do you assess their use in the classroom in terms of whether or not they should or should not have a place in a teacher's management plan?
3. How do you think that a teacher can truly prepare himself or herself to only react to a student's misbehavior as opposed to react to the student as a person?
4. How would you go about helping a student understand the difference between sharing information with the teacher in order to be helpful, or even prevent a problem from occurring, and tattling?

5. If you were a teacher who recognized that a colleague was having problems in getting students to complete work primarily because the work that was being assigned was simply too difficult for the students, how would you help your colleague come to realize that this was the case? How can a teacher maintain high standards in assignments and still adjust to a variety of ability levels or levels of understanding in the classroom?

REFERENCES

Adams. R., & Biddle, B. (1970). *Realities of teaching: Explorations with video tape.* New York: Holt.

Benton, J., & Hacker, H. (2007). Analysis shows TAKS cheating rampant. Retrieved June 8, 2007, from www.dalasnews.com/sharedcontent.

Borich, G. (2006). *Effective teaching methods: Research based practice* (6th ed.). Upper Saddle River, NJ: Merrill/Prentice-Hall.

Borich, G., & Tombari, M. (1997). *Educational psychology: A contemporary approach* (2nd ed.). New York: Longman.

Brophy, J., & McCaslin, M. (1992). Teachers report of how they perceive and cope with problem students. *Elementary School Journal, 93*(1), 3–68.

Charles, C. (1976). *Educational psychology: The instructional endeavor* (2nd ed.). St. Louis, MO: C.V. Mosby.

Cotton, K. (1999). *Research you can use to improve results.* Alexandria, VA: Association for Supervision and Curriculum Development.

Emmer, E., Evertson, C., & Worsham, M. (2006). *Classroom management for secondary teachers* (7th ed.). Needham Heights, MA: Allyn & Bacon.

Evertson, C., Emmer, E., & Worsham, M. (2005). *Classroom management for elementary teachers* (7th ed.). Boston: Allyn & Bacon.

Freiberg, H., & Driscoll, A. (2004). *Universal teaching strategies* (4th ed.). Boston: Allyn & Bacon.

French, J., & Raven, B. (1959). The bases of social power. In D. Cartwright (Ed.), *Studies in social power* (pp. 150–168). Ann Arbor, MI: University of Michigan Press.

Glasser, W. (1986). *Control theory in the classroom.* New York: Harper & Row.

Glasser, W. (1998). *The quality school teacher.* New York: Harper Perennial.

Good, T., & Brophy, J. (2007). *Looking in classrooms* (10th ed.). New York: Addison Wesley Longman.

Goodlad, J. (1984). *A place called school.* New York: McGraw-Hill.

Gootman, M. (2001). *The caring teacher's guide to discipline: Helping young students learn self-control, responsibility, and respect* (2nd ed.). Thousand Oaks, CA: Corwin Press.

Hunt, G., & Bedwell, L. (1982). An axiom for classroom management. *The High School Journal, 66*(1), 10–13.

Hunt, G., Touzel, T., & Wiseman, D. (1999). *Effective teaching: Preparation and implementation* (3rd ed.). Springfield, IL: Charles C Thomas.

Jones, V., & Jones, L. (2007). *Comprehensive classroom management: Creating communities of support and solving problems.* Boston: Pearson Education.

Kohn, A. (1993). *Punished by rewards: The trouble with gold stars, incentive plans, A's, praise, and other bribes.* New York: Houghton Mifflin.

Kounin, J. (1983). *Classrooms: Individual or behavior settings? Micrographs in teaching and learning* (General Series No. 1). Bloomington, IN: Indiana University School of Education. (ERIC Document Reproduction Service No. 240 070).

Kounin, J. (1970). *Discipline and group management in classrooms.* New York: Holt, Rhinehart & Winston.

Kummer, F. (2006). Leaders aim to curb cheating on tests. Retrieved October 26, 2006, from www.philly.com/mld/philly/living/education.

Levin, J., & Nolan, J. (2007). *Principles of classroom management: A professional decision-making model* (5th ed.). Boston: Pearson Education.

Marzano, R., Pickering, D., & Pollock, J. (2001). *Classroom instruction that works: Research-based strategies for increasing student achievement.* Alexandria, VA: Association for Supervision and Curriculum Development.

McCormick, C., & Pressley, M. (1997). *Educational psychology: Learning, instruction, assessment.* New York: Longman.

Nissman, B. (2006). *Teacher-tested classroom management strategies.* Upper Saddle River, NJ: Pearson Prentice-Hall.

Noguchi, S. (2006). Schools fight cheaters who use tech tools. Retrieved September 26, 2006, from www.mercury news.com.

Schlechty, P. (1976). *Teaching and social behavior: Toward an organizational theory of instruction.* Boston: Allyn & Bacon.

Sixty percent of U.S. high school students cheat, 28% steal, study finds. (2006). Retrieved October 17, 2006, from www.financialexpress.com.

Weiner, B. (1985). An attributional theory of achievement motivation and emotion. *Psychological Review, 92*(4), 548–573.

Weinstein, C., & Mignano, A. (2007). *Elementary classroom management: Lessons from research and practice* (4th ed.). New York: McGraw-Hill.

Chapter 7

CASE STUDIES FOR ANALYSIS IN STUDENT MOTIVATION AND CLASSROOM MANAGEMENT

As this text has been developed, the foundation that has been laid has identified that effective teachers must work as informed reflective educators. While it is recognized that effective teaching can be defined in different ways, when the term effective teaching is used here, effective is in reference to teaching practices that bring about increased levels of student achievement. And, with respect to effective teachers being informed reflective educators, informed in this context includes the teacher's knowledge and/or abilities in five key areas. These are the teacher's:

1. understanding of his or her students to include their abilities, interests, and background characteristics,
2. understanding of what is known through educational research regarding the body of knowledge related to student motivation,
3. understanding of what is known through educational research regarding the body of knowledge related to classroom management,
4. understanding of what is known through educational research regarding the body of knowledge related to best teaching practices, and
5. ability to be a reasoned decision maker who uses relevant information and a logical and systematic approach to solving problems of student motivation and classroom management that will result in higher levels of student achievement.

Detailed information has been presented through the previous chapters in this text regarding each of these five areas of knowledge and/or ability. Of special importance has been reference to the use of the Model for Reflection and Inquiry introduced in Chapter 1. This model has been referred to throughout the text to reinforce and illustrate the importance of effective teachers being logical problem solvers. It is included again in this chapter in Figure 7.1. The focus of the remainder of the text will be on using the model in exploring specific student problem behavior situations in the classroom which represent problems of student motivation and/or classroom management.

Model for Reflection and Inquiry

1. **Statement of the Problem**

   The problem is identified and clarified; the problem should be meaningful and manageable.

2. **Development of a Hypothesis(es)**

   A hypothesis or educated guess regarding a solution to the problem is formulated; there may be more than one hypothesis.

3. **Collection of Relevant Data**

   Data or pertinent information relevant to the problem is collected and/or identified; references or sources of information are considered and reviewed.

4. **Analysis of Data**

   Clarifications are made as to information collected; sources of data are considered and perhaps reconsidered. Relationships should be identified among data collected and data should be clearly organized and analyzed as to how this information relates to the problem.

5. **Interpretation and Reporting of Results, Drawing Conclusions and Making Generalizations**

   Conclusions should be drawn and relevant generalizations made related to the accuracy of the original hypothesis.

Figure 7.1. Model for Reflection and Inquiry.

Reflective educators are able to use information in a logical manner to solve the problems that they encounter in working with their students. In cases where additional information is needed for the problem to be solved, beyond that which is immediately available, reflective educators also have the ability to acquire this additional information and appropriately apply it to the decision-making process. Teachers are confronted with numerous problems needing resolutions on a daily basis. It is their ability to solve these problems efficiently and effectively, and learn from the problems that they have solved, which in large measure determines their effectiveness as teachers.

The remainder of Chapter 7 will focus on the application of the Model for Reflection and Inquiry as a systematic problem solving approach recommended for use in addressing nine different types of student misbehaviors commonly found in schools today. Eight of these types of misbehaviors were introduced and discussed at some length in Chapter 6. The behavior of bullying was introduced in Chapter 5. Behavior case studies are provided that represent the following types of student misbehaviors: *inattention, disruptive talking, attention-seeking, chronic avoidance of work, dishonesty, unruliness, defiance, aggression, and bullying.* Two case studies for analysis are presented for each type of misbehavior. One case study focuses on the problem as it may be encountered at the primary-elementary grade level with the second case study illustrating the problem at the middle-secondary level. Looking upon logical problem solving as representing a reasoning process that involves asking and then finding answers to a series of questions, the following questions are offered as a guide to the analysis of each case study presented. Consider the following questions that a teacher should ask himself or herself, and then apply them to the case studies that follow:

Guiding Questions for Classroom Problem Analysis

1. Exactly what is the problem that I am dealing with?
2. What might be a possible solution that I could use to effectively address the problem?
3. What additional information do I need to have that will impact the effectiveness of my solution? For example:
   a. What information is needed about the student(s)?
   b. What information is needed about my teaching?

    c. What information is needed about the specific problem in general?
    d. What information is needed from other teachers?
    e. What information is needed from family members?
4. How will I know if my solution was effective?
5. What should I do if my solution is not effective?
6. How can I best decide when or perhaps where this particular solution will work in the future?

After reading each case study and keeping the questions listed here in mind, apply the Model for Reflection and Inquiry to develop an acceptable solution to each problem situation that follows.

INATTENTION (PRIMARY-ELEMENTARY GRADES)

Suki's Inattention

Suki is a fourth-grade student who does not care for school; school seems boring to her. At least that is how Ms. Graves, Suki's teacher, sees it. According to Ms. Graves, what Suki appears to do best is sit next to the window and watch other students on the playground as they play games and enjoy other activities. She likes going to the playground for Ms. White's physical education class, and Ms. White says that Suki has good physical abilities. When the students select teams, she is usually one of the first ones chosen. She also enjoys arts and crafts class taught once a week by Mr. Brown. Mr. Brown indicates that Suki has a kind of "creative flair" in art. She is especially good in sketching with her pencil and working with clay. Mr. Brown says that she has the ability to envision things on her own rather than only do the assignments that she is given.

However, Ms. Graves sees Suki as someone who just cannot stay focused in class. This is especially the case when she is talking to the entire class. In her opinion, a fourth grade student should be acting more maturely. Besides looking out the window, sometimes she just draws or doodles at her desk. She also has an annoying habit of tapping her pencil on her desk and humming quietly to herself. Suki has a history of poor grades and lately has shown some behaviors that are not acceptable to Ms. Graves. Suki's inattentive behavior can also be distracting to the other students as well. She is sorry to admit it, but she has come to a point where she prefers Suki's daydreaming rather than some other misbehaviors that she might exhibit. At least she is not being a disruptive force when "she is in her own world."

Still, Ms. Graves has become especially concerned with Suki and a few other students like her as her school district has become very focused on the importance of raising test scores. Her principal makes more and more frequent visits to her classroom to see just how things are going and to check up on whether or not everyone is on task. Suki, sadly, is often not on task.

Ms. Graves spoke to Suki's mother about her inattention at the last parent conference and she said that she would speak to her about it. So far, though, Suki's inattentive behavior has not changed at all. Ms. Graves just doesn't know what she should try next, but she knows that she has to do something. What should she do?

INATTENTION (MIDDLE-SECONDARY GRADES)

Javier's Inattention

Ms. Thomas, Javier's seventh grade math teacher, finds Javier to be a polite young man. Javier is always well dressed in the current fashion and quite popular with his classmates. When he answers questions in class, which isn't all that often, he speaks clearly and uses correct grammar. While she sees Javier as a pleasant student, she feels strongly that he doesn't pay enough attention to what is going on in the classroom to get the most out of it. She often notices him looking at magazines that he has brought with him to school or writing short poems or song lyrics in his notebook rather than paying attention to what she is saying. She has heard him play his guitar in the lunchroom and, in her opinion, he is quite talented.

Sometimes, when she is teaching, she observes Javier just staring out into space. He often doesn't seem to know what is expected of him. She doesn't think that he is really misbehaving badly in class but, she does see his inattention as a definite problem. Up to this point Javier's behavior hasn't proven to be a problem for other students, but she is worried that some of them might begin to do what Javier is doing. He is very popular and some of the other students even seem to look up to him. She has seen other occasions in the classroom where, when one student began to do something, others then began to follow.

She is aware that Javier has lived in the United States for about four years and that he and his parents moved to this country from Mexico. He has one older brother in the twelfth grade and a younger sister in the second grade. Javier's older brother has received an academic scholarship to attend the local university next year. It is a very prestigious scholarship, and he plans to major in government in preparation to one day become a lawyer. Javier has made average grades all through elementary school, not excelling or doing poorly in any one subject. In her class, however, he is barely keeping up. Javier's mother stays at home and doesn't work. His father works as a salesman at a local automobile dealership. Ms. Thomas has never had a conversation with Javier's parents, but she has seen them at some of the Parent-Teacher Association meetings.

Although Javier's not paying attention isn't the greatest problem in the world, it is creating difficulty for Ms. Thomas, and she is sure that he isn't learning as much as he can from her teaching. She, however, wants to reach all of her students but isn't sure just what to do in this situation. What should she do?

DISRUPTIVE TALKING (PRIMARY-ELEMENTARY GRADES)

Sierra's Disruptive Talking

Sierra is a third-grade student in Ms. Jackson's classroom. Sierra is an excellent student who has never made a grade below "A" since she began school. She is very proud of her record and seems to be pleased that other students are aware of it as well. She has indicated that her parents always give her a special reward for getting such good grades on her report card. Getting good grades in school seems to come easy for her.

Her best friend is Beth who is also a good student, yet not as excelled as Sierra. Although Beth is a good student, her grades have been getting worse in recent weeks. She only infrequently completes the assignments that Ms. Jackson has made and often does not follow the instructions and examples that Ms. Jackson provides. Ms. Jackson has noticed that Sierra usually finishes her work before anyone else in the class and then spends time talking to Beth. She feels that this has been a part of the drop that she has seen in Beth's performance. When it got to the point that Sierra was consistently talking while Ms. Jackson was explaining lessons to the class, Beth and Sierra were asked to change their seats as far from one another as possible. This bothered Beth a good deal because Sierra now has become best friends with Rachel, whom she now sits beside. In fact, Sierra now spends much of the class time talking with Rachel, whose work is beginning to suffer. In turn, Beth now has begun talking in class with Clifford instead of completing her own work.

Ms. Jackson's effort to help Beth's grades improve by moving her away from Sierra has not been effective. Rather, Beth has begun her own disruptive talking behavior and is now having a negative impact on Clifford. Too, Sierra's disruptive talking has actually continued even with the use of the new seating arrangement as she now talks to Rachel after she completes her assignments.

Ms. Jackson has spoken to her about her problem with talking, and Sierra has promised to stop. She told Sierra that when she talks that it is distracting to her when she is teaching, and this is frustrating. She also thought about lowering Sierra's grade because of her talking but decided not to mention this possibility to her at that point. Ms. Jackson was prepared to speak to Sierra's parents about the problem at the last parent-teacher conference that they had scheduled, but they didn't show up for the conference as planned. She isn't sure what step to take next. What should she do?

DISRUPTIVE TALKING (MIDDLE-SECONDARY GRADES)

Kelli's Disruptive Talking

Kelli is one of those students who seems to be happy one day and sad the next. One day she is prepared with her homework, and the next time homework is due, she hasn't done it. The one thing that Mr. Howard, Kelli's tenth-grade science teacher can predict, however, is that he can tell every time Kelli is in the classroom because she seems to be constantly talking when she is there. He has spoken to her about her talking on more than one occasion because he finds it to be quite distracting to his teaching. Sometimes, she talks to other students when he is trying to teach and often just calls out answers to questions that he is asking, even when he is about to call on another student for an answer. She even makes remarks about what he is talking about during his lesson to seemingly no one at all. It is as though when an idea comes into her head, she just says whatever comes to mind. When she talks, he focuses on her talking, and loses track of where he is. This upsets him, and he thinks that Kelli and the other students can tell when he gets upset.

To Mr. Howard, Kelli hasn't outgrown a behavior that he thought was more common to elementary school students. One thing that adds to his frustration is that Kelli almost always receives some of the highest grades in the class. He really can't figure out how she does it when he knows that she isn't giving his teaching her undivided attention. Kelli's talking is also distracting to the other students who sit near her. Some students don't want to be her lab partner because they know that it is difficult for them to concentrate and get their work done when she is nearby.

He has heard that Kelli is from a large family, but he really doesn't know anything specific about her home life. He can't recall ever speaking to anyone from her family. The more he thinks about it, she is actually somewhat of a mystery to him. He can't remember if he has ever seen Kelli with any other students outside of class on any regular basis.

He knows that he has to do something about Kelli's disruptive talking. He just isn't sure, though, how he can find out what he needs to know and what to do in order to make things better. What should he do?

ATTENTION-SEEKING (PRIMARY-ELEMENTARY GRADES)

Bridget's Attention-Seeking

Bridget, although she comes from a disadvantaged background, makes very good grades in her fifth-grade classroom. Yet, Ms. Wilson, her teacher, is very concerned about Bridget's behavior problems. While it is easy for her to recognize that Bridget has what many call a "sound mind," she also often acts in a fashion that Ms. Wilson feels is immature for a child her age. Bridget, for example, is known by her classmates as a "tattler" who frequently goes to Ms. Wilson to tell her of some instance when a classmate broke a rule while the teacher was not watching. Not only does this make her classmates angry, this constant behavior, more common to younger children, has started to get on Ms. Wilson's nerves. It certainly interrupts her instruction when Bridget does this. Moreover, Bridget tries to dominate Ms. Wilson's time, even pretending to not understand things just so Ms. Wilson will come and sit beside her desk. At the beginning of the school year, Bridget "clowned around" and tried to be funny in class seemingly as a way to get attention. She hasn't done this for some time, though, as many of the other students laughed at her in a way that was not the "type of laugh" that she was seeking.

Ms. Wilson finds it difficult to give the necessary attention to the other students in the class because of Bridget's constant demands. During a conference, Ms. Wilson found that, although Bridget is living with an aunt who seems to care for her very much, she has been in three different homes over the past five years. Bridget's birth father, who didn't live with her long, has now left the area and has not been heard from for over a year. Bridget's birth mother has four other children and has asked her sister, Bridget's aunt, if she could care for her. She has tried to care for Bridget, but her circumstances are also difficult; and she is away at work in the late afternoons and evenings during the week. In all, Ms. Wilson has discovered that Bridget is one of those many children who, in large part, are raising themselves. It is no wonder that Bridget craves attention from her as she gets little positive attention away from school. Still, Bridget's behaviors are both interrupting to her instruction as well as not age-appropriate, she feels, for a student in the fifth grade.

Ms. Wilson wants to help Bridget as she does all of her students, and she recognizes her learning potential. However, she cannot continue to accept Bridget's attention-seeking behaviors. She is uncertain about how to approach the problem. What should she do?

ATTENTION-SEEKING (MIDDLE-SECONDARY GRADES)

Jennifer's Attention-seeking

Jennifer is in Mr. Winslow's tenth-grade Spanish II class. This is an unusual class because, of the twenty-four students in the class, only five are females. Mr. Winslow noticed early on in the term that Jennifer frequently did things to bring attention to herself. Sometimes she would just act out in a disturbing way and other times she would do something to try to look funny. Once or twice, she even came to Mr. Winslow to tell him something that seemed unnecessary about another student in the class. Not only is her behavior annoying, it is also disturbing to him and the rest of the students.

Mr. Winslow thinks that Jennifer is really struggling to keep up with the other students and wonders if maybe this could be a reason for her attention-seeking. Maybe, she is trying to hide that she isn't doing very well. But, when he asked some of the other teachers in the school who had Jennifer in class, he learned that this was how she acted in their classes too. One of the other teachers added that Jennifer lived with her mother and a younger brother who attended the middle school.

Mr. Winslow is worried about Jennifer for a number of reasons. First, her clowning around and drawing attention to herself is distracting to him and other students. Second, her coming to him and telling him things about other students, he thinks, is not really a typical or appropriate behavior for a student her age. It certainly isn't earning her any friends in the class. Finally, he is concerned that Jennifer isn't being successful as a student. Except for trying to draw attention to herself, she is friendly, attractive, dresses well, speaks clearly, uses good grammar, and gets along fairly well with the other students. Through some of his investigation, he learned that Jennifer is a cheerleader and that she has been in some of the school plays. On the surface, she seems far better off, at least financially, than some of the other students whom he is teaching. But, he has been teaching long enough to know that what might be apparent on the surface might not represent the complete situation. He knows that, when students seek attention on a regular basis, this can represent a problem.

He wants to help Jennifer, but he just doesn't know how to go about it. One thing he knows for sure is that he needs to know more about her. What should he do?

CHRONIC AVOIDANCE OF WORK (PRIMARY-ELEMENTARY GRADES)

Tabitha's Chronic Avoidance of Work

Tabitha, at times, can be one of the most cooperative students in the class and other times she can just act as though nothing in the class has any importance to her. Mr. Waverly is Tabitha's fifth-grade teacher, and he has observed her behavior with interest. Lately, what has become especially bothersome for him is that Tabitha seldom turns back in to him the work that he has assigned. He does a lot of whole group instruction as well as cooperative learning activities, and it doesn't seem to matter. For the past two months it has been virtually impossible for him to receive any schoolwork from Tabitha. It seems that it is almost weekly that he asks her about her work that is due, and she always has some comment to make about it. Sometimes it is in her mother's car. Other times she and her parents had gone out to eat the night before, and she didn't have a chance to get it done. Frequently, she just shrugs her shoulders and says that she has simply forgotten to do it but that she will bring it in the next day. The next day, Tabitha never seems to have her work.

Mr. Waverly is very concerned about Tabitha's behavior; it has happened before but has not lasted so long. At this point, Tabitha is falling further and further behind the rest of the students in the class. The school has a parent-teacher conference scheduled in about two weeks, but Mr. Waverly isn't sure that he can wait that long to speak to Tabitha's parents. He knows that both of them work and that it might be hard for them to help her regularly with her schoolwork. He has spoken to the teachers who had Tabitha in class in the second and third grades, and they indicated that this was not typical behavior for her. Although they did not remember Tabitha as being a high-performing student, they did remember her as a student who was solidly in the average range and who was cooperative and helpful in class. She also got along well with other students.

This description of Tabitha doesn't remind Mr. Waverly of the Tabitha that he knows. His Tabitha is neither cooperative nor dependable. Sometimes, she seems downright moody. He also doesn't see her getting along well with other students or even regularly associating with them. Even with just this brief history, Mr. Waverly knows that he has a problem that he needs to deal with. Tabitha's behavior needs to change in terms of her schoolwork, and, if she is having other problems, he needs to be prepared to help her there as well. But, what should he do next?

CHRONIC AVOIDANCE OF WORK
(MIDDLE-SECONDARY GRADES)

Jay's Chronic Avoidance of Work

Ms. Davis is Jay's ninth-grade English teacher. She has been closely following his progress, or perhaps his lack of progress, for the past three weeks. It is difficult for her to know just what Jay is able to do because he so seldom completes and turns in the work that she has assigned. To reinforce the high expectations that she has for her students, she regularly gives writing and some other question-completion assignments each week. Jay hardly ever turns in the work that she has given.

Ms. Davis knows that things have been pretty rough for Jay. He is in the ninth-grade when most of his friends are in the tenth-grade. Jay repeated seventh-grade. That had been a difficult year for him as his mother died that year. She has thought about pulling his record to see how he did in school before that year, but she hasn't had the time. Jay lives with his father and three younger sisters. She hasn't visited his home, but she knows that Jay's father works at the local electronics plant. It has to be hard for him raising three young girls and Jay.

Still, Jay is behind the other students in the class and falling further behind with each assignment that she gives. She asked him a couple of times why he hadn't completed his work, and all that he said was that he hadn't had the time. Once he said that he didn't understand what he was supposed to do and really didn't see the point in it anyway. She doesn't understand how he can't know what she wants. She gives her assignments in a very regular and predictable way. He has many chances to ask questions if he is not sure what she wants.

Fortunately, Jay's behavior in class doesn't seem to be a problem. He is quiet and keeps to himself. She isn't sure if he has any real friends in the class or not. She usually teaches the class as a large group and hasn't seen him talking to any of the other students for any length of time. She has so many students in her classes throughout the day that she hasn't had time to get to know Jay very well. She feels bad about this, but that is just the way it is.

She doesn't want to give Jay poor grades, but she can't just ignore his not completing his work. After all, she has her standards to think about. She does recognize that she has a problem. But, she isn't sure what to do. What should she do?

DISHONESTY (PRIMARY-ELEMENTARY GRADES)

Thom's Dishonesty

Ms. Gore has been teaching fourth grade for ten years and is considered an excellent teacher by both parents and fellow educators. However, never in her ten years of teaching has she had the type of problem that she has had this year. The problem began when Terry reported that he had some money missing from his desk. He said that it was a couple of dollars. Two days later Lakisha said that part of her lunch had been taken. Within the next week, almost every student in the classroom reported that they had been the victim of something having been taken. Ms. Gore knows that some of the reports are not factual. Some children are simply mistaken, and others have gotten caught up in the moment. However, she is certain some things are being taken; in fact, someone went so far as to steal money from her own desk. But now, students are accusing other students without having any proof.

Ms. Gore finds it amazing that a fourth-grade class can take on all the primary characteristics of what she thinks of as an unruly mob. Fingers are being pointed and innocent students are being hurt by false accusations. She even got two calls one evening and one email last week from parents asking what was going on in the class. Their children had said that some things had been taken from them. While the parents didn't actually seem angry, she could tell that they wanted to know more about the problem and what was being done about it. All she could say was that she was looking into it. Getting calls from parents makes her think that things are truly getting out of control.

Then, a most amazing thing happens. She finds some of the things that have been taken in Thom's desk. When confronted in private, Thom admits to taking everything. Ms. Gore is very confused because Thom's parents are known to be wealthy and generous people. Thom does not "need" to steal. Thom tells her that he is sorry he has stolen and that it will never happen again. He also begs her not to tell his parents about what he has done.

Ms. Gore, although an experienced teacher, is not sure just how to handle the situation. It won't take long for the other students in the class to find out that it is Thom who has been taking things. After that, their parents will soon know. She has a lot to think about and some important decisions to make. What should she do?

DISHONESTY (MIDDLE-SECONDARY GRADES)

Shekiah's Dishonesty

Mr. Gallagher sees himself as someone who can handle most any problem in the classroom. He teaches eighth-grade social studies and tries to have his class operate as though it is a small, democratic community. Everyone has a chance for input into making the "rules" and deciding how the community will operate. He has the class meet regularly to talk about how things are going. Communities are governed by laws, and he thinks that having his students meet on a regular basis will help reinforce this fact. This also helps him see what is on the minds of his students and shows them that he cares about their ideas and their lives. He is glad that he has a positive relationship with his students because he is facing a difficult problem. Over the past month, some students have told him that they have had things missing. Some of the missing items have been pens and pencils, but some have been make-up kits, perfume, and even money. He also thinks that he has had some cheating on his last two tests. The students who told him about the stealing even named another student in the class, Shekiah, as the thief. He also believes that Shekiah has been cheating on his tests. Stealing affects other students in that their property is lost. Cheating also affects other students in that it can make a difference in the grades that they receive. Cheating also may be symptomatic of other, even deeper problems.

Mr. Gallagher doesn't know much about Shekiah except that she doesn't seem to him like someone who would steal and cheat. She has only been in his class for about two months as she has just recently started attending the school. She interacts well with the other students and seems bright and alert. He has seen both of her parents at school functions, and they both came for the parent-teacher conferences that had been held just two weeks ago. Stealing and cheating are very serious problems. The class meetings that he has held so far have not gotten into anything like this. Should he bring up the problem of stealing and cheating to the students at a class meeting? Maybe he is wrong about Shekiah. But, what if he is right, and she really is doing these things? This is a problem that has to be dealt with.

There are issues here that are important not only because of the acts that have been committed, but also because they have been formally brought to his attention by some of the students. The problem is pretty much out in the open and needs to be dealt with. He has to take action, but it has to be the right action. What should he do?

UNRULINESS (PRIMARY-ELEMENTARY GRADES)

Billy's Unruliness

Billy is a second-grade student who has little self-control. One of his favorite things to do is run down the hallway at school making motor sounds with his mouth while pretending to shift gears with his right hand. Although Billy thinks this is great fun, Ms. Lee, his teacher, finds this behavior unacceptable. So do other teachers in the school. Billy's classmates often find Billy annoying because he frequently gets too loud and out of control when the class is involved in one of Ms. Lee's many fun activities. Actually, Ms. Lee views Billy as the kind of child who usually means to please; in fact, Billy is a good learner and makes above average grades as a rule. However, more than once Billy has embarrassed her by his behaviors like running and talking too loudly in the cafeteria and knocking on each teacher's door as he goes by on his way to the restroom.

At first, Billy's behavior seemed as though it might just be the behavior of a very energetic boy. Billy almost always seems happy and alert when he comes to school. The fact that he does make good grades has indicated to Ms. Lee that he has a sound mind and is able to comprehend what is expected of him. He seems to be one of the stronger students in the class in science and math. His repeated behaviors that just seem too loud, too physical at times, and too much playground-like, however, have proven to be a problem for what Ms. Lee is trying to accomplish in her teaching. His behavior, she feels, also has impacted negatively on the learning of the other students in the class.

Ms. Lee has spoken to Billy on more than one occasion about his overly rambunctious behavior, and his response has always been that he will try to do better. In fact, Ms. Lee feels as though Billy actually has tried to do better but has just been unsuccessful in his attempts. Her view is that, if he can learn science and math, then he can learn to act properly in the classroom and school. She has even thought about having Billy meet with the assistant principal, hoping he might be able to offer assistance. So far she hasn't done this nor has she spoken to Billy's parents about his behavior.

Ms. Lee has always been the kind of teacher who desires to "solve her own problems" whenever they occur. Billy's behavior, though, seems to be getting worse and not better. Ms. Lee needs to try something else, but what?

UNRULINESS (MIDDLE-SECONDARY GRADES)

Kendrick's Unruliness

Kendrick is a handful for Ms. Singh. Ms. Singh is Kendrick's eleventh grade social studies teacher, or at least tries to be. She has all but given up on Kendrick ever being well behaved in class or being a good student. He is too loud and boisterous. He probably thinks that he is funny, but she thinks that he is trouble to have around. About every time that she seems to have things going well, he does something to distract her and the rest of the class. Sometimes, he will just get out of his seat and walk around the room; other times, he will talk to the other students who sit near him. She doesn't think that he knows how to whisper. She can hear him talking all the way from the back of the room where he usually sits. She doesn't use assigned seats for her students as it is her opinion that students this age should be able to pick where they want to sit in the class.

Ms. Singh considers herself to be a dedicated and flexible teacher, but her way just isn't connecting with Kendrick. She knows that he is popular in school and thinks that this is because he is on the basketball team. She has never been to one of the games, but she has heard other students talk about how many points he always scores. She has even heard that there may be some college scouts looking at him for a basketball scholarship. Her view of him, though, is that he simply is undisciplined.

As a student, Kendrick is struggling. His work is below average, and his mind really appears to be "somewhere else" when she is teaching. Ms. Singh has become very frustrated because she believes that Kendrick is getting the best of her. His behavior is distracting to her and to the other students; he simply seems immature when compared to the rest of the class. She has looked in his file and knows that he lives with his mother and four brothers and sisters. He has had a poor track record in school over the years and is barely making the grade to be able to play basketball. As she sees it, basketball is one of the only things that keeps him coming to school and doing any work at all.

Ms. Singh feels that, when Kendrick acts out in class, this makes her look bad in the eyes of the other students. If she allows him to "get away with it," other students eventually will try to do the same thing. She knows that a lot of students simply aren't interested in social studies, and that surprises and disappoints her as she finds social studies very interesting. He certainly hasn't learned very much from her teaching up to this point. In her opinion, the situation has to change. What should she do?

DEFIANCE (PRIMARY-ELEMENTARY GRADES)

Maggie's Defiance

Maggie is a second-grade student who has had a personal problem during the current school year. Mr. Ray, her teacher, is aware that Maggie's parents recently divorced and that Maggie has become very upset by the fact that her father has moved to a new dwelling with another women and her children. Maggie continues to live with her mother and her older sister who will graduate from high school at the end of the year. The source of Maggie's frustration seems obvious. Immediately after the divorce, there appeared to be little change in Maggie's behavior. Over the past month, however, her behavior has changed significantly in a negative way.

Mr. Ray is concerned that on three occasions in the last two weeks Maggie has refused to do as he has requested and has told him in front of other students that she did not have to what he told her to do. These incidents have taken place in such a way that he feels his ability to control his class has been threatened or at least definitely challenged. The public nature of this challenge has been especially bothersome to him. At first, he was shocked at Maggie's behavior and her remarks and just tried to coax her to do what he had asked. Fortunately, she did. On another occasion, when he asked his students to work together in pairs, Maggie and the student that she was paired with got into a big argument about who was going to do what on the project that he assigned. When he talked to them about it, the other student just said that Maggie didn't want to cooperate and share the materials that he had passed out.

Mr. Ray feels sorry for Maggie and knows that she is suffering. The changes in her home conditions must be traumatic for her. Still, he does not feel that he can continue to allow her to talk to him as she has and challenge his authority, especially in front of other students. With Maggie's parents' divorce being final, there is no chance that her lifestyle will return to being the way it was. Mr. Ray, who is a first-year teacher, is uneasy about going to his principal for advice because he wants to appear as though he can manage his own classroom problems.

He recalls some discussions in college that dealt with managing classrooms but doesn't remember that this particular kind of situation was presented. He recognizes that he has a problem. Now, he must find the solution. What should he do?

DEFIANCE (MIDDLE-SECONDARY GRADES)

Eric's Defiance

Ms. Hutton is in her first year of teaching. She feels fortunate that she has been able to get a job given that she graduated in December and that there are not as many teaching positions open in the middle of the school year as there are at the beginning of the year. The part that she doesn't feel so fortunate about is that the position that she has accepted is at the high school level when she wanted to teach younger students. The school is also in a rather rough neighborhood. Still, she pledged to herself that she was going to be the best health teacher that she could be. One thing that she learned early on is that some of the students in the school come from very difficult home backgrounds. At times, some of them are hard to manage.

Eric is one such student. Up to this point, Ms. Hutton has not had any major problems with Eric though she has made every effort to avoid them too. Eric seems to be one of those students who tries to push the envelope as the popular expression goes. He hardly ever acts as though he wants to be involved in the activities that she has planned and almost dares her to see if she can get him to participate. Once or twice he even has made what she thinks are "smart remarks" about what she is having the students do. Even though she has a good relationship with most of the students, she still feels very new to being a teacher. Maybe things have gone fairly well up to this point just because she has shown a lot of flexibility in what she asks her students to do and when she asks them to do it. From listening to some of the other teachers talk, she wonders if she is being too flexible.

Today, Ms. Hutton has given her students what she thinks will be an interesting assignment that her students will enjoy doing. When Eric gets the assignment sheet, Ms. Hutton can tell that he doesn't want to do it. As she is walking by his desk, he just wads it up and drops it on the floor. He says, "this is the most stupid thing I have ever been asked to do, and I'm not gonna do it." Ms. Hutton knows that she is facing one the most difficult moments in her short teaching career. She can't let Eric talk to her like this in the classroom, and she also knows the problem is bigger than just this one assignment.

How can she best deal with the problem of the moment as well as help things be better in the long run? What should she do?

AGGRESSION (PRIMARY-ELEMENTARY GRADES)

Julian's Aggression

Julian is a kindergarten student whose behavior has been a concern to both his parents and his teacher, Mr. Woo. Julian seems to be advanced in his learning as compared to some of the other students in the class. His mother, a former first-grade teacher, spent a great deal of time with him before he began school which resulted in his being a very good reader when he started kindergarten. He also does well in beginning writing and in certain computation skills activities. In fact, Julian's parents wanted to have him placed in the first grade this year with children a year older because of his advanced learning abilities. They both value education highly and, as Julian is their only child, they are very focused on his development and eventual accomplishments. The accelerated placement to first grade, however, was not made.

Although Julian's academic skills are much like a student in the first grade, Mr. Woo recognizes that Julian's social and emotional characteristics are actually less developed than those of even the average kindergarten child's. When playing on the playground with other students, Julian often becomes angry and hits or bites his classmates. When Mr. Woo tries to control Julian, Julian frequently screams and even kicks at him. Additionally, Julian's aggressive behavior is not relegated only to the playground. He displays similar behaviors in the cafeteria, the hallways, and sometimes even in the classroom. While there is room for other students to avoid him on the playground, this is not the case in the classroom. On more than one occasion, classroom activities have had to be adjusted because of his behavior. Over the past month, some parents have even complained to the principal that they did not want their children in the same class with Julian because they feared for their safety.

When in a conference with Mr. Woo, Julian's parents voiced their opinion that Julian gets frustrated because the other students are not as advanced as he is which results in his angry outbursts. Since the beginning of the school year, they have continued to feel that Julian should have be been placed in the first grade. Mr. Woo shared with them that he has tried to talk to Julian and work closely with him, but that his aggressive behavior is a definite problem for him and the other students.

Mr. Woo isn't sure just what to do next. He likes Julian and recognizes that he definitely has learning potential, but his behavior needs to change. What should he do?

AGGRESSION (MIDDLE-SECONDARY GRADES)

Sebastian's Aggression

Mr. Allen is embarrassed to say it, but he has come to the point where he is glad when Sebastian is absent from school. Mr. Allen teaches seventh grade math, and Sebastian is one of his students. The school year started out all right, but it started without Sebastian. It is now early December, and Sebastian joined the school and his class in late October. It has been a rough month and a half. Sebastian is just a very aggressive person. He has already been in two fights and come close on a number of other occasions. When Sebastian is around, the tension in the class seems to rise.

Sebastian actually is physically smaller than many of the other students and has had a difficult time catching up to them academically. Mr. Allen hasn't had a chance to see the file that has been sent from Sebastian's last school, but, at least in the math area, Sebastian is far behind. Sebastian also has had a difficult time adjusting to the rest of the students in the class as well as to his teaching style which Mr. Allen sees as being very straightforward.

He doesn't believe that Sebastian is a bully in that Sebastian doesn't regularly start fights with other students. But, he is quick to say things that offend other students or something that most people consider uncalled for and inappropriate. He sees Sebastian as a loner; he doesn't appear to have any friends in the class. Sebastian was always eating by himself the few times that he saw him in the school cafeteria. The more he thinks about it, the more he actually feels sorry for him. He is in a new community and a new school and is behind the other students in his class. This must make him feel very out of place. Maybe, he is doing the best that he can do.

One day, all of the good feelings that Mr. Allen had about reaching Sebastian seemed far away as he saw Sebastian and another student standing face to face, perhaps squaring off, in the back of the room. Class hadn't started, but it was supposed to in just a few minutes. Mr. Allen's attention was attracted to the back of the room when he heard two students say "Sebastian shouldn't have said that to him," and "I'll bet Sebastian is gonna get it good."

Mr. Allen knows that he has at least two problems to deal with. First, what is he going to do about the fight that is about to take place in his classroom? Second, what can he do to help Sebastian not be involved in such situations in the future? What is the answer to each of these questions?

BULLYING (PRIMARY-ELEMENTARY GRADES)

Jose's Bullying Problem

Ms. Howard is a third-grade teacher in a mid-size elementary school. While she has encountered different and sometimes difficult problems in her teaching each year, she has been able to resolve them satisfactorily. This year, though, she has been confronted with a new problem, at least new to her, that she has yet to resolve. Ms. Howard's school year began with twenty-three students in her classroom, but now that number has grown to twenty-four with the addition of Jose about a month ago. Her initial impression of Jose was quite positive as he was polite, quiet, completed his work, seemed cooperative, and generally kept to himself. Now, however, Ms. Howard has developed another view, one that has become troublesome.

As she has observed Jose in her classroom and in other areas of the school, she has seen more closely his relationship with other students. In particular, this has involved two of her other students, Marcus and Charles. She has been both troubled and surprised by what she has observed. Marcus and Charles have been two of her favorite students. Now she thinks that she may be seeing a different side to them.

Over the last three weeks, she has seen one or both of them tease and make fun of Jose. At times they have walked by his desk and knocked his books, papers and pencils to the floor. At other times, they have shoved him out of line in the lunch room. At still other times, they have actually punched him at recess when they thought that no one was looking. One of the other third-grade teachers who was on playground supervision said that she had heard them call Jose some very ugly names and say some very mean things to him.

The end result has been that Jose has become more quiet than usual, missed days of school, and become inconsistent and sloppy in his school work. To make things worse, she has heard some of the other students in the class laugh when the two boys played their tricks on him. Ms. Howard had come to think of her classroom as a small community where all of the members got along and watched out for each other. Now she isn't so sure. Marcus and Charles come from what she thinks of as good homes. They have grown up together in the same community and moved through the grades in the same classes. Why would they be doing these things?

Ms. Howard is well aware of many of the issues in schools that involve bullying, but she has never encountered it firsthand. Obviously this situation cannot continue and she knows that she has a responsibility to take some action. She is not sure, however, just what that action should be. What should she do?

BULLYING (MIDDLE-SECONDARY GRADES)

Keith's Bullying Problem

Keith is in the tenth grade and very anxious for the school year to end. Actually, he is anxious for his high school years to end so that he can get away from one particular student, Junior. Junior also is in the tenth grade and, for some reason that Keith can't understand, Junior has taken it upon himself to make his life miserable. Junior stands about 6' 2" and weighs around 200 pounds. Keith is a modest 5'9" and barely 150 pounds.

Although Keith and Junior only have one class together, it seems that each day Junior has something in store for him. So far, Junior has trashed his gym locker as well as his locker in the main part of the school, let the air out of the tires on his car in the school parking lot, and in the lunchroom, walked by and dropped a dirty rag onto his plate of food. Sometimes he just walks by and bumps into him, hard, and makes comments about the way he dresses, how he smells, or how he has his hair cut. Junior has also made threatening remarks to him such as "I'm looking forward to finding you alone some day after school." Keith is even afraid to go into the restroom alone. School is no longer a place for learning, but merely a place for surviving.

Keith's favorite teacher is Mr. Jeffries, his social studies teacher. He has shared some of his concerns with him but isn't sure just what will come of it. Mr. Jeffries said that he should tell a school administrator, but he doesn't want a reputation of telling on other students and getting another student in trouble. He knows that other students have seen how Junior has been after him, but no one seems to be interested in getting involved. Most just look on for the entertainment or turn their heads and walk away.

Last Friday, when he was ready to leave school for the weekend, he saw Junior in the parking lot just leaning on his car so he decided to stay in the school until Junior went away. That took about an hour. Some teachers walked by while he was waiting, including Mr. Jeffries, but no one said anything. He has decided that when he comes back to school on Monday, if he comes back, it might be a good idea to bring something to protect himself.

In all, he simply doesn't know what to do. He thinks that Mr. Jeffries understands his situation, but he doesn't believe that any help will come from him. He doesn't know if he should try to stand up to Junior or just try to stay out of his way. In the meantime, his grades are terrible and he is a nervous wreck. What should Keith do? What should Mr. Jeffries do?

CONCLUSION

In spite of the many rules and procedures that teachers have established, many of the problems that they face each day have no one right answer or solution. Most are specific to the particular situation where they arise and to the student or students involved and require analysis within that context. Through guided problem solving based on a strong knowledge base of information related to best practice in teaching, student motivation, and classroom management, however, teachers can identify patterns in the various problems that they are called on to deal with and learn from one problem to another. While each situation needs to be analyzed individually, common patterns and plausible solutions will emerge. It is because of this that it is critical that teachers learn from each situation that they encounter so that they can more quickly find effective solutions to the problems that they will be faced with in the future.

The case studies presented here for analysis serve to illustrate this point. Teachers can learn from their successes, as well as from their mistakes, if they are willing and able to analyze them in a systematic, informed, and objective manner. Whether the teacher is dealing with a problem of dishonesty in the second grade or defiance in the tenth grade, a logical approach should be followed to address the problem. Chapter 7 offered a number of realistic problems for review. By addressing each problem as a situation where certain questions must be answered for the problem to be resolved effectively, the positive impact of the use of a logical problem-solving model in problem resolution can be seen. Through the disciplined use of the model in these hypothetical situations, the transfer can more easily and successfully be made to the real-life problems that teachers face each day in their schools and classrooms.

GLOSSARY

academic learning time. That portion of the classroom time where students are engaged in meaningful learning activities and are successful during this engagement.

academic organization. The teacher's means of ordering and arranging information for instruction so that students will be better able to understand the information communicated, e.g., diagrams, outlines, hierarchies, etc.

active listening. Specific approach to listening where the teacher gives full attention to both the emotional as well as intellectual meaning of what the student is saying; often involves mirroring back what a student has said or otherwise confirming that one is attentive, interested and nonjudgmental.

advance organizer. Described by David Ausubel as the teacher's use of introductory statements or activities that frame the new content to be taught as a part of the lesson focus.

advancework. The process of preventing problems before they begin rather than reacting to problems after they have already occurred.

aggression. A serious behavior problem in that the possibility exists that one or more students may be injured; fighting is the ultimate form of aggression though aggression may also include pushing and shoving, overly physical play, name-calling or other verbal attacks.

allocated time. The amount of time a particular teacher or school designates to an identified course topic or activity.

anticipatory set. Mental or attitudinal foundation established by the teacher for the students at the beginning of the instructional experience that helps students to understand what they may anticipate in the instruction which will follow.

antisocial behavior. A behavior directed toward bringing about a negative consequence for someone or something.

Applied Behavior Analysis. An approach to behavior management based on the work of B.F. Skinner's operant conditioning theory; a rewards-based approach to modifying student behavior.

anxiety. Feeling of apprehension, worry, tension, or nervousness.

Assertive Discipline. Management theory promoted by Lee and Marlene Canter that focuses on the tenet that teachers have the right to teach while students have the right to learn, and no one has the right to disrupt the learning environment; clear rules are established along with clear consequences for students who choose to break established rules.

attainment value. Value determined by how a task or domain fulfills a person's needs; it concerns the relevance of an activity to a person's actual or ideal self concept.

attention-seeking. Student behavior problem often exhibited by tattling and showing off; teachers are advised that there are reasons behind the displaying of attention-seeking behaviors and these reasons need to be ascertained by the teacher to appropriately deal with the behavior.

attribution theory. Cognitive theory that involves the student's views of the causes of outcomes and how these views influence his or her expectations and behaviors.

autonomy. In self-determination theory, independence and the ability to alter the environment when necessary.

behavior modification. Associated with the work of B.F. Skinner, now more popularly called Applied Behavior Analysis; management approach that utilizes rewards for modifying student behavior.

Behaviorism. Theory of motivation that focuses on the use of reinforcements or rewards to modify student behavior.

bullying. A negative behavior which is intentionally designed to cause real, or threatening injury or discomfort to another individual that may reflect physical harm, psychological harm, or both.

chronic avoidance of work. Potentially a serious student behavior problem where a student consistently fails to complete his or her assigned work following repeated teacher effort to get the work completed.

clarity. Important teacher characteristic in being able to be clear in communications with students so that they understand the different teacher messages used during instruction, how the instruction will be conducted and what is expected of them.

class meeting. Management strategy recommended by William Glasser where the teacher meets regularly with students as a way to involve students in establishing guidelines for acceptable behavior and as a forum for collaborative problem solving.

closure. Type of review that occurs at the end of the instructional episode or period that enables the student to end the lesson with a better understanding of the topic and a place to build on in the future.

coercive strategies. Behavior strategies used by the teacher in maintaining a well-managed classroom that are based on the power of punishment.

cognitive memory level question. Question at the lowest level of cognition that asks students to recall previously learned and memorized information; behaviors such as recalling, recognizing, and reporting are typically involved.

cognitive theories. Theories of motivation that stress the student's need for order, predictability, and the understanding of events around him.

competence. In self-determination theory, the ability to function effectively in the environment.

Conflict Resolution. Management strategy developed by David and Roger Johnson that relies on training students to deal with their own problems and those of their fellow students; peer mediation is an important part of this strategy.

connected discourse. Ability to communicate so that it is clear to students that the teacher's presentation is thematically well connected and leads to a goal, going point by point.

convergent level question. Question at the second lowest level of cognition that asks students to put facts or concepts together in order to obtain the single correct answer; questions may require students to make comparisons, explain facts or concepts, state or describe relationships, or solve problems using learned procedures.

criterion material. The information that students will be held accountable for which has been communicated to them prior to instruction; the criteria or standard upon which the teacher will base student success.

debilitating anxiety. Anxiety so extreme that it gets in the way of successful student performance.

defiance. A serious form of student misbehavior where the student refuses to do what the teacher asks or boldly talks back to the teacher in a hostile or threatening way.

deficiency needs. Needs at the lower levels of Abraham Maslow's Hierarchy of Needs including survival, safety, belonging, and self-esteem.

desists. The use of verbal or nonverbal communications by teachers for the purpose of stopping student misconduct or misbehavior.

discipline. Action taken on the part of the teacher to enforce rules and respond to student misbehavior.

disequilibrium. State of being out-of-balance.

dishonesty. Considered by some to be the most serious form of student misconduct often exhibited through cheating and/or stealing and telling untruths and lying.

disruptive talking. Student behavior problem through talking that interferes with the learning process by interrupting the teacher while teaching, students as they are listening to the teacher, or as they are involved in completing activities that the teacher has assigned.

divergent level question. Question that asks students to engage in divergence of thought and produce a response that is original for that student; questions may require students to predict, hypothesize, or infer.

diversity. In the school or classroom, pertains to the variety of backgrounds or circumstances from which students come as they enter the schooling environment.

emphasis. An element of communication where the teacher specifically identifies for students important points to be remembered, e.g., through the use of such statements as "this is important" or "be sure to remember this."

engaged time. The portion of instructional time that students actually spend directly involved in learning activities; often referred to as time-on-task.

enthusiasm. The amount of energy and vigor shown by the teacher; felt to communicate to students the degree to which the teacher enjoys teaching and the degree to which the teacher believes that the students will be successful in their learning.

equilibration. The process of searching for order or balance, i.e., equilibrium, and, in so doing, testing one's understanding against the real world.

equilibrium. Being in a state of balance.

equitable distribution. A recommended approach to asking questions where all students are called on as equally as possible.

expectancy X value theory. Theory that students are motivated to engage in a learning task to the extent that they expect to succeed on the task and the degree to which they value achievement on the task or other potential outcomes that may come as a result of task achievement.

expulsion. Process exercised by a school district's governing authority, generally the school board, of banning a student from attending school for the remainder of the school year or the remainder of the school year plus an additional period of time carried over into the next school year.

external locus of control. When students feel that forces external to or outside themselves control their lives.

extrinsic motivation. Motivation to become involved in an activity as a means to an end; to receive a reward, praise, or some other recognition.

evaluation level question. Question at the highest level of cognition that asks students to make judgments based on logically derived evidence; students must defend or explain their judgments based on criteria that they designate or which have been established by others.

facilitating anxiety. Anxiety in such a small amount that it may actually help to improve student performance.

feedback. Information provided students by teachers, generally in oral or written form, that lets them know the status of their learning progress; the more specific, regular, and in depth the feedback the better.

focus. The attention given to and maintained on the important points to be made during instruction; when teachers have good focus, students clearly understand what will take place during instruction and what will be expected of them as learners.

frequency. Important aspect of question-asking that deals with the number of questions that the teacher asks; generally the more questions the better.

goal. That which an individual is striving to achieve or accomplish; in teaching, goals are generally broad as opposed to narrow and more long-term as opposed to short-term in nature.

group focus. On-task behavior where all students in the classroom attend to the teacher or activities that the teacher has assigned.

growth needs. Needs at the higher levels of Abraham Maslow's Hierarchy of Needs including intellectual achievement, aesthetic appreciation, and self-actualization.

Hierarchy of Needs. Humanistic theory of motivation developed by Abraham Maslow that identifies a hierarchy of needs associated with underlying reasons for human behavior; needs are identified as deficiency or growth needs.

Humanism. Theory of motivation that views behavior as an individual's effort to satisfy or fulfill his ultimate potential as a human being.

I message. Three-part communication from the teacher to the student delineating the student's undesired behavior, describing the effect the behavior has on the teacher or the classroom, and relating how the teacher feels when the behavior occurs.

inattention. Student behavior seen as the least severe management problem; students may engage in daydreaming, staring into space, doing unrelated work, etc., as examples of not being involved in the learning process.

indirect teaching. Approach to teaching that focuses heavily on the use of student ideas and student active participation in the learning process.

instructional time. The portion of allocated time that is actually devoted to learning activities.

instructional variety. The consistent utilization of a number of different instructional techniques or strategies by the teacher in instruction rather than relying on only a very few; see also variability.

inquiry. Logical approach to problem solving that includes the statement of the problem, development of a hypothesis, collection and analysis of data, and the drawing of conclusions.

internal locus of control. When students feel that they are responsible for what happens to them.

intrinsic motivation. Motivation to become involved in an activity for its own sake.

intrinsic value. A value reflected by the immediate enjoyment one gets from doing a task.

learned helplessness. Feeling on the part of students when they come to believe that no amount of effort on their part will produce success.

learner-focused classroom. Classroom where emphasis is given to a focus on student learning as opposed to student performance with special attention given to student self-regulation, climate, teacher characteristics, and instruction.

learning goal. Also referred to as mastery goal; goal that emphasizes the challenge of learning and the mastery of a task as opposed to performance.

locus of control. The degree to which students perceive that both positive and negative events in their lives are under their control.

logical consequences. Recommended by both Rudolph Dreikurs and William Glasser as representing understandings on the part of students that when certain behaviors are exhibited certain responses or consequences will follow.

management. A system of organization that addresses all elements of the classroom (i.e., students, space, time, materials, and behavioral rules and procedures) in order to reach optimum levels of instruction and learning.

management organization. The general organizational structure used by the teacher to coordinate the classroom, e.g., starting on time, having specific learning routines, etc.

mastery goal. Also referred to as learning goal; goal that emphasizes the challenge of learning and the mastery of a task as opposed to performance.

misbehavior. Student behavior seen as being unacceptable or inappropriate for the setting or situation in which it occurs.

Model for Reflection and Inquiry. Five-step model for logical problem solving recommended for teachers to use as they analyze problems with student management and motivation; the model includes the statement of the problem, development of a hypothesis, collection of relevant data, analysis of data, and the interpretation and reporting of results, drawing conclusions and making generalizations.

modeling. Being able to see someone else perform a particular task successfully influences the observer to do the same; use of demonstration to assist students in the learning process.

motivation. An internal state that arouses students to action, directs them to certain behaviors, and assists them in maintaining their arousal and action with regard to behaviors important and appropriate to the learning environment.

motivation to learn. Motivation represented by the quality of a student's cognitive engagement in a learning task or activity.

no-lose approach. Approach to helping students resolve their own conflicts or problems in such a way that all students involved feel positive about the resolution.

normative strategies. Behavior strategies used by the teacher in maintaining a well-managed classroom based on all involved doing what is traditionally expected of them, e.g., teachers are expected to ask certain things of students, and students are expected to do what they are asked by their teachers.

operant conditioning. A form of learning where an observable response changes in frequency or duration as a result of a consequence; the response increases in frequency as a result of its being followed by reinforcement.

pedagogical content knowledge. Knowledge of teaching methods and approaches that are specific to the particular subject, or the application of certain strategies in a special way, that the teacher teaches; this includes an understanding of the content in order to teach it in a variety of ways, drawing on the cultural backgrounds and prior knowledge and experiences of the students.

pedagogical knowledge. Knowledge that includes the general concepts, theories, methods, and research about effective teaching, no matter the content area.

peer mediation. Important aspect of the Conflict Resolution approach to behavior management where students, after formal training, lead the problem solving process by helping each other (i.e., peers) reach acceptable solutions to problems that they have experienced.

performance goal. Goal that emphasizes the demonstration of high ability and the avoidance of failure.

potency. The strength or power of a reinforcer, reward, praise or criticism, to change behavior.

power-seeking. Student behavior problem where the student seeks to control the teacher instead of being directed by the teacher; the student could use such strategies as refusing to follow directions, lying, arguing, and throwing temper tantrums.

precise terminology. Clarity in communication that eliminates vague and ambiguous words and phrases from presentations and interactions with students.

Premack principle. The principle that a high-probability or desired activity or behavior can serve as a reinforcer for a low-probability or perhaps less desired activity or behavior; the principle can be a helpful guide for choosing the most effective reinforcers.

primary reinforcer. A reinforcer that meets a basic physiological need such as food, water, and safety.

principle of least intervention. Principle that, when dealing with routine classroom behavior, misbehaviors should be corrected with the simplest, least intrusive intervention that will work.

proactive teacher. A teacher who, through prior planning and knowledge gained, has the ability to "head off" most management problems before they occur and respond to management problems when they occur in such a way that sets the stage for learning to continue in the future.

probing behaviors. Verbal techniques used by teachers, typically through question-asking, that request in a nonthreatening way that a student go deeper into an answer given or comment made and reflect on his or her ideas.

professional knowledge. Knowledge about teaching in general; this includes knowledge about learning, diversity, technology, schooling and education, and the profession of teaching as a whole.

prompting. Question-asking strategy that helps students respond to questions by providing cues after an incorrect or incomplete answer or silence.

prosocial behavior. A behavior directed toward promoting the well-being of someone else.

proximity control. Control exercised by the teacher based on the teacher's nearness to or distance from the student; generally, the nearer the teacher is to a student, the less likelihood there will be for the student to display inappropriate behaviors.

psychological membership. The feeling of membership in a group that is determined by the degree to which students feel personally accepted, respected, included, and supported.

psychological state. Emotional or attitudinal state of a student with respect to performing a task, e.g., tired, anxious, or fearful students will experience a lowered level of self-efficacy.

punishers. Consequences used by a teacher to weaken an undesired student behavior or decrease the likelihood of it recurring in the future.

punishment. The process of using punishers to decrease behavior.

reactive teacher. Teacher whose behavior is characterized by reacting or responding to classroom management and motivation problems after they have occurred rather than ascertaining the causes of such problems and, through prior planning and the use of relevant information, reduce the likelihood that they will ever take place.

Reality Therapy. Management approach recommended by William Glasser, now more popularly referred to as Choice theory, where students play an active role in the decision-making processes in the classroom.

reflection. A way of thinking about educational matters that involves the ability to make rational choices and to assume responsibility for those choices; it requires that the teacher be introspective, open-minded, and willing to accept responsibility for decisions and actions.

reflective practitioner. Educator who regularly utilizes formal problem solving strategies to develop solutions to problems related to motivation, management, and instruction.

reinforcer. Something given or a consequence that, depending on whether it is positive or negative, either adds to or reduces the frequency or length of a behavior.

relatedness. In self-determination theory, the feeling of being connected to others in one's social environment and feeling worthy of love and respect.

remunerative strategies. Behavior strategies used by the teacher in maintaining a well-managed classroom that are based on the power of rewards.

resilience. The ability to recover quickly from some type of misfortune or adversity; resilience results in a heightened likelihood of success in school and in other aspects of life, despite environmental adversities.

resilient self-efficacy. The belief that one can perform a task successfully even after experiencing setbacks with the recognition that effort and perseverance are essential for success.

revenge-seeking. Student behavior problem where a student may do something to cause other students to be punished to "get back at them."

review. Instructional procedure that may occur at different points during a lesson where the teacher summarizes important information from previous work in helping students to link what has been learned to what will be taught in the future.

ripple effect. The effect on other students in the classroom when the teacher reinforces or corrects particular students for their behavior.

sane messages. Recommended by Hiam Ginott as a way for teachers to communicate to students by focusing on their undesired behaviors and not on them as individuals on a personal level.

secondary reinforcer. A reinforcer that may address a particular psychological need such as praise, grades, and money.

self-actualization. The full development or use of one's potential.

self-determination. The process of deciding how to act on one's environment.

self-efficacy. Learners' beliefs about their capability of succeeding on specific tasks.

self-fulfilling prophecy. Phenomenon that a student's performance is greatly influenced when a teacher holds certain beliefs about the student's ability to perform.

self-regulation. The process of using one's own thoughts and actions to reach academic learning goals and to govern one's own behaviors; includes taking responsibility for learning by using one's own thoughts and actions to identify goals, develop strategies for reaching them, and monitoring progress toward their attainment.

shaping. The practice of gradually changing a student's unwanted actions to more acceptable behavior over time through the use of reinforcements.

state anxiety. Anxiety brought about through the presence of a certain situation that typically results in a sense of fear, concern, or threat.

structuring comments. Verbal statements used by the teacher, normally at the beginning of the instructional experience, that alerts students to the events which are to follow and the important points that they should focus on during the instruction.

student success rate. The rate at which students gain an understanding of and correctly complete their work.

suspension. Removal of a student from the regular school environment for a stated period of time for the breaking of identified school rules; most schools have both in-school as well as out-of-school suspension programs.

task-oriented/business-like behavior. Manner of conducting classroom instruction where the teacher is business-like and task oriented in his or her demeanor and approach to teaching, communicating to students that there is a clear and important goal to be achieved and that students will stay on task during that period of time needed to reach the goal.

teacher burnout. Point of teacher extreme stress where a teacher has lost his or her enthusiasm for teaching and has little energy to focus on helping students learn.

Teacher Effectiveness Training (TET). Developed by Thomas Gordon as a model for classroom management focusing on problem solving, active listening, and assisting students to resolve their own conflicts through no-lose processes.

teacher efficacy. The teacher's belief in his or her ability to be successful in getting students to learn.

teacher expectation. What a teacher expects or thinks a particular student will be able to accomplish.

time-on-task. See engaged time.

trait anxiety. Type of anxiety where students appear to be anxious even in circumstances that should not normally be thought of as threatening.

transition signals. The use of specific communication signals in blending one topic with the next that follows so that the flow of the instruction will be smooth and not abrupt.

You message. As opposed to an *I message*, a statement used by a teacher with a student that blames or attacks the student personally for a problem that has been identified, whereas the *I message* focuses on the behavior as the problem, not on the student as the problem.

unruliness. Serious behavior problem where the student exhibits a lack of self-control; unruliness may be exhibited by talking loudly, running in hallways, using unacceptable language, etc.

utility value. Value that focuses on the usefulness of a task as a means to achieve goals that might not be related to the task itself.

variability. Important teacher quality related to student achievement that is represented by the teacher's diversity of information-sending techniques or strategies used during the presentation of lessons; see also instructional variety.

wait-time. The amount of time the teacher allows after asking a question before speaking again; average wait time is about one second; a minimum of three seconds is recommended to increase student achievement.

withitness. When a teacher displays the ability to have an ongoing awareness of events throughout the entire classroom and not just one area of the setting.

zero tolerance. Policy for managing student behavior, usually adopted on a school district-wide basis, represented by the use of certain predetermined consequences when particular rules are broken; the consequences are applied automatically regardless of the circumstances surrounding the rule being broken.

zone of proximal development. A range of tasks that a student cannot yet do alone but can accomplish when assisted by a more skilled partner.

INDEX

299